O9-BTM-818

FICTIONS
AND EVENTS

BY THE AUTHOR

The Example of Melville

The Ferment of Realism

Edmund Wilson

WARNER BERTHOFF

FICTIONS AND EVENTS

Essays in Criticism
and Literary History

E. P. DUTTON & CO., INC. | NEW YORK | 1971

MIDDLEBURY COLLEGE
LIBRARY

12/1971
Eng.

The author wishes to thank the editors and publishers of *College English, The Massachusetts Review, The New England Quarterly, New Literary History* and *American Literature* for kindly allowing him to reprint essays and reviews first appearing in their pages.

Grateful acknowledgment is also made to the following for permission to use copyright material:

Basic Books, Inc., for "The Confidence Man," Chapter 11 of *Landmarks of American Writing,* edited by Hennig Cohen, © 1969

Chandler Publishing Company for the Introduction to the Chandler Facsimile Edition of Ralph Waldo Emerson's *Nature,* © 1968

Harvard University Press for "Fiction, History, Myth," *Harvard English Studies 1,* © 1970 by the President and Fellows of Harvard College

Pantheon Books, a division of Random House, Inc., for two paragraphs from Boris Pasternak, *Doctor Zhivago,* translated by Max Hayward and Manya Harari, © 1958

University of Minnesota Press for several paragraphs from *Edmund Wilson,* University of Minnesota Pamphlets on American Writers No. 67, © 1968 by the University of Minnesota

Viking Press, Inc., for passages from Iris Murdoch, *The Red and the Green,* © 1965

Copyright © 1971 by Warner Berthoff
All rights reserved. Printed in the U.S.A.
First Edition

No part of this publication may be reproduced or transmitted in any form or by any means, electronic or mechanical, including photocopy, recording, or any information storage and retrieval system now known or to be invented, without permission in writing from the publisher, except by a reviewer who wishes to quote brief passages in connection with a review written for inclusion in a magazine, newspaper or broadcast.

Published simultaneously in Canada by Clarke, Irwin & Company Limited, Toronto and Vancouver

Library of Congress Catalog Card Number: 78-133582

SBN 0-525-10470-4

PS
121
B53

For Felix Gilbert, Joseph Frank, Charles Mitchell, Sherman Paul, Edward Morris, Robert Burlin, Hugues Leblanc, Eugene Schneider, Peter Bachrach, colleagues and friends.

"Now there are diversities of gifts, but the same Spirit. . . . For to one is given by the Spirit the word of wisdom; to another the word of knowledge by the same Spirit; to another faith by the same Spirit; to another the gifts of healing by the same Spirit; to another the working of miracles; to another prophecy; to another discerning of spirits; to another divers kinds of tongues; to another the interpretation of tongues: But all these worketh that one and the self-same Spirit, dividing to each man severally as he will."

—I Corinthians 12: 4, 8–11.

PREFACE

The essays in this collection were written for a variety of occasions and were not meant to form a single continuous argument. Yet the process by which we willingly respond to some occasions and not others can have its own incremental logic, in which the developing claims of interest and conviction may provide as good a way as any of consolidating a supportable critical outlook or frame of judgment and putting it freshly to the proof as the need arises.

The unity I would claim for the collection is in a certain reasoned attitude toward, at once, the phenomenon of "literature" and the practical obligations of those who have to do with it. My title proposes a first definition of this attitude. We inhabit a world of events, unintermitting, numberless, intermerging and reciprocal; the event is the fundamental unit of conscious, sentient existence, whether in the form of the willed and fabricated actions by which we substantially interfere in the continuum of actual being or of the crystallizing fatalities which bear down on us as the sum of past occurrences. The constructed event, or fiction, that constitutes "literature" takes its place within this lived, historic continuum, which it thereby augments. At the same time it essentially and expressly exemplifies the common way in which, as creatures of language, sentiment, civil aspiration and memory, we participate in life; that is, it has the distinctive characteristic of proposing clarifications and explanations of the form and manner of this generic participation. I would not say that individual writers necessarily address themselves to their work in these grand terms, only that this is the "meaning" that matters most, the efficient cause by which all accessory meanings and values are secured.

In this view a shared fiction of "literature" and its uses underlies every particular literary performance, every new venture at fictive creation. And in an era of epidemic disorder and confusion challenging, or so we feel, the legitimacy of every consensual undertaking, we not only have to rethink common assumptions about what literature, among other activities, may be good for. The survival and reconstitution of the thing itself becomes a first concern, the survival, that is, of the effective community of writers and readers in which literature practically exists and from which its special influence spreads. The essays in the first half of this collection, on general themes and issues, are my own puzzled tribute to the unnerving disturbances of present history. If the argument should seem affirmative and hopeful on one page and near a kind of despair on the next, I can only plead that this reflects accurately enough the deep uncertainty of all our prospects.

The essays in the second half are concentrated on American subjects because these are what I mainly deal with as a university teacher, what also I know most familiarly by the accident of birth and rearing. Otherwise, for the collection as a whole, the writers and books individually treated all embody, as I read them, some element or force that has seemed to me vital to the very existence of an effective literature, and my hope in each case is simply to have fixed attention on this essential virtue. Thus, I have admired and wished to celebrate in Emerson that seriousness to the point of self-denial in the pursuit of truthfulness which kept his power of encouragement alive to so many later writers and artists; the unsparing absorption in measuring out the tale to be told that gives objective firmness to the work of a minor figure like Sarah Orne Jewett and a prophetic grandeur and authority to a Melville's, a Pasternak's; the generous satisfaction in the mere existence of literature which has lent Edmund Wilson's journalism a value transcending the work of measurably finer critical intelligences; the pride of formed eloquence that fires Hart Crane's best verse-stanzas, and Stevens' and Cummings'; the exceptional nerviness and purposefulness of invention that in a singularly treacherous era has been displayed by Iris Murdoch in English writing, by Norman Mailer in the United States.

The list is not meant to be exhaustive; these are simply writers I happen to have written about to some purpose at one time or another. Let them stand here for the whole company of those we prize. In a bad time our sense of indebtedness to them can only be the more compelling—and the more worth trying to make explicit.

CONTENTS

The Study of Literature and the Recovery of the Historical

> . . . what it is that inspires an art effort is not easily determined,
> much less classified.
> —Charles Ives, *Essays Before a Sonata*

> When a classification does not ideally exhaust its object,
> haphazard classifications are altogether preferable; they set
> imagination in motion.
> —Kierkegaard, *Repetition*

What knowledge are we in search of when we "study" literature? Or, to renew American scholarship's historic first question (as Emerson asked it in 1837), "what would we really know the meaning of?"

It will be observed that the question is not, "why do we read works of literature?"—classics, subclassics, classics emergent, or any recommended and promising work that others are reading—nor is it, "what are the uses and functions of literature?" Answers here, if wanted, are easy to come by. All we commonly ask is that they not be too narrowly or shrilly utilitarian, too meanly sentimental-therapeutic. We have been conned too often with requests to subscribe to one or another reappraisal of the literary past on grounds that what is displayed will "clarify today's situation" or show us "what it means to be human and extant" (I quote from two recent texts for college use) not to have grown suspicious of the familiar decayed-humanist claims. There have been too many declarations of faith in the power of poetry to "save us"— "*sauve qui peut,*" we say, not altogether cynically, and go back to reading what we like: when young, what will feed us; when older, rationing our excitements, what we can still bear. It is

Reprinted from *College English*, April, 1967.

a fact that we read books because we have always read them, have grown up reading them, belong to the community of those who read for a living; because we find ourselves needing them (and many other experiences) ; because we are unregenerately curious, restless, suspicious, envious, willful, distractible, sentimental, hopeful, visionary, and most of all, perhaps, because we are forgetful; because we are always in search of clues as to where we stand (and by what reason of things we came there), what our present task is, and what unconscionable thing the future may have in store for us. But at our best we read books because they are "there," which is to say because they have been created and creative power properly attracts us; it encourages us and makes us glad (so Emerson told the astonishing new poet of *Leaves of Grass*, in a deservedly famous letter), allowing us to bask or to prosper, as we prefer, in its extraordinary presence.

Yet we may learn to take our pleasures as seriously as anything else, so that we can eventually say in all conscience that, reading for our pleasure, we are in fact defending the natural integrity of literature, helping to keep its peculiar virtue alive and available in the matrix of consciousness—a historical matrix, it will be a main purpose of this essay to suggest. The confusion of literature with scripture and legislation, or merely with "school," as Robert Frost sourly called it: that is the thing we resist, without in the least denying the power of books to change our minds and lives. It is in fact the erosion of precisely this power that disheartens us. If Ezra Pound's "thought of what America would be like/ If the Classics had a wide circulation" troubles our sleep as he claimed it did his, it is not with visions of some brilliant Confucian millennium administered by clear-spirited makar-kings but only with the depressing awareness of what is likely to remain of the influence of even the best books after the scheduled procedures of American education have conscientiously engorged them.

Moreover, reading seriously for our pleasure, we do not turn aside from common obligations as souls and as citizens. For it is in the very nature of our growth into life, as long as it continues to be growth, that the active pursuit of pleasure is increasingly disciplined by the sense of what is fitting and customary (or honorable, or healthy, or just), so that in due course we discover the creaturely logic of Coleridge's twin assertions about the uses of literature, which I take to be axiomatic: that there is "no delight, either in kind or degree, equal to that which accompanies the distinct perception of a fundamental truth relative to our moral being," and that the authors who bring us to such delight may be said in effect to have brought "the whole soul of man into activity, with the subordination of its faculties, according to their relative worth and dignity."

"Although literature is one thing and morality a quite different thing, at the heart of the aesthetic imperative we discern the moral imperative": how neatly Sartre's blunt continental idiom complements the Anglo-evangelical refinement of Coleridge's.

The great function of literature is to open the heart and increase wisdom. Or it is, in Dr. Johnson's plain phrase, "to bring realities to mind," and incidentally to indicate how they are to be dealt with; also to remind us that knowledge of realities does not come at a whistle but must be labored after with much pain and disappointment. But beyond these modest claims, claims to the possibility of certain useful inward transactions, we feel that it is probably wise not to go; we prefer, nowadays, deflation and irony. It is not that we now positively disbelieve what Ben Jonson once believed and what Emerson, repeating Jonson with full approval, still believed: that "the principal end of poetry is to inform men in the just reason of living." We are simply less secure, less inward, with the words "just" and "reason," and obsessed with the invasion of the business of "informing" by electronic retrieval and transmission systems. If, in our post-Christian, post-European, egalitarian and anthropological times, we are still sure of anything, it is that there is more than one way of defining such words and of translating them into conduct. It is true that in defense of professional privilege we still find ourselves speaking rather grandly in public—*litterae humaniores* and the modern university curriculum as the secure repository of the human spirit's capital gains: our parliamentary half-truth—but we grow uncomfortable in this vein and fall back with relief on more guarded and practical maxims: on some such position, for example, as that propaedeutically advanced by William

Empson, that "the central purpose of reading imaginative literature is to accustom yourself to this basic fact . . . that there is more than one code of morals in the world." Yes, our happiest criticism now is anthropological: literature as the inexhaustible man-show and witness-feast (conveniently structured, or made talkaboutable, as William James would say) of our common life.

Delight in books, hunger for their contents and for the power they symbolize, and a presumptuous readiness to imitate them and compete with them in new books, poems, novels, plays, parodies, journals, manifestoes: what is more natural to the aroused young? Their capacity for education, and so for becoming accomplices in schemes of civilization, is a biological gift.

But is the *study* of literature really natural to the young? I am less and less persuaded that it is.* At least its real peculiarity should be acknowledged and faced up to. The standard disciplines of learning deal with positive knowledge (even philosophy, which deals with classifiable propositions) and seek to construct patterns of positive knowledge which may be applied to further circumstances or occasions of the same generic kind. But imaginative literature, as an object of study, itself consists of concluded patterns of knowledge. More precisely, it consists of patterns or sequences of the action of knowing, the writer's act of knowing first of all; patterns which in their totality are indeterminate and untranslatable and which, moreover, describe nothing more exactly than their own creation, so that they can be known in their full reach and bearing only through a kind of ideal re-creation. The whole character of literature, as it is known to us, corresponds: it is not "like" other elected disciplines of knowledge but "like" historical life. It is at once artificial and accidental, imperiously self-assertive but also self-enclosed, self-parasitic, self-terminating (biol: *metagenetic*), extraordinarily complex and inclusive yet open-ended and uncompletable, constituting a set of

---

* Of course I am not talking here of the usefulness of positive information: names, titles, careers and life histories, technical data, facts of language and idiom, the contents of that ideal reference library which, one can argue, appears rather further from completion than it did fifty or sixty years ago.

inconceivable further possibilities as well as of registered accomplishments. So too, one might equally say, literature offers patterns of ignorance and limitation; it displays that lapse into existential compromise which, nicknamed "the fall," has been attributed to both human and divine life; it is a propitiatory holding off of darkness and chaos—a "stay against confusion," Frost said—which are nevertheless the more vividly shown to be real darkness, real chaos, real confusion, by any spiritual or civil measure.

The very success of literature abashes us. More than theme or representational truthfulness, though we respond prejudicially to these, it is the internal progressions of the work that hold us to it and, while we are occupied with it, win acceptance. It is sentence upon sentence, event after event. Yet these felt progressions are the one thing we can never reproduce for examination and verification. It would be easier to memorize *Paradise Lost* than to keep in mind how it works. (And would it be less worthwhile?) That serial coherence-in-complexity which actively charms consciousness (in infinitely varying degrees according to the singularities of the writer's performance and our condition of readiness) exists *in* consciousness only as we ourselves are actively following it forward, as we freely, generously, alertly collaborate in its renewal. Then we lose touch with it—and have no guarantee that the experience is recoverable or communicable.

What critic of novels or plays can even summarize the story, the plain succession of significant events, to any other's satisfaction? The critic himself may hardly understand his own summary ten years later. "We do not see the same Stavrogin or the same Charlus at forty that we saw at twenty," Iris Murdoch remarks—nor do we hear the same story or carry away the same interior meaning.

Forced back into modesty in these high matters, we sensibly call the critical study of literature a "common pursuit." We see that it has always to be corrected, always to be reestablished. Or, to change the metaphor, we see that it is a holding action; the most strenuous countermeasures are required merely to keep within reach of what is lost even while it is being won, which is a knowledge of the active virtue in the created objects we have in view. But again, are holding actions the proper work of the young? This is the strategic question that our formed vocation as scholar-teachers regularly conspires to keep us from asking, and yet it is fundamental to our whole institutionalized existence. For the young make wonderful shock troops; with only a little encouragement they drag us forward into the treacherous, indifferent future; but their tactics are reckless and wasteful; left to themselves they may keep nothing in reserve; they labor to repeat all our notorious mistakes; they would gain positions all day and lose the field itself by evening. And it is the best trained among them, the most knowledgeably ambitious, who, stimulated by the priestly approval of their prize-awarding, succession-jealous elders, become the leading agents of this continuous lapse. "Will the fashion for prize pupils in contemporary literature last much longer?" Proust once asked, himself just at the point of beginning to see past the literary ambitions he had casually inherited toward the long wearing process of discovering his own extraordinary lifework. "It would be a great pity."*

Is it indeed our prize pupils who are the sacrifices exacted by our aggrandizing scrutiny of masterworks of the past and by the classificational, and competitive, wars of truth so prized by the academy? That would be a savage irony truly. But why should we deny the disordering effect upon insufficiently prepared minds (by which I mean the generality of well-schooled minds of any era, the gifted examination-passing and rule-abiding apprentice Pharisees who become the necessary placemen of literate civilization) of great creative achievement too long and too scrupulously attended to? At best, as objects of contemplation, great works of literature increase and substantiate our knowledge of our essential ignorance. They mock the determined studiousness that sent us out to take practical command of their fugitive lessons; indeed they mock all studiousness except that aimed at some comparable act of creation. As a result, the more intense our response to them, the more they shorten our patience with the ordinary expedient scramble of conscious life. They end not in worldly action—the

---

* "Contre la jeune école": the title is of course ironic and, in its severe way, compassionate. Its tone is well caught, I think, by Sylvia Townsend Warner's translation, "Against the Young Writers of the Day."

great aim of the untried sociable young, whose proper occupation is pillaging and using up—but in silence and inert admiration. Beyond some initial quickness of response and readiness of common sympathy, which are the mind's birthright, great works of literature, taken as objects of scheduled understanding, require fine judgment, resolute disinterest, the patience of the obsessed, and a superflux of imaginative and expressive discretion that the widest experience and most approved education cannot guarantee. But these in any case are the mind's latest and most precarious acquisitions; they are not the natural equipment of the young. How they are won or how maintained and renewed, no one can say convincingly: hence the essentially tautological notion of *genius*, the myth, an analytic philosopher's myth, of the visitations of the *daimon*.

Yet great works of literature also bring us as effectively as any experience we know into the presence of just these extraordinary capacities of mind. Such works have the power to surprise and excite of any greatly generous and original action; they have also the unique power to explain themselves. I hope it is clear that I am not arguing for withholding them from circulation or making them inaccessible to anybody at any time. On the contrary we can never publicize them enough. For in them we see directly, perhaps more directly and more conveniently than in any other way, how an informed power of mind may give order and consequence to the random successions of active experience and to the fitful inventiveness and absorptiveness of human intellect. We trace out in them perfected examples of intellectual and imaginative mastery—and may remember Rilke's prophetic maxim that "every perfect instance of mastery furthers mastery in general."

For what we are shown through works of literature is how a collective wisdom (concentrated first of all in sentence and anecdote, which are at once the prime units of literary meaning and the essential idiom of continuing civilization) can operate for the duration of a deliberated creative effort within a single intelligence—and can act thereafter as a new cause, an instrument of unpredictable change and transcendence. That is, we are shown the fundamental pattern of the *historical*, by which I mean that indeterminate successional dimension of existence (and of the knowledge of existence) which, so far as we know, belongs to man alone in the scheme of creation, and belongs to him (and is the element that defines his coming into existence) by virtue of his freedom, his inventiveness. And as literature is first of all a category of human invention, it signifies and posits first of all the renewal of man's singular identity, as the creature who lives historically, in a milieu of his own progressive making. To be man is to have freedom; to be free is to choose; to choose, as Sartre says, is to invent—that is, to bring about, for good or ill, sequences of effect that otherwise would not take place *and could not be specifically imagined.* In other words, it is to create "history." I might say, to create "human history," but that would really be redundant, man being the history-making creature. What I speak of as "the historical" is the sequential acting out, in private and simple as well as in vast collective forms, of the human condition, the condition of inventiveness, freedom, unanticipatable consequence, and hence, too, of both satisfaction and remorse. Literature, also structurally sequential, imitates or "recovers" the historical, so defined. I believe Aristotle said this too, though more efficiently.

Thus in the serial structure of works of literature, the basic form of human or historical existence, a form of action and consequence incessantly multiplying, is revealed in a provisionally completed segment.* It is the generic progression of our lives that literature finds out. We live by an immense complicity, and we are not born knowing this but discover it only through being told and told and told of it in incessant stories, anecdotes, serial participations. But only gradually and laboriously do we begin to see how all this happens, how millions of individual lives, acts, words, silences, mistakes, conspiracies of invisible preparation and undeserved enfranchisement support every step we take, every thought we move through; and the greatest function of literature and its rational yet gratuitous fictions is to establish free ceremonies of impli-

---

* I assume it is understood that feeling, too, is a form of invented and sequential action and has its history; that it is, moreover, the history that is particularly open to us as each other's "others" to share within our own actual being; so that it is just our deepest, most intimate experience of feeling which is most collaborative and plagiaristic—otherwise it would not be so overwhelming. It takes us a long time to learn this, however.

cation and participation in this definitive truth about the character of our historical lives.

Of course the concrete materials out of which works of literature may be composed, the circumstances and details of the revealed action, the articulation of interior relationships, are infinitely variable. We can observe within this mass of particulars certain distinctive types and recurrences—narrative, rhetorical and organizational, imaginative and symbolic—but even these are far more numerous, and more unstable within individual works, than classification customarily allows; the higher criticism of our busy century has hardly begun to identify them. Moreover, though tenacious and persistent in the traceable history of literature, these observed types and recurrences cannot be proved to be of the nature of literature itself.* But some basic formal series of predication and resolution, which we call "plot" or "argument," is always there. It may stand our ordinary sense of sequence quite on its head; yet an unfamiliar or seemingly chaotic structure is still, in any made thing, a structure; in time, as it finds an audience, it can become a convention like any other. We require this of what we recognize as literature not simply because it soothes anxiety or furnishes a manageable symmetry of design but because it is "true"—true to our life as in our own unintermitting and progressive histories we come to know it, or see that in the fulfillments of time it might reasonably be known; true to the sense that rises with our coming-of-age, our hard-won and

---

* Modern archetypal and generic criticism has much increased awareness of the subtlety and historical persistence of genres and expressive forms. But especially as criticism of this kind has been occupied chiefly with matters of content (story alignments, motifs, images and symbols) it has proved not less vulnerable than earlier schools of essentially substantive criticism to sectarian bias and premature schematization. What may be residual and contributory—for example, the element of Biblical specification in the literature of 1830–1930, the literature of "modernism"—may be regularly taken as formative and essential, since it retains so remarkable a power of implication; whereas a prime question for critical understanding will be to determine whether this is in fact the case. Students of the archetypal and generic are like students anywhere; they may learn to exclude, to rationalize those necessary habits of imperception in which, as students, they seek shelter from the onslaught of the knowable, before they learn to grasp and understand; in particular, they confuse temporal survival and persistence with universality. They find it as hard as anybody to "know their knowledge," in Coleridge's always challenging phrase.

imperfect second birth into the historical, that one thing does, always, lead to another and to just that other thing, moreover, which nothing else has ever led to.

Thus the distinctive use of literature, among all conceivable incidental uses, is to mirror and confirm our creaturely participation in the dimension of the historical, the dimension of elected and continuing human life. This is true in a double way. Literature "imitates" history; that is, it rehearses unique actions, concrete and successional. But as it registers first of all the process of its own creation, literature also exists in and belongs to history; and it is as phenomena of historical existence that works of literature can be "studied." The *study* of literature, as of art, of religion, of war, of commerce, of every form of the civil and communal, is the study of a special sector and type of historical existence, and the knowledge proper to this study is "historical" knowledge, in the sense of the word advanced in this essay. The great central purpose of the study of literature is consequently twofold. It is to re-create an imaginable past, in reasoned conceptions of the fundamental effort and action of mind, individual and collective, that works of literature embody and signalize. It is also to join this knowledge as both cause and critical measure to the tasks of our present life: those tasks in the conduct of which our precarious collective effort to pass not altogether barbarously into the fatalities of our created historical future will succeed or fail.

But that the proper *study* of literature is historical is no more than what common sense has regularly understood for at least two hundred years, even when it has seemed necessary to insist as if absolutely on the autonomy of literature and to campaign for its liberation from all time-serving requirements. The history of individual writers, as persons, as men of letters; the history of their opportunities, including on the one hand the history of the formation and descent of literary genres and conventions and on the other the history of the corresponding social habituations and acceptances; the history of ideas, of religion, of science and philosophy, of technology, of social crises and transformations: any or all of these have been seen as appropriate objects of knowledge, or adjuncts to knowledge, according to the case in hand. In particular we have come to appreciate the importance for imaginative literature of parallel structures of expression and argument (subliterary, preliterary, antiliterary) from jokes, curses, riddles, and raw anecdotes to highly formalized scientific and philosophic modes of inquiry. For literature does not emerge without mediation from creaturely experience. It derives its ways of explanation from already established systems of explanation—some seemingly inherent in the very existence of language and discourse—in which it is possible for writers to be drilled to a very high competence before they quite know what they are doing. Syntax, definition, all the basic structures of linguistic address, are themselves narrative and fabulous and exert some measure of *formal* authority however they are filled out.* Literary creation, we see, is inherent in articulate expression, and is inherently parodistic. Some other familiar way of saying is always assumed and is openly or covertly referred to or else negated. For the more complex structures of high literature, more sophisticated antecedents may play a special formative role, as the Bible does for much of the literature of the Christian Era. Some of the most widely instructive critical studies in recent times have been those, as by Rosamund Tuve and Louis Martz, showing in convincing detail how certain argumentative structures of humanist logic and rhetoric or the controlled exercises of devotional meditation were "imitated" in the Middle Ages and the Renaissance in secular poetry. Comparable work has yet to be done for Romantic and modern literature: putting it in relation, for example, to the more self-concealing but hardly less influential forms of discourse and address developed within the intense convocations of post-Reformation sectarianism. In some respects, in fact, serious historical work on the literature of the past two centuries has hardly begun, as is fairly plain to anyone comparing the later volumes of the *Oxford History* to most of the earlier ones.

But it is also a historical fact that literature, though in-

---

* One suspects, without knowing how to argue the case, that mathematical equations are a kind of simple narrative—metamorphic riddles, perhaps, predicating archetypal changes of state, or, more obviously, antimetamorphic (i.e. tautological) conundrums thrown in the face of both nature and history—and would thus find their place in any ideal encyclopedia of fictions.

separable from the historical totality of linguistic culture and experience, is nevertheless distinct in function and aim, being, within these wide limits, self-serving and self-engendering. What more than anything else it imitates, or parodies, is other literature. We may come to feel that literary history is a kind of immense echo-chamber in which the same utterances are endlessly renewed, though in gradually altering tones and vocabularies. Literature repeats and repeats—yet each new author does so in his own way, each work that finds a place in the commemorated series of literature is unique in its manner of self-completion.

As a consequence two specific kinds of knowledge are fundamental to the "historical" study of literature, so defined:

1. The long history of the continuing emergence of literature-as-such, with its free, rational, self-reflective elements of parody and commentary as well as those of imaginative and mythical projection and with its ultimate drive toward artistic transcendence; an emergence which, as we know it in its later and documented stages, is in some measure recapitulated by every individual writer and sometimes by whole provinces or epochs of literary enterprise. All studies of literature in terms of cycles of creative purpose, of formal conventions and genres, and of archetypal images and recurrent myths, contribute to this first kind of knowledge and increase our understanding of the nature of the thing we seek to know.

2. The history of particular works of literature—and this not only in the recoverable circumstances of their making (for which, beyond an established text, early drafts, personal statements, demonstrable parallels and sources may all provide evidence) but also in their historical continuance: their effect on the work of other and later authors, and their whole second life as causative agents in the consciousness, in particular the literary consciousness, of posterity. All criticism assumes the possibility of this second and continuing life, and all effective criticism helps to extend it.

Thus, all literature in its concrete historical existence—its creation and then its continuance as an object of measured participatory knowledge—has the character of a rite, a ceremonial acting out of the collectively realized inheritance and present condition of its communicants, commemorating the past performance of such rites and positing their future renewal. It proceeds from a particular action of mind (and is the deserving beneficiary of many contributing actions of mind which, in proportion as it is generously conducted, it somewhat reorganizes and confirms). It rehearses and concretely projects a particular action of mind, which is that of its making (and once we are beyond the stage of primitive illusion, we are always conscious of this; we say not only, what a happy couple they are now, or, what terrible suffering and retribution—if only we could stop it!—but also, how well that passage was managed, what an absolute tragic climax, what a stylish conclusion). And it invites and encourages further actions of mind, being in its deepest character dependent on them; though it may recognize no other responsibility, it thus creates its own future.

The rites or ceremonies of literature in its historical existence, thus defined, are threefold, and the article of critical belief this essay rests on is that every individual work of literature lends itself to them all or eventually loses acceptance.

First, rites of association: the work's communion with its audience, acting through expressive conventions—all that establishes tone—to secure the illusion of effective community and forestall the sense of isolation or (literally) absurdity in human existence. In the service of these rites we prize style (or voice), coherence of language and address, eloquence and precision of statement, rhetorical mastery.

Second, rites of propitiation or placation: the work's communion with the world of subjects and materials (including the inheritance of myth), acting through symbols and other invocational figures to charm some part of the universe of otherness by which we are surrounded, and which our own lives continually augment, into a semblance of harmony and compliance. In the service of these rites we prize generous perception and truthful representation, coherence—and amplitude—of reference, imaginative resourcefulness and tact.

Third, rites of power: the work's progressive communion with itself and with the force of mind through which it emerges, acting under its own propulsions to secure an illusion of efficacy and consequence in the world of free, rational, elected human performance. In the service of these rites we prize energy and inventiveness, organization and an internal coherence—and completeness—of structure, all in short that makes for compositional, i.e., argumentative, authority.

As with any ritual activity there are, in the minds of communicants, true and false forms of participation and a constant danger of formalism and decadence (or of "bureau-cratization," Kenneth Burke's alarming word). The conduct of particular rites and their authority over our consciousness cannot escape being affected by the general set and direction of the common culture; and in the present age the disorderly rites of contemporary life—of salesmanship and leisure-class indulgence; of production and consumption for their own sake; of social intimidation and intellectual submission to neutralize the risks of an explosively open and unstable society; of public violence that has become not only aberration but elected state policy; of disaffection, the refuge of the young (as insensibility becomes the refuge of their elders)—have invaded the civil insti-tution of literature to an unprecedented degree. All that puts civility in peril puts every free, rational, creative effort of mind in peril, too. The increasingly preposterous obstacle course of authorized growth and development that besets the uncommit-ted young (its gaps and voids worse than its established barriers) certainly does not clear itself away when they make a com-mitment to literature. But these conditions only make the thing itself the more precious to us, and our best conception of it and of its uses the more compelling. Wherever the par-ticular enterprise of art persists, it retains its character, which is not so much independent as gratuitous, giving off its own superfluous pictures and rehearsals, its own habit of inquiry, its own examples of fundamental progression and consequence, and yet convincing us of their precise relevance to the life we know and seek to know. And wherever this enterprise persists, it gives to literary creation its distinctive end or goal, which is, in Sartre's beautiful formulation, "to recover [or restore: *ré-cupérer*] this world by giving it to be seen as it is, but as if it had its source in human freedom." For this is an end, Sartre continues, that can be secured only by the free, responsible collaboration, the ritual communion, of author and reader:

> Since what the author creates takes on objective reality only in the eyes of the spectator, this restoration is consecrated by the ceremony of the spectacle—and particularly of reading.*

At this point abstract argument must give way to other forms of encouragement—to primary acts and renewals, as the chance develops. It must remain a standing reproach to professional "students" of literature, an invitation to humility, that nothing we do can equal, in its power to restore life and health to the rite we serve, the thing itself: the emergence of some new work originally conceived and resourcefully executed that speaks its own language, discovers its own truth, and accomplishes its own design, and that can find its own responsive audience. This is what maintains literature in its historical existence, and in its historical uses and historical continuance; and this is the historical possibility we are called to serve, which defines for us our duty as students, scholars, critics, editors, lecturers, reviewers, teachers, promoters, and recommenders wherever placed—and above all and primarily as readers and participants. Like all education, like life itself (for what is education but an attempt to put to good use a convulsive and chancy biosocial process?) the study of literature is an act of corresponsive faith; and the point I have wanted to make in this essay is simply that the nearer it brings us to reimagining the real historical accretion of the thing it attaches to, the better.

---

* This is why we always "get more" out of a work—more pleasure, more significance—when someone we trust or admire or wish to please has recommended it to us, when we meet it in the course of some already approved pattern of experience. Not just the music pleases and nourishes us when we go to a concert, Delacroix shrewdly and civilly remarked, but the whole enterprise "of dressing, going out, even being distracted from important business, in order to listen to the music. . . ." "To find oneself in an appointed place and among people who have come together out of a common desire to enjoy something in one another's company, even the boredom of hearing certain pieces and certain virtuosi, all combine without our realizing it to add to the effect of a lovely work. If that beautiful symphony had been played for me in my studio I should probably not have retained the same memory of it." (*Journal,* Sunday, March 11, 1849.)

Fiction, History, Myth:
Notes Toward the Discrimination
of Narrative Forms

Theory of fiction absorbs our attention currently—and not merely that professional part we struggle, as "scholars," to keep free of day-to-day, month-by-month institutional crisis; for there, too, we have learned to speak of scripts and scenarios, and we ruefully confess the power of various presumptive fictions of reformation or of reprisal that, put in action, can turn any civil community of learning into a theater of cruelties. The latest forms of university disorder, these ritualized winter's tales and spring festivals of mutually punitive confrontation, may well reinforce our professional hope that the critical study of fictions and fiction-making is an activity possessing "relevance." Common apprehensions do put their stamp on learned judgments. A troubled sense of the complicity of several twentieth-century masters—preparers, it had seemed, of a saving new order of literary mythmaking—in the political and ideological barbarism of modern history has already set the terms for one recent round of critical reappraisals. Consider Yeats, for example. It became disconcerting to realize that the mythopoeic imagination that produced "Among School Children" and the Byzantium poems should also have given visionary blessing to a repressive land system and have

Reprinted from *Harvard English Studies* 1, 1970.

flirted, though briefly, with fascist solutions in civil life. It could lead to the thought that "there may even be a real relation between certain kinds of effectiveness in literature and totalitarianism in politics" (Frank Kermode, *The Sense of an Ending*, p. 39). Yet there could be reassurance in remembering that the same poet had set down in verse, in a time of actual civil violence, a singularly compact diagnosis of the whole disturbing syndrome. "We had fed the heart on fantasies,/ The heart's grown brutal from the fare"—so at least in one eloquent instance of self-reflection this conspicuously "masterful" creator of extreme fictions proved to have understood well enough the common dangers of living by them. Yeats's unremitting concern with his own dubious case as an artist was, we can say, what saved him for greatness; a means of imaginative restraint and self-correction as well as of aggrandizement. So, too, in general, the self-absorption of modernist writing, its preoccupation with its own formative processes, has not necessarily involved the abdication of ordinary responsibilities. It may instead have been the necessary modern way of fulfilling the old humane command to "show the very age and body of the time his form and pressure"—in an age, that is, which has been taught to see itself as living, as in games theory, by its choices among competing playbooks.

❋ ❋ ❋

The recent multiplication of "studies in the theory of fiction" (subtitle of Professor Kermode's valuable book) is a sign of the times. Like other branches of learning, the study of literature has its own significant history, its own contingent succession of imperatives and responses.

It is a sign, first, of a continuing effort to establish literary criticism and classification, including evaluation, on a more systematic basis. Most "students" of literature are teachers and university scholars and prefer not to be excluded from the circle of serious academic approval. When one after another accredited science of human behavior has become absorbed in devising fundamental grammars, the impulse of literature professors to follow suit is not surprising. All traceable literary history involves the composing and transforming of particular

fictions; that is the tautology—fiction: a making—that circum-
scribes the subject; and what richer or more comprehensive
topic of inquiry can there be than the anatomical norms by
which the historically emergent body of composed fictions
holds together as a generated species? For that inquiry the
rapid development of structuralist analysis in other fields of
humane learning—philosophy, linguistics, anthropology—provides practical models as well as competitive challenge and
provocation.

What is also signified is a widening recognition of the
definite end of the great modernist renaissance in art and
speculative thought, coinciding, it seems, with the closing out
of the liberal-bourgeois hegemony in cultural valuation. This
creative renaissance—lasting from the era of Romanticism with,
in poetry, its revolutionary new figurations of the writer's
essential character and performance, through the 1930's and
early 1940's, when Musil, Faulkner, Yeats (also Freud, Cassirer,
Wittgenstein) were completing their major work and Pasternak was planning *Doctor Zhivago*—was the historical force
around which, until quite recently, the best of modern literary
scholarship shaped its understanding of its distinctive task. A
continuing outflow of original masterwork had required, and
coincidentally enabled, a companion effort of critical affirmation, apology, exegesis, that did not need wider justification.*
Moreover it had *not* required abandoning—though with each
new step it seemingly threatened to—older humanistic notions
of the uses of literature. Literary scholarship needed only to
serve the practical cause of removing obstacles to informed
understanding; for traditionalists and modernists alike the
function of criticism could be defined as simply, in Eliot's
formula of 1923, "elucidation and the correction of taste." The
good critic merely helped willing readers join forces with
writings that on the point of justification were quite able to
look after themselves.

---

* This secondary scholarly effort was of course not limited to the study of
modern writing. My point is rather that the major expository and synthesizing work on earlier literatures, too, and the intellectual confidence
with which it was carried out were equally indebted to that immense
primary stimulus—whether or not the debt was acknowledged.

Now that long splendid era (in which the intellectual carriers of modernism could still see the shape of the future prefigured in their thinking) is past—and common trust in the doctrines of critical humanism, which could survive one tactical revolution after another but not a drying up of invention itself in the old sense, has passed with it. As a consequence, or so one feels, the ambitious present effort to establish a general theory of fiction carries, is perhaps largely carried by, an intensifying factor of nostalgia and anxiety: nostalgia for the great days when the exhilarating task was the defense of certain particular books and authors, past as well as present, Donne as well as Joyce, and their assimilation into the grander traditions of literary virtuousness; anxiety that no such new epoch appears in the making or is even any longer quite conceivable, and that knowledge of a splendid past is no guarantee of renewal in the present or future. As with anthropological studies of certain exotic cultures, the moment when analysis becomes really systematic and complete is also the moment when the system of behavior under examination enters, sadly, the phase of final dissolution.

* * *

Instead, then, of being a kind of vital proof that to occupy oneself systematically with imaginative literature is to open access to a unique source of energy and authority, this last withdrawing galaxy of modernist masters and masterpieces now mocks us with our own deepening exclusion from whatever imaginative economy produced them and is no more. We are left behind with the classifier's job of sorting out a chapter of history the vital principle of which we hardly know where to look for, since nothing so richly encouraging can be detected within our own horizon. Both factors—estrangement from a heroic near-past, the absence of stable signs of renewal and continuation—are at work in our expanding awareness that in back of the most fundamental professional issues of historical definition and critical precepting stand even more fundamental issues concerning the very character and possibility of the *event*, the *activity*, in human life, of fiction-making. To deal with these issues, students of literature are forced to become psychologists, epistemologists (or phenomenologists), cultural anthropologists, theorists of the life sequences of civilization, as well as, on their own particular ground, experts on narrational formulas and the morphology of themes.

But of course it is in just this intimidating enlargement of the critical task, if anywhere, that motive and stimulus are to be found for continuing it at all; it is by this self-imposition of new, unaccustomed burdens that a way may be opened past the breakdown of the older insulated humanism of great-books and great-subjects learning to a tougher and deeper humanism of mind itself, in which, at the least, our own working lives and fortunes are seen to be in hazard with every professional choice we make. If the study of narrative forms takes us this deep, it would seem worth keeping up.

Predictably, certain late-modernist writers of fiction can be found pointing the way—and it seems fitting that the two novelists I am about to cite in this regard should also be writers professionally competent outside the conventional scope of novelistic and literary-critical understanding: one by training both engineer and philosopher and for a time a scientific adviser to the Austrian War Ministry, the other a philosophically educated theorist of music, painting, mathematics, and the calligraphy of landscape. Thus to Robert Musil the very "law of this life"—that fundamental law "for which one yearns, overburdened as one is and at the same time dreaming of simplicity"—"is none other than that of narrative order" (*The Man Without Qualities,* chap. cxxii). To which Michel Butor has added the needful corollaries: that the essential medium and stuff of our knowledge of life, the stuff of human understanding, is also narrative ("Le Roman comme recherche"), and that to "work on" narrative—that incessant rehearsal-in-sequence of proposed statements and actions which surrounds us from first consciousness and which the highest extensions of scientific thought are only an extraordinary refinement of—and to work on it "tirelessly, methodically," as an unending vocation, is the one way in which as language users we truly approach an objective reality and productively confront "what we habitually say with what we see and with the information we continually receive" ("Recherches sur la technique du roman") .*

* * *

Considerations this lofty surely dignify a theoretical concern with the study of literary fictions and fiction-making, or of narrative, the more elemental term fixed on by Musil and Butor. But they are hardly to be treated properly in a short essay. What is needed in any case is a certain agreement on the character of the subject and the primary terms and categories to be used in speaking about it. A rough survey of current works on the theory of fiction does not uncover any such agreement, and the notes that follow are only an attempt to contribute to that limited end. But one can no more pretend to neutrality in defining basic terms than in any other activity of mind. Even dull terminological speculation is controlled by apprehensions and hopes about the present condition of things, and in the end our discriminations will invariably point to an estimate of literature's (and the imagination's) practical chances in the foreseeable future.

* * *

The fundamental forms of our knowledge being (in the nature of our common rearing) narrative and fabulous, particular

---

* If we are thinking of fiction primarily as an *activity,* then we think of the maker of works of fiction as being supported in his intention, sustained in his choice of this or that line of development, by the recollection (having, always, a narrative form) of a multiplicity of concrete events and episodes and an even greater multiplicity of reports and recitations of events and episodes—including of course many earlier works of fiction, which he plagiarizes and parodies. If we are thinking of works of fiction primarily as *objects* for critical and historical assessment, then we draw on our own comparable recollection, disciplined and expanded by study, in placing and rating them. In either case critical recollection is the means of knowing, choosing, deciding, inventing. ("Toute invention est une critique," writes M. Butor helpfully; "toute critique est invention.") On the other hand, the very effort of either novelist or critic to have his say effectively operates as a generative incitement to this agency of recollection—but also, when intelligence falters, may merely force-feed it.

narrative modes have a cognitive basis. They communicate a certain knowledge of experience; they do so by imitating and parodying established modes of entertaining and communicating knowledge. The simpler of these modes—grammatical statement, household anecdote—we have from early life an unreflecting mastery of, more or less; they are the way our apprehension of experience, and first of all of the uses of language, grows in us. The more complex ones we are educated into, and these include, as a common bond between writers and readers, the developed conventions of standard literature. Particular narrative modes have also a functional basis in the common order of life. Here the matter becomes more problematic, though also, I think, more casually discussible. The question is: what civil and imaginative end is this or that species of narrative being made to serve? what kind of experience is it meant to gain a purchase on? what kind of address does it make to such experience? how is it commonly performed, and heard, and used?

Three basic modes of narrative are to be distinguished: fiction, history, myth. (I would argue that the several narrative genres we are customarily occupied with in literary commentary are all forms of *fiction*—the choice among them representing essentially rhetorical or social strategies—but that they may be best defined by their appropriation of primary qualities from these other two basic modes. Thus: *Allegory* is a branch of fiction dominated by homiletic or, to use a word recently proposed by Kenneth Burke, pontifical purposes; it establishes an exemplary connection between one meditated sphere of existence and another and facilitates passage between them. *Pastoral* is a branch of fiction dominated by nostalgia for the imaginative satisfactions that, in the perspective of economic disorder, certain benign myth-constructs are remembered as providing. The *chronicle-novel*, on the other hand, moves in the direction of certified history and the kind of credence owing to that. And among all other forms, *epic* gains its peculiar grandeur by assimilating both the detailed particularity of histories and the drive toward absoluteness—completeness, autonomy, immunity to neglected contingencies—characteristic of myth. But this kind of classification too easily degenerates into wordplay.) There is considerable duplication of functions among these three modes: in particular, an impulse in the grander practice of history and fiction to enter into competition with the mysterious authority of the mythic. Our vernacular use of the word *story* for all three is symptomatic of such complications, which will emerge as they must while our main definitions go forward.

* * *

The functional differences between these three basic narrative modes can be most directly indicated by examining our common words for them. Etymological definition is not foolproof, but it has the merit of pointing up practical distinctions in usage which may be taken as important until positively proved otherwise.

Fiction is the plainest case. The word's derivation flaunts the fact that it describes something made up, and as we apply it in talking about literary narrative, we have in mind works about which we usually know (or would know if we had the evidence) who did the making up; we assume the presence, we recognize the workmanship, of an individual maker. His variations and elaborations on the story materials he exploits interest us as much, in reading, as the particular human action he rehearses, since his rehearsal of it is itself an action of comparable significance; it tells us, acts out for us, how this or that species of experience may be absorbed into consciousness, how it is to be talked about and lived with. Our ordinary familiarity with gossip and talebearing confirms this; we grow impatient hearing really interesting news from someone who, either by short-circuiting its imaginable structure of linkages or by displacing these with the armature of his own personality, cannot bring it to plausible life in the detail.

* * *

With *history* ambiguities develop, though on the whole they are manageable ones. The word refers less directly than *fiction* to the process by which narrative structures so designated come into being; and the variety of uses we have for it reflects this displacement. *History* serves not only as (1) the generic name for a species of narrative discourse ("a work of history") but also as the particular name for (2) a single piece of work in this mode (*A History of the Eighth Air Force in World War II*), (3) the general aggregate of past events ("human history," "the history of creation"), (4) any one finite sequence of events ("I am Stubb, and Stubb has his history"), and (5) the discipline of inquiry, cognition, and explanation that deals with such sequences ("the method of history," "the philosophy of history").

It is this last element—systematic inquiry in search of an explainable sequence of evidence—that is primarily conveyed in the word itself. The Greek verb ἱστορέω means to make inquiry and, by extension, to give a systematic account of what is learned through such inquiry. The noun ἱστορία means, first, knowledge or information obtained in this way, and, second, a written presentation of such knowledge. (The root appears to be the Indo-European morpheme for the kind of *knowing* that comes by *learning*.) Thus, *history* is reserved for that species of narrative in which we try to describe something that has happened according to the discoverable testimony about it and by means of certifiable techniques for gathering and identifying such testimony. The practice of history, so defined, seems a more recent development than myth and fiction. (How and why modern historiography developed, and what was involved in the emergence in Europe of a specifically historicist consciousness, is not to the point here.) It would seem to be a technological development, requiring the stabilization of some sort of graphic or monumental means of statement; you cannot find out the history of things, perhaps you cannot see that there is a history to be found out, until durable records of one kind or another have been constructed and identified as such. (In this regard a collection-in-series of battle trophies or a hillside of patriarchal tombs would do as well as written documents; and if some prehistoricist New Guinea tribe learned from its anthropological or military acquaintance that the construction of documented histories was a virtuous activity, its university wits could set to work constructing their own—though there would be arguments about the quotient of reliability in what resulted.)

✳ ✳ ✳

History, in brief, is the story of happenings that are, or might be, otherwise knowable.* Here is the evidence we have collected and the design we think it composes; but if we had a set of eyewitness accounts or some other source and order of evidence, then we would know these things better; at least we would know them in a somewhat different way. *Fiction,* by contrast, gives us stories—a particular author telling us in his own fashion about made-up events—which are otherwise unknowable and which cannot otherwise exist, except by an accident the chances of which are interesting only to a few mathematicians. If we did not have one history of the French Revolution we would have another; we have in fact a great many and more are to come. But if Henry Fielding had not written *The History of Tom Jones, A Foundling,* if Charles Dickens had not written *The Posthumous Papers of the Pickwick Club,* there would be no others, and "Tom Jones" and "Mr. Pickwick" would be unknown to us, though there would be plenty of fictional foundlings and peripatetic old bachelors. Nor would there be any conceivable way of recovering them; it would not be understood that there was anything to recover.

Anyone can write a new history of an old topic, so long as evidence of some sort remains accessible; such evidence will include, of course, previous histories. But no one can write a second *Tom Jones* or *Pickwick,* only imitations.

✳ ✳ ✳

Ideally, then, *history* is descriptive, and its problem is verification. *Fiction* is constitutive or inventive, and its problem

---

* It is fundamentally *story* insofar as its basic unit of consideration is the event, in contrast to sociology, which is fundamentally analytic and concerned with the unit of the institution. The best sociology, however, is historical, analyzing the structure of institutions in the perspective of their temporal continuance.

is veracity. Both, as modes of narrative, are composed. But in the first case the order of the narrative is meant to reveal a preexistent order of actuality; in the second, though the narrative may imitate the form of a history, it is known from the first to be a particular writer's invention.

* * *

In modern literature the interesting fact is that these two modes, as we now understand them, have flourished together and have undergone crises of confidence together, as at present. In their strongest realizations they have shared, perhaps, the same essential audience: that conventionally educated elite, in the modern era a bourgeois elite, habituated to the discriminating consumption of certified goods and services (including intellectual entertainment) and relatively secure in position, leisure, and self-regard, which imagined that what it read and approved mattered not a little to the civil future. There was a brief time when it was thought that systematic history might replace fiction, as well as myth and a good deal of standard philosophy, in literate acceptance, as photography might replace painting or the scientific imagination, the religious. Rather the opposite has proved to be the case. Not only did the separate prestige and advance of historical inquiry help to liberate fiction from certain demands for reportorial and statistical realism; the latter-day failures of history to accomplish its own ambitious program for the accurate and comprehensive description of human activity in the dimension of time and change has even licensed a certain overconfident waywardness and libertinism of imagination among postmodernist writers of fiction. Whatever their artistic durability, their long-run capacity for truthfulness, the post-Hitler novels of Günter Grass and the plays of Rolf Hochhuth and Peter Weiss have rather provocatively undertaken a job that historians have hardly begun to contemplate doing: to provide an audience-that-matters with the common, sensible truth about its own immediate past.

The practice of fiction, for its part, has proved remarkably adaptable to various new formal opportunities for impressive statement that have opened to it in modern times, that is, that have been forged by other systems of explanation. One rival system it has skillfully assimilated is, of course, history, including the religious and, later, the psychiatric case history. A great deal of modern fiction has been, in the most literal way, "feigned history," Bacon's name for poetry; such feigning of the forms and assurances of historical narration has been a standard means of fulfilling fiction's wish to be known as seriously truthful. The two novels mentioned above, of Fielding and Dickens, are notable instances of the imitation of a specifically historical rendering of events—or so their titles pointedly advertise. *Tom Jones,* a "history" which is also a "comic epic in prose," which borrows theatrical devices for scene-building, and which comes equipped with its own anthology of critical justifications, manages to wear several different formal costumes. Like *Moby-Dick*—which fits the specifications for, at once, epic, tragedy, romance, encyclopedia, and chronicle of spiritual growth—Fielding's masterpiece gains authority by virtue of being, as to form, a perfect *mélange adultère de tout.* Writers of fiction have even borrowed from the special occupational anxiety of modern historians the theme of despair at ever accomplishing their ideal of perfected explanation—a theme independently invented, we recall, by the author of *The Life and Opinions of Tristram Shandy.* Gide's *Counterfeiters,* Faulkner's *Absalom, Absalom!,* Butor's *Degrees* are major examples of the formative use of this theme, each asserting the presence of a real and decisive history behind the broken story that conventional narration can put together.

✳ ✳ ✳

For historians, positivist illusions about a kind of descriptive exposition of past events that would have the authority over human understanding of scientific law (and therefore over future human action: philosophy teaching by incontestably certified example) increasingly seem only an incomprehensible memory. Not everything important that happens in human life gets recorded, even where there is widespread agreement on what should be. At the same time, records now multiply beyond any conceivable power we have of assimilating them. In fact, in a record-keeping age, measures are systematically taken by those conscious of participating in "history" to stay off the record whenever possible and to leave behind instead a pseudo-record that will tell their story according to their own preferred vision of it. Furthermore, not everything that we can imagine happening has yet happened— so we particularly think in an epoch of fantastically rapid and abrupt public transformations—and changes must be anticipated for which recorded history offers no sort of sensible model.*

In short, the mode, strictly practiced, of historical inquiry and explanation is inadequate to our narration-ordered consciousness of reality, though it remains essential to our moral and sentimental concern for verification. It is inadequate both with regard to the business of reconstructing an intelligible past and with regard to our desire, our need, to maintain awareness in some way of the full present possibilities of corporate human life.

In consequence, history is trapped into competition with fiction (and myth) in order to arrive at its own models of completeness.† The work of great narrative historians is thus as susceptible to literary analysis (phenomenological, structuralist) as the work of poets and fabulists. In professional circles the study of the various fictions of historical explanation may become wholly preoccupying and supersede standard tasks. The truth is that historians, too, participate in that "romance of order" which the young critic Laura Krugman has specified as the "novelist's privilege": the generic means by which the courage-establishing hypothesis is maintained that the world is, to intelligence, "controllable" and by which readers are given "the illusion of human potency" even in the face of those "forces of life that elude human will." In the

---

* Thus, perhaps, the success, from Mary Shelley to Arthur C. Clarke, of so formally crude and repetitive a genre as science fiction; and thus, too, the substitution, in think tanks and computer warrens, of game-playing for common historical wisdom.

† More immediately, it is trapped by a public demand for such models into competition with that useful species of retrospective journalism which offers the self-appointed public-that-matters comprehensive narratives of recent events accepted by this public as having special importance: the outbreak of war in 1914, the administrative development of the second Roosevelt Presidency, the fortunes of the House of Krupp.

long run the most durable historians, those whose work best survives fundamental changes in the realm of evidence, are those in whose work this "romance of order" is most firmly and shrewdly philosophical in its articulation. Professional historians nowadays pay little attention to David Hume; but if he is not the most perfect writer of historical narrative in the English language, who is?

✻ ✻ ✻

To sum up: *fiction* is the body of synthetic and, in detail, idiosyncratic narrative of imagined events, composed by identifiable authors. *History* is the body of synthetic and, in detail, self-duplicating narrative describing events presumed to have actually occurred, as recovered by inquiry and assembled according to some cohering fiction (in the nonnarrative sense) of intelligibility.

✻ ✻ ✻

What, last, of *myth?* Consideration here becomes more problematical still, for there is noticeably less agreement on the proper meaning and use of the word itself. Professor Northrop Frye, who has done much to rationalize the critical discussion of myth in literature, calls it, first, "a certain kind of narrative," or "a certain type of story" ("Myth, Fiction and Displacement" in *Fables of Identity*) . But he then rather confuses the matter by offering one prominent but by no means constant or exclusive feature of mythical narrative as definitive of the species as a whole. A myth, he writes, is "a story in which some of the chief characters are gods or other beings larger in power than humanity." The trouble with this is not that it does not precisely fit all or even most members of the class in question, though in fact it does not, but that it also fits a great deal of fiction, as here defined. It particularly fits that kind of fiction which is consciously devoted to the imitation or reactivation—the parody—of certain great myths.

The root meaning of the word makes a better starting point. Μῦθος, as is commonly known, means simply the thing said—the word, saying, or speech, but also (in the modality of narrative) the basic sequence of utterance required to set out the indispensable agents and occurrences of the story. The verb μῡθέομαι means "speak" or "tell," and there is an interesting Homeric cognate, μῡθολογενειν (*Odyssey,* xii, 450), which has the sense of repeating in so many words a tale that has been told before.

The emphasis lodged in this derivation thus falls on the way in which the special mode of mythical narrative exists in the consciousness of users. Works of fiction, we have every reason to think, are *composed,* and we know or might know who composed them (though some authors of fiction will claim to have done their composing under supernatural dictation). Myths, however, are *told,* and we do not know their particular origin. Histories, to complete the triad, are reassembled. That is, we do not know myth as a making, only as a telling; and there is, with myth, an element of unchangeability in the structure of the telling, the basic terms of which, as spoken, heard, repeated, have the authority of the ritually stabilized. Aristotle's special use of μῡθος in the *Poetics,* as that part of the imitated action which cannot be changed, though the poet may choose one or another segment of it to develop dramatically, fixes on this point. Myths, in fact, are not to be known or encountered directly but only through the performance of tellers, only, that is, in fictive versions, retellings. Is it possible to recognize the existence of a myth until several different tellings give us the means of detecting it as a common structural factor or presence? Perhaps the highest use of fiction is as a way of knowing and replenishing the consciousness of the mythic. But there is always this essential difference between fiction and myth, that in the one mode we know or can imagine an individual maker and in the other we cannot.* Myth— the very word insists—is in its mode of existence a species of narrative fundamentally different from composed fiction. It

---

* By this reckoning the Euhemerist fallacy is not primarily that there must be historical prototypes for mythical constructs but that such constructs are composed, constituted, in the same way as fictions; that they, too, are stories of which we may not know the name of the originator or formulator but would know if proper records existed. The Euhemerist doctrine also neglects the probability that the historical occurrence taken to be the source of a particular myth was itself directed and shaped by its agents' consciousness of mythical patterns, not to say imperatives.

is primarily collective, in the same way (as Ernst Cassirer powerfully argued) that language is collective, and indeed is best thought of by direct analogy to linguistic behavior. Most probably it is intrinsic to linguistic behavior; myth in this view is a primary constitutive structure of language use. It shares with language the quality of being knowable not in itself but only through the behavior it sponsors and is maintained by—which is, for both language and myth, the collective activity of uttering and reuttering (with all manner of local, idiomatic variation) certain relatively unchanging formulas of statement.

* * *

The topic stretches one's wits and needs always to be moored to commonest experience. I sometimes think that we never come nearer the praxis of myth than in the circulation of jokes, rumors, and odd stories, which all have both the structural unchangeability of the mythic and a mystifyingly potent element of collective endorsement and refinement. Among standard literary forms, ballads, with their fixity of main narrative terms and their surrealistic accretions and elisions of connective detail, bring us close to the mythic, perhaps even closer than folktales, since the music, the singing, intensify and stabilize the rites of their continuance, and since music itself is, in the behavior it exists by, a sequential language directly comparable to the narrative (and tonal) language of myth.*

* * *

Cassirer's association of language and myth, and of both with the fundamental process of human thought, has become prescriptive in contemporary thinking, and is regularly confirmed by the findings of cultural anthropology. Cassirer himself spoke of his work on language, myth, and symbolization as a "philosophical anthropology." In recent years Professor Lévi-

---

* For a fresh discussion of this resemblance, see Claude Lévi-Strauss, *Le Cru et le cuit*, chap. i.

Strauss in particular has deepened understanding of the role of myth in the constitution of human society and human thought; and though his formulations are not designed to serve literary analysis, they seem to me directly applicable to the description of myth as a basic modality of literary statement.

In *La Pensée sauvage* Lévi-Strauss identifies myths as "constitutive units," or "classificatory schemes," for the ongoing business of dealing with (thinking about, or upon, or into) the perceived universe, natural and social. They function, with respect to thought, as "synthesizing operators between ideas and facts, thereby turning the latter into *signs*."* But the purpose of this significatory classification is not merely to control or exorcize, one by one, the constituents of an impinging world of contingency. It is at least equally, and perhaps primarily, to stabilize and extend classification itself and the activity of formulaic speaking by which it is secured. That is to say, myth explains not so much what to think about events and objects but in what direction and with what degree of force to think and how precisely to situate the constituents of the thinkable. It tells what kind and degree of seriousness to attribute to the various elements of the self-constituting, self-organizing, self-maintaining world of human discourse. Taking the particular case of the mass of Amerindian myths concerning the origin of clan and tribal names, Lévi-Strauss concludes: "Their role seems to be demarcative, rather than aetiological; they do not really explain an origin or indicate a cause." Rather, we might add here, they serve to attribute to the species of fact in question the element or quality of the causative, or of causativeness, that is, *generic* origination. Such myths define, by the selection-and-arrangement of appropriate terms that constitutes their form, that species or class of importance peculiar to the occasion they embrace and thus indicate, formally, the appropriate gravity and respect to be

---

* Professor Lévi-Strauss is a remarkable master of discursive prose, and his terminology frequently has an imaginative suggestiveness that both stimulates and puzzles. Does his choice of *opérateur* deliberately recall the word's use to describe the medium in occultist exercises? Does it allude, further, to Mallarmé's appropriation of this term for the character and function of poets?

accorded them by their audience. They thus control, as norms of consciousness, the ceremony of their own continuance. Certain myths are to be told or spoken only at certain hours or seasons, and each one has its proper performative sequence and scope. Myth, in fact, is inseparable from ritual, and it appears to have a correspondingly intimate association with religious life, where the binding of men to each other and of speech ("the word") to action and perception is at its most intense.*

*   *   *

It cannot be said too often that what we have to do with in discussing myth is really another way of *thinking* than the systematic propositional reasoning we usually have in mind in affirming that prized function of human intelligence. Simplifying hugely, we may say that there are two related sources of common confusion on the subject. One is the assumption that the object of thought is always production of a definite quantum of positive knowledge, an assumption that has not been discouraged by the explosive advance of modern technological science. The other is the assumption that for human affairs the proper end-result of thinking is belief, that is, a

---

* This was Cassirer's conclusion, but in writing about the matter he sometimes failed to keep pace with his own philosophical pioneering, as occasionally in ascribing priority to the one over the other, ritual over myth. In *The Myth of the State*, a late work, he wrote, "It has become clear that rite is a deeper and much more perdurable element in man's religious life than myth" (p. 24) , and later, "mythical stories of gods or heroes . . . . are nothing but the interpretations of rites" (p. 28). But there is neither categorical nor experimental ground for either of these assertions, which deal with facts of human development that appear to be unknowable. Hierarchical nineteenth-century concepts of evolutionary sequence did not easily give way, not even in the thought of a writer as instrumental as Cassirer was in overthrowing them. Another formulation in the same passage is more satisfactory, in simply attributing to myth and ritual different—and complementary—practical functions: "Myth is the *epic* element in primitive religious life; rite is the *dramatic* element" (p. 28). In the one we tell out, in the other we act out, a structure of sacred consciousness. But of course the ceremony of the telling is itself a rite, and the performance of rites accords, so to speak, with mythical scripts. Man is the language-using animal and, some physiological functions aside, nowhere acts—not even, it is now argued, in the darkness of the unconscious—without recourse to formulas of speech.

propositional fix or tenet system that we can put more credit in, with regard to behavioral necessities, than any other like it, an assumption that is in large part a consequence of the prolonged contest for ideological and political dominance, since the Reformation, among rival churches, sects, estates, and national societies. It hardly seems an accident that the slow philosophic correction or transcendence of these errors has taken place alongside the intensive anthropological study of non-European cultures—not to speak of the widening rejection, in a period of obvious breakdown, of the exigencies of Western politics as normative for human choice and value.

It is not possible here to do more than identify these further considerations, which are philosophical and political, perhaps also religious. But the probability is that differences on issues of specifically literary analysis and classification cannot be settled or even understood without reference to them.

*　*　*

To distinguish the special character of mythical thought from propositional or ideological thinking, Lévi-Strauss (in *La Pensée sauvage,* chap. i) draws an amusing contrast between two kinds of workman, the engineer and the *bricoleur* (a term which defies translation: it combines the sense of someone who does odd jobs in an unsystematic, pottering way and someone who introduces antic and extraneous elements into sports and games) . The engineer defines a project, assembles the precise equipment or "instrumental set" needed for it, and carries it through in the most efficient way, rather as a mathematician aims at the minimal formula in which the solution to a given problem may be fully stated. The *bricoleur,* occupying himself with a comparable project, is not comparably direct in his treatment of it but positively devious and refractory. He uses not a limited set of instruments appropriate to that one job but everything he has at hand; a set of instruments, that is, which "bears no precise relation to the current project, or indeed to any particular project, but is the contingent result of all the occasions there have been to renew or enrich the stock or to maintain it with the remains of previous constructions or destructions."

The *bricoleur's* performance is as much ceremonial as practical, and it includes a built-in principle of expansion and elaboration that rejects shortcuts or time-and-effort-saving steps; for some of his tools and materials have indeed been "collected or retained on the principle that 'they may always be of use.'" It is not, however, purely ceremonial; the *bricoleur* does perform real work. But he does it the long way round, as in a game the object of which is not to win but to try out all known strokes and engage to their own satisfaction all available personnel. So with any one task the *bricoleur* first "interrogates all the heteroclite objects of which his treasury is composed to discover what each of them could 'signify,'" thus contributing to the definition of a new set that differs from a purely instrumental one by the principle according to which its parts are disposed and by the refusal to exclude anything for reasons of efficiency.*

The analogy makes concrete this basic truth about the mythic mode of knowing and the operation of mythical narration: they are fundamentally comprehensive and plenary, or accruent. Professor Frye touches on this point in speaking of "an odd tendency" in myths "to stick together and build up bigger structures" ("Myth, Fiction and Displacement"). This tendency is not odd at all but of the essence. More than anything else, more certainly than any assumption that the events of myth "really happened," it is what puts myth into "the special category of seriousness" by which Frye usefully distinguishes myth from folktale. The full reference of myth is always to the conscionable totality of identified experience, and the story told should be understood as making complete sense only when placed in combination with all other myths. At any one time this ultimate combination is a *terminus ad quem* rather than a manageable achievement. The instinct for it, however, controls our actual reading experience more than analytic criticism commonly recognizes: do we not begin to compose, for example, an ideal narrative universe in which

---

* The distinction corresponds, incidentally, to Marx's differentiation of two basic kinds of work: that in which the performer makes controlling use of the "working conditions" and that (held to be characteristic of all capitalist and machine-age production) in which "the working conditions make use of the worker."

events in the career of Hamlet or Ishmael and events in the career of any other significant human agent whom literature or history makes impressive to us in some way coexist?* The basic function or purpose of myth is thus not *explanation* (in the sense of interpretation) but *recovery, preservation, organization, continuance.* It is to bring the multiplicity of things that are known about, and the speech terms by which they are known, into an order in which they will continue to exist and be serviceable. There is a principle of generosity in this that the myths of literary criticism regularly stand in need of. The essential character of myth is plenitude and accommodation, above all the accommodation of the collective mind of men to their own incessant experience.

* * *

For practical criticism it is important to keep in mind the modal differences and also the points of contact, the functional symbiosis, between myth and fiction. Professor Kermode's stimulating inquiry in *The Sense of an Ending*, for example, seems to me unnecessarily obstructed early on by a wrong-angled opposition of these terms that derives, it appears, from political considerations ("ethical" is the author's word), specifically an honorable concern to express political disgust and fear. Myth, to Kermode, is what the controlled structures of fiction "degenerate into . . . whenever they are not consciously held to be fictive." The example provided, however, makes clear that this definition is quite arbitrary, or outer-directed. (It entails, I think, a grossly oversimplified psychology of assent, according to which the mind operates either by blind faith or by a fully knowledgeable critical, and self-critical, skepticism.) "In this sense," the passage continues, "anti-Semitism is a degenerate fiction, a myth; and *Lear* is a fiction." In a world haunted by Buchenwald, counterinvective can be a virtue, and there is certainly a need to name and denounce any metaphysical agency of so great a horror as un-

---

* All this remains true even if particular myths, like particular elements in the *bricoleur*'s backyard, are mislaid or wear out or accidentally get welded into others. Myth is not, as narrative, of the type of history, but it indubitably has its history—if only we knew it.

equivocally as possible, even if that agency appears in other functions to have high-placed defenders and virtuous-seeming apologists. But "myth"—if there is any truth at all in the descriptions offered above—is not the word for what engineered the death camps.* If mythical assertion is comprehensive and plenary, then the "fiction" of anti-Semitism is "degenerate" exactly because it involves a false, viciously reductive interpretation of a body of life-death, kinship-alien mythology. It is not a myth but a maniacal delusion—and the strongest warning yet of what can happen when the conservative and accommodating economy of the mythic (the sum of the narrational habituations of living culture) is subverted by an ideologically fueled struggle for power and revenge, and by the runaway timetable of modern technological systematization. As a fiction, its relation to myth is exactly the opposite to that given in Kermode's formula; that is, it is a fiction which has murderously failed to fulfill the highest potentiality of fiction-making—the replenishing of the expansive consciousness of the mythic.

* * *

If *fiction* gives us stories, more or less truthful, of what might have happened or could happen in any given human instance, *myth* is story in which the uttered sequence of happenings remains open to the fullest collective apprehension of the universe of causes and effects. Fiction is closed programmatic thinking—but can be more or less generously, answeringly, conducted, and that more-or-less makes a great difference. It is what evaluative criticism is properly concerned with. Myth is open and absorptive narrative thinking, generous by definition; and the strongest cultural obstacle to the murderous narrowing down of fictitious explanation represented by anti-

---

* Thinking so leads Kermode inexorably into his own version of the guardian's suspicion which he has effectively criticized in others: the suspicion that the practice of imaginative literature, precisely in proportion to its seriousness and ambitiousness, is not only incompatible with the pursuit of justice but a major cause of injustice, and worse. It may of course be just that. So may every other elected human activity. The relevant doctrine here is possibly that of Original Sin, or, in modern terms, Original Alienation.

Semitism or by race and class hatred of any kind is the persistence and extension of myth, so understood. In these terms the ultimate justification of pluralistic as opposed to merely egalitarian democracy would be that it contributes better than other civil systems to this persistence.

* * *

The organized plenitude of myth requires social, behavioral mediation, and in the anthropologist's view everything that takes place among persons is engaged in such mediation. As an object of understanding this plenitude is, to repeat, an ideal. But it is an ideal that may provide the best objective criterion for the critical discrimination of the structures of fiction. Let us apply it to criticism of the novel (to concentrate on modern literature's major compositional form). Historically the novel has proceeded by a series of tactical departures from its own formal inheritance, and these departures have regularly been in the direction of a wider or a more intense truthfulness. Each time this happens we find an apparent rejection of the novel-as-found—the work of "mere fiction," according to prevailing conventions—and a corresponding effort to recover some measure of the expansive truthfulness, the "seriousness," of myth. The major history of the novel has been in large part the history of a series of cognitively expansive antinovels. Let me cite an instance that may not immediately come to mind. In his "advertisement" for *The Antiquary,* the "Waverley" author apologized for having broken with established proprieties of form in fiction. "I have been more solicitous to describe manners minutely," he wrote, "than to arrange in any case an artificial and combined narrative, and have but to regret that I felt myself unable to unite these two requisites of a good Novel." The self-deprecation seems sincere. No doubt Scott felt, as a naturally deferential and conservative man, that he was at fault in having sacrificed to his own special ends the kind of formal organization ("artificial and combined") he so admired in Fielding and in his remarkable contemporary Jane Austen. Yet he here speaks directly to the set of compositional decisions that were to make him a revolutionary force throughout the European world, and not only in the writing of prose fiction. For by "describing manners minutely" he meant nothing less than introducing into his novel—through his concrete allegiance to the data of Scottish history, folklore, balladry, social habituation, and linguistic usage, and through the sheer pedantry of his respect for the ways of speaking by which all these things lived in ordinary consciousness—a plenary treatment of available materials that has, in the performance, the very character of the mythic. It richly supported, in this instance, the new nineteenth-century mythology of organic nationalism; also the new humanitarian concern for social justice. Even the absence of stylistic distinction in Scott reflects this opening out of fiction to myth, for myths, unlike fictions, have no particular locutionary style; their distinctive properties are structural.

Scott's apology is the apology of all those forced back, for whatever reason, from the restrictive compromisings of settled fictional convention to the open, outreaching sprawl and voluminousness—the largesse—of mythic narration. His impact on the consciousness of his age may be taken as a measure of the complicity of the mythic in the profoundest organization of civil society. The case suggests, to repeat, the possibility of an objective criterion of value in fictional form —and does so all the better for *not* involving a writer who, as we say, wrote like an angel, with that mysterious charm of voice and of artistic coherence which always commands respect even if impressive in no other signal way and for which daimonic possession has not yet been wholly displaced as the most satisfactory explanation. Scott's gracelessness as a craftsman meant that his practical influence on the composition of fiction would be short-lived and diffusionary, and essentially unrecoverable to later times—compare him to Dickens in this respect—but it also serves to isolate more effectively the substantive or constitutive aspect of form I am dealing with here.

This criterion may be stated fairly briefly. That work of fiction will have an extraordinary interest and importance, a grander capacity to persuade, in which the author has put into combination a greater rather than lesser multiplicity of familiar ways of speaking—more precisely, of the familiar *substances* of human speech and discourse, the "things that are said," in love, school, politics, the market, gossip, superstition and fantasy, law, philosophy, standard literature, work, games, ritual, prayer. It must of course be a new combination, though every element in it traces to a traditional and recognizable source.* And it must be carried through in a way that substantially respects the locutionary character of each of its components, and that at the same time can take quick and regular advantage of the opportunities thus created for refreshing any one of these components by putting it in relation with another or others having special appropriateness. The tonal blend resulting will vary, like the choice of formal genre, according to the governing rhetorical intention. It may, for example, be mainly critical and corrective, an ironic counterpointing meant to deflate spurious and falsely valued expressive currencies. Or it may be optative and celebratory, aiming at a richer expressive harmony, a symbolic concord. The true masterworks of our literature almost invariably do both things, simultaneously correcting and reaffirming the "things said" at the complementary centers of human experience. But whatever special tactics are used, it is this element of combinative resourcefulness in a great work of fiction, rather than lexical fanciness or ingenuities in story arrangement, that permanently arrests interest and makes changes in the history of literate consciousness.

That work of fiction, in brief, has most authority which most abundantly opens itself to the modality of the mythic. But to be a mythmaker, to move toward myth, is not simply to invent new fictions, including exploratory or ironic reconstructions of famous individual myths. It is rather to compose by way of continuously refreshing the substance of what people characteristically say in each other's presence up and down the whole range, or some great part of it, of purposeful human utterance. Joyce, for example, is not a great writer simply because he reasserted the Ulysses schema (among others), recognizing its singular applicability to modern social and spiritual life, but because, in addition, he was a master twice over of

---

* The more solidly traditional and commonly recognizable, the better. So Proust: "For there is a stronger analogy between the instinctive life of the mass of persons and the talent of a great writer, which is only an instinct religiously hearkened to in the midst of silence, an instinct perfected and understood, than with the superficial verbiage and fluctuating standards of the certified judges." (*Le Temps retrouvé*, chap. iii.)

languages, of narrational formulas and dialects; he had a superb ear, and he systematically applied it over an extraordinary scale of speech quantities, not omitting those formalized by special disciplines of science and scholarship. It is no accident that he flourished when he did; he is the great novelist of the anthropological breakthrough in human understanding.

* * *

The sanctifying example of this creative and re-creative use of narrative form in Western literature is contained in the story written out in the four Gospels. In accordance with its transcendent seriousness, it is offered there as a true history, a scripture; but what in fact gives it its sequential authority over our understanding is its unbroken command of the characteristic largesse of mythical narration. Thus we hear it as above all a new music. So at least it was said by the author of the last great triumph of the modernist insurgence in European literature, *Doctor Zhivago,* in a choric passage that, among other things, sublimates the myth of Orpheus into the commemorated ministry of Jesus, which is seen as an irresistible narrative reconnaissance into the very substance of common human life. Zhivago's uncle is speaking:

> Wait, I will tell you what I think. I think that if the beast drowsing within man could be held in check by prisons or by threats of retribution beyond the grave, then the supreme emblem of humanity would be the lion tamer in the circus with his whip and not the prophet who sacrificed himself. But that's just the point—what has for centuries been raising man above the animal and carrying him upwards is not the cudgel but a music: the irresistibility of unarmed truth, the attraction of its example. Until now it has been assumed that what is most important in the Gospels are the ethical maxims and the rules contained in the commandments; but for me the most important thing is that Christ speaks in parables taken from daily life, that he explains the truth in terms of the everyday world. At the base of this lies the idea that it is communion between mortals that is immortal and that the whole of life is symbolic because it is meaningful. (Chap. ii, sec. 10).

It may be worth observing that this declaration comes early in the novel and that the socially concerned man (a dogmatic Tolstoyan) to whom it is spoken can make no sense of it.

Literature
and the Measure of "Reality"

> When our sensations have no self-assurance, everything must
> be a lens.
> —Robert Lowell, after Montale, "News from Mount Amiata"

"Realism" is so unstable a critical concept and has been used
to characterize or defend so many schemes for replacing one
type of literary artifice with another that, except for one inconvenient historical fact, the sensible course at this point
might well be to scrap it altogether. Merely by its long survival, a slogan word since the middle of the nineteenth century, it has become as obstructive a scandal for anyone devoted
to the clarification of terminology as "romanticism" ever was.
That fact, however, makes all the difference. It is simply that
writers themselves have gone on invoking an idea of "realism,"
or seeking to reestablish it in some new way, or inventing programmatic locutions to take its place, as if indeed it had some
positive meaning. Since first being adopted for use—coincidentally, we may note, with the widening establishment of a
free manufacturers' economy and the invention of shoddy as
a licensed class of merchandise—"realism" has served certain

An invitation to join a humanities conference on literary realism at York
University, Toronto, November 1-2, 1968, produced the present discourse,
which is less a statement on the topic specified than a reconnaissance
patrol in search of issues that stand nearer the actual choices forced on
writers, and critics, in a time of unchecked civil crisis. An imminent
national election below the border, as well as the deepening abomination
of the Indochina war, nagged at the consciousness of everyone present and
intruded more than once upon conference business.

purposes of product identification and discrimination which outweigh the word's essential indefiniteness. Writers and critics, feeling its practical force, have taken this indefiniteness in stride and have written drafts against it with the assurance of market insiders as to its remittance value, as Ezra Pound did when he chose to praise an odd new book of poems called *Prufrock and Other Observations* "for its fine tone, its humanity, and its realism," adding, with a wave of the hand, "for all good art is realism of one sort or another."

Insofar as criticism, whatever philosophic rigor it properly aspires to, is dependent on the primary existence of another species of discourse—the discourse of authors whose first purpose is not category-making but invention and generation—it must resign itself to this stubborn currency. The student of literature must simply accept the persistence of "realism" as a practical standard. In this instance as in others, he will be wise to abide by Veblen's rule, as it deserves to be known, about the use of "unsophisticated vulgar concepts, with whatever content of prejudice and sentiment they carry," when talking about the real world of ordinary behavior. If one is to avoid mandarin irrelevance and paralogistic deception in describing actual human institutions, Veblen wrote, "one must resort to words and concepts that express the thoughts of the men whose habits of thought constitute the institutions in question."* The institution in question here is a body of literature, modern literature, in which, through innumerable variations of style and strategy, "realism of one sort or another" has remained a generating intention and the substantial presence or absence of "reality" a principal measure of virtue.

Of course confusion over what specifically "realism"

---

* "Mr. Cummings's Strictures on 'The Theory of the Leisure Class'" (1899), reprinted in *Essays in Our Changing Order* (1934).

Fifty years further along, the philosopher J. L. Austin spoke to roughly the same point when he observed that such commonly and freely used words are those most deserving of respectful attention. For they embody "all the distinctions men have found worth drawing, and the connexions they have found worth marking, in the lifetime of many generations," and therefore are likely to be "more sound, since they have stood up to the long test of the survival of the fittest, and more subtle, at least in all ordinary and reasonably practical matters, than any you or I are likely to think up in our arm-chairs of an afternoon—the most favored alternative method." ("A Plea for Excuses," *Philosophical Papers*, p. 130.)

means is increased, as in the preceding sentence, by the fact that "reality" is, unavoidably, a first cognate. If we use this vocabulary at all, it seems colloquially reasonable to say that those works of literature are realistic which have more rather than less of reality about them, which are more directly expressive than not of the character of things-as-they-are, the *res extensae* of the given world. But postulations about "reality" are likely to be even more diverse and problematical than critical appeals to a standard of "realism." The one clear post-Kantian principle is that "reality," however deployed as a linguistic term, cannot belong exclusively to objective conditions as such. Certainly in the pragmatic fabrications of art, "reality" is always a factor of consciousness first of all; that is to say, it is always symbolic, and what it symbolizes is a particular apprehension of the norms and conditions prevailing in the world of behavior (including all relations between knower and things known, transacting agents and the circumstances acted into or against) that is posited, imaginatively and dialectically, through the writer's extended performance. "Reality" in literature has never been merely descriptive or reflective but moral and creative, a function of the writer's own essential behavior and not simply of policy decisions concerning the management of some stockpile of available subject matter.

Two broad historical propositions may be useful at this point:

1. The more we look into the matter, the more we are compelled to agree that "realism" has always been a relative term. The indefiniteness of what is involved in any particular appeal to it follows from its invariably having primary reference to something other than the precise definition of its own formal character. We understand it best by seeing what it opposes. As a measure of virtue "realism" has regularly been put forward in response to a sentiment of something acutely unsatisfactory in existing literary conventions and hence also of something repugnant in the settled contemporary practice of the *activity* of literature within the vast institutional conspiracy that at any given moment we call society.

2. Consequently the fact that "realism" has survived so long as a procedural imperative may be taken as a sign of a pro-

longed and continuing crisis in the civil standing of literature and of the concrete events constituting literary history. In the modern era this has meant in particular the ordered context of classical and humanist learning and the cultural habituations supporting it, which is to say that context of thought and attitude within which the great received works in our recognized literary tradition have mostly emerged and within which they are officially "studied," as we say. It is not the performed substance and design of past masterpieces from which moral admiration keeps falling away—for masterpieces by definition are works which remain formally beautiful and admirable to us even when we can no longer imagine anyone's proposing to write them in that particular way—but rather the sense of what sort of civil order must have fostered their creation and also their public continuance as objects of prestige and consequence; the sense, too, of what kinds of personal behavior, what complicities and connivances, were required of those who produced them and may still be required of those whose occupation is to profess them or celebrate them. This prolonged crisis is, in a word, a crisis of vocation; it requires writers, and critics, not simply to learn how to do good work of some defined and accepted type but to discover in the first place (like anyone living in revolutionary times) "what is to be done" and then to justify doing it; and it is the matter I have chiefly in mind in this paper. The reality of such a crisis and the need to come to terms with it are the chief premise in everything that follows.

Academic discussions of "realism" and the footing of literature in "reality" have in the main taken a different tack. The concern is with problems of expressive intention and technique (what structures of actual life, natural, social, psychological, moral and historical, does the writer mean to call our attention to, and what formal tactics does he use to represent them?) or with underlying philosophical issues of truthfulness and validity in representation (what is meant by saying that a work possesses "the air of reality" or that it is "true to life"?) . This is probably because it is mainly in the academy that "realism" is felt to need systematic description. For it is in the academy that the bullying competition of other modern systems for grasping structures of reality is most intensely felt: the various systems of scientific inquiry, with their authoritative procedures of experimental classification and validation, and the broad system of historical and sociological investigation, professionally committed to a species of documentary or descriptive positivism and also to demonstrating the legitimacy of the documentary-empirical method itself as a preferred discipline.

Looking back, we can see that all three of these reality-seeking systems of discourse—literary realism, experimental science, the documentary-empirical method for doing history and sociology—came into general practice at about the same time; they are part and parcel of what we mean by "modern" in the history of thought. We see also that an element of theoretical naïveté was present in all three systems from the start, though this did not prevent the carrying through of a lot of fine work; perhaps it was essential to their taking hold as systems and becoming institutionalized. In any event much of the subsequent inner history of each system has involved revisionist efforts to displace such naïveté with a more sophisticated understanding of method, only to have it return unnoticed in new disguises. We may even speculate that its persistence in some form, its power to impose itself (in the minds of new generations of students and practitioners) even on those structures of critical thought devised specifically to overthrow it, is normative in the life of the mind; an inevitable part of the ebb and flow, the natural dialectic, of critical awareness. Certainly naïveté of this kind in the working assumptions supporting the inherited practice of literature has provided contemporary writing with a high proportion of its prime target-occasions: all those manifestos attacking the pretensions of the "old" novel to explain or penetrate the real world of experience and claiming to substitute a new mode of fictive creation that builds on some bare undeluded encounter with phenomenal and occupational realities; all those Borges-tinted fables, dear to writers from provinces like Argentina or Poland or the American university campus where real civil existence *is* fantastic and absurd, luxuriating in the discovery that "fiction" is always and inevitably a mere making-things-up.

The gross fictiveness of fiction, the practical absurdity of its grander pretensions, have long been appreciated as offering a first-rate subject for novelists; consider Cervantes, or Sterne. For modern novelists this issue has become the lion in the path. The novelist Edouard in Gide's *Les Faux-monnayeurs* (1925) is a famous case of the naïve realist and the reckoning reserved for him, Edouard's by no means simple-minded or unreasoned ambition to put "everything" into his own novel running aground on the gratuitous tragedy of young Boris's suicide, an "indecency," as he says, that he is unable to use.* Another is the protagonist of Michel Butor's fine novel *Degrés* (1960), with his self-destroying scheme for composing a record of the totality of life, all persons, events, relationships, materials of discourse, causes and ongoing vibrations, during one class hour in a Paris *lycée*. Another is the heroine of Doris Lessing's *The Golden Notebook* (1963), also a failed novelist, in desperation attempting to write down the totality of events during a single day of her life; this scheme, too, ends in a disorder that engulfs its initiator.

Yet another (the list could be made very long) is the author of the ultimate in unfinishable books who is described in Peter Weiss's story "Abschied von den Eltern" (1961), the ex-mathematician-engineer-economist Hieronymus. The work that occupies him is a "universal book," a book comprehending "all aspects of everyday life" and hence making all other books "superfluous." In fact he is not writing but compiling it, a giant collage containing "countless units he had cut out of the mountains of old books and magazines"—and crammed shoe boxes and fragment-stuffed card indexes—that have turned his living quarters into an immense disordered landscape. Yet it is a book "destined to remain incomplete," which in any case is "only a sideline" for him (though he is totally absorbed in it), the thing that really interests him being the problem of *lasting*, of surviving through the chaos of actual existence by, in his case, translating the whole of it into literature. The scheme is mad, of course. Yet it is not madder than that modern pattern of "everyday life" it

---

* Yet this ambition is nobly conceived and reminds us that any significant "realism" must aim not only at an incidental accuracy of treatment but at fullness and completeness as well.

seeks to put in order; moreover from the point of view of literary history, we can say for it that it merely re-creates on the side of an insupportably exhaustive prose realism the rational purity of Mallarmé's antirealist formula for the creation of a supreme poetry: "Tout au monde existe pour aboutir à un livre."*

This running together of the program for descriptive realism, stretched into absurdity, and the historic antithesis represented by Mallarmé's abstracting and purifying symbolism, underscores my initial point: that the matter of "realism," in literature, is a cover for a deeper concern with the behavioral and ethical reality of the writer's vocation. To concentrate on questions of technique, or upon underlying philosophic problems of validating the writer's special apprehension, is to miss something fundamental to the way in which the standard of realism was actually raised. Practitioners of literary realism have themselves rarely shown any fine methodological scrupulousness about descriptive consistency and verifiability. Their work, it is commonly realized, can be as fantasy-ridden, as full of subjective distortion, as anything in the Romantic or Gothic modes. This is why, for example, realist and naturalist fiction proves so wonderfully available to psychoanalytic readings, a carnival, as with Zola or Henry James, of phallic or uterine shapes, fecal accumulations, castration traumas and reified death projections.

Further, when we go back to the original manifestoes of realism, we find them, too, curiously haphazard about formal principles. Ezra Pound, interested as always in clearing the way for essential tasks, once declared that "the whole case for realism" was stated in the Goncourts' preface to *Germinie Lacerteux* (1865) and there was no need to spend more time on it; "one can not improve the statement." A good tip, perhaps, but when we look it up, what do we find? The "roman vrai," say the Goncourts, is first of all one that comes off the

---

* Hieronymus' work-in-progress resembles the "new Bible" being planned by Boris and the author in *Tropic of Cancer:* a book to be written "anonymously" with contributions from "all those who have anything to say" and to be called *The Last Book.*

common street, that brings "les basses classes" into the narrative light. In an age professing egalitarian social principles, do not these fellow beings of ours—"ce monde sous le monde" —also have a right to effective representation, in our novels as in the political order? Other elements are proposed by the way, a "clinical" treatment of love, a style of emotional and social analysis that borrows from the objectivity of modern science, a concern for the actual moral history of present times; but the principal question for the Goncourts is one of common justice, the right even of the least of persons to have their lives and fortunes brought into the circle of public sympathy, and thus the further advancement of the modern religion of humanity. It is a question, in brief, of literature's responsibility to the general life of the human community.

And in this regard it may well appear that the standard of "realism" in literary matters makes most sense, or at least can be most precisely defined, as a standard for criticism, including the critical element in all creative effort. It is characteristic of the beginnings of the realist epoch in literature that a general principle of reflective intelligence was seen to be involved. We find this principle stated plainly, and twice over, at the beginning of a famous text not usually grouped among the manifestos of "realism," Matthew Arnolds' great essay on "The Function of Criticism at the Present Time," published, as it happens, in the same decade as the Goncourts' preface. "It is the business of the critical power," Arnold declared, "in all branches of knowledge, theology, philosophy, history, art, science, to see the object as in itself it really is." Not an activity, he added, for which the mass of men or their popular leaders will ever show much zeal, being caught up as they must be in "the rush and roar of practical life" and the warping compulsions of *interest.* But it is just that separation of critical reality-seeking from the ordinary compromises of social interest that can give it its unique value.

Matthew Arnold's understanding of the service to be performed by criticism was based squarely on the old quasi-clerical "humanist" conception (which it brilliantly refreshed) of how cultural health and value are generated and maintained in society, by what "disinterested" enterprise of enlightened and discriminating "propagation," to use his key terms.

A century later this stands as an elitist conception, in the catchword of present-day cultural radicalism, though the elite thus defined is no doubt nobly dedicated. The assertion of disinterestedness makes us uneasy nowadays in policy arguments; we are not merely giving in to cynicism if we feel that it cannot be accepted as a basis for claiming special prerogatives and exemptions, even while we understand that the illusion of possessing it may well be the great constitutive fantasy of every professionalized branch of knowledge. But the unadorned principle Arnold proposed transcends, as it is stated, the apostolic or treasure-house theory of culture he joined it to. Times and ideologies have changed and changed again in the intervening century; yet this modern principle of seeing the thing, event, activity, as it "really is" is the one we still swear by—philosophically indefinite as it may be—if only for want of conscionable alternatives.

Just at present it is a principle that most frequently results in the subordination of technical and formal issues to broader considerations of social usage and consequence. Contemporary anthropology (daughter, Lévi-Strauss has said, to the whole modern era of programmed exploitation and rationalized violence, on a global scale), not less than Marxist or communitarian radicalism, directs us with fresh urgency to look for the social contract or compromise that is served by every customary practice, the practice of literature included. Our understanding of what any given object "really is" becomes inseparable from our understanding of how it exists and has functioned in civil practice. With literary objects this means the full range of its common social uses, for the writer who creates it, the business establishment that publishes him and the particular social community that composes his readership, and also the larger civil community in which writing, publishing, bookselling, reading books, are licensed and rewarded activities like any other that can somehow buy its way.

One of the purest instances I have seen recently of a critical statement determined in just this fashion to "see the object as in itself it really is" is a review of Sol Yurick's new novel, *The Bag*, written by Carl Oglesby, a founder of SDS and, within the circuit of my own awareness, one of a small number of embattled contemporaries whose struggle to secure a just vocation, as writer and citizen, may prove exemplary for our era. It is a review notable for the completeness of its disengagement from the fiction of disinterestedness. The hero of Yurick's story is a novelist haunted by the gap between literary ideals of an uncompromising honesty of witness and the cynicism of a social order that will market his book for him whatever line of argument it takes and support him as it supports anybody who can divert it a little while observing, however grudgingly, certain basic rules of behavior. The fact that the book amounts to a critical rejection of this social order only makes things worse. Carl Oglesby sums up as follows the occupational "bag" Yurick's novelist is in (characteristically placing himself there, too, though his review is being written, all uncompromisingly, for the radical journal *Ramparts*) :

> Novel writing (like reviewing) implies a continuity of culture via its institutions. The novel surrounds itself with tacit assumptions by embedding itself in an actual world of publishers, distribution systems, agents, contracts, stores, buyers, critics, etc. It becomes a social commodity and hence an implicit affirmation of the society's institutional powers of veto and approval. It reifies the concrete world order in which novel writing is one job among others. When the novel comes forward to attack that very world, the artist is forced to recognize himself in a relation of duplicity: form affirming what content negates, gesture undercut by the ground on which it is made. (*Ramparts*, August 24, 1968.)

And the critic is compelled to observe that Sol Yurick himself, unlike his hero, has not withdrawn *his* manuscript but adds that this contradictory surrender to the rules of the game has not been dishonestly camouflaged. At least, Oglesby remarks, the author has not tried to joke his way out in the evasive manner of black humor; he has not equivocated by means of special story contrivances, magical escape-hatches, an appeal to the presumptive sanctions of satire or parody; "he has taken the measure"—and fairly—"of his own servitude."

Implicitly in the Goncourts' preface, directly in Carl Oglesby's review, the critical issue has become this: in a society riddled with inequities, corrupted beyond reversion by its own ruling system of production and consumption, what turn must the writer's work take to justify his occupational existence? What effort of mind and spirit must it embody to gain reality, within the order that materially sustains it, not merely as a commodity in trade but as a new force, an extension and perhaps enhancement—beyond routine accommodation—of the common fortune? Accepting the civil and behavioral coordinates thus erected, I should like to try to say with some preliminary definiteness what it might mean to speak of a literary work, or of any social activity, as satisfying the test of "reality," as being in itself "real" or "unreal." For in a commonsense fashion we know that these words can indeed stand for something in experience that is palpable and, by appropriate means, measurable, something hard to speak of so plainly in any other way; can indicate judgments which provide a rational basis for further action or choice—as when a poet cries out, "Unreal City," or a sensible woman tells us, unspitefully, of another, "but she's a real woman."

For reasons not guaranteed to be untainted by numerological magic my formulation will be threefold:

1. A first measure of "reality" is objective, or pragmatic. That has "reality," we may say, which attracts people to participate actively in it, to contribute their own assenting being to its being. In a rough way, short of any Kantian universality, a rule of numbers applies here; also, more decisively, a rule of intensity and continuance. In politics, for example, by the rule of numbers it may well turn out next Tuesday that enough Americans of voting age will actively endorse the presumption that the Republican candidate really is conceivable as a President of the United States to make that presumption the constitutional reality. But by the rule of participatory intensity the numbed resignation with which great masses of the electorate appear to be moving to this decision signifies that, whatever the constitutional outcome, the thing itself may remain quite extraordinarily in doubt. The reality that will be demonstrated is merely that, through force of habit, or want of alternatives, there is still a degree of belief in the magic of elections.* So in the circumstance of literature, there

---

* The 1968 presidential election was to take place the Tuesday following. It may be remembered how the palpable unreality of what seemed about

must be a certain intensity of responsive absorption among the readers of a work, whatever their numbers—an imaginative quickening within the act of reading—in order for it really to be "read" at all and hence to enter into real existence as a work of literature.

2. A second measure is phenomenological and symbolic. (It will be noticed that these three categories of the "real" overflow one another as phases of a single condition or process of being.) That has "reality" for us which actively corresponds to our residual sense of the conformations of experience and to the coded rhythms of creaturely life: the short-term sensory and emotional rhythms, more extended seasonal and biological rhythms (including those of memory), the moral rhythms of the relationships we participate in and our progressive language-borne consciousness of them. In literature and the arts, all that charms us, all that makes for affective recognition and assent—for self-recognition, as it may be—is involved in this attribution of "reality."

3. A third test is collective or social, but in another way than the pragmatic test of a tangible consent. We may define all literature as having to do with how human beings deal with each other and how they deal with a world in which one being exists only because others exist. In such terms that work or performance will have "reality" which incites us to recognition of the reality of other beings; which enables us more or less distinctly to conceive of their real existence (i.e., as real as our own) and hence of the community of being we share with them; which thus makes it possible for us to imagine, and reimagine, the act of living with them. The special importance of imaginative literature is that among the arts it is

---

to happen—more this, one would argue, than any greater credibility achieved by either of his rivals—nearly overcame the wide lead the very-well-known Republican candidate had been given in public-opinion polls up until the very end of the campaign.

As a further contribution to the interesting question whether Mr. Nixon is in reality a President, a remarkable essay by John H. Schaar and Sheldon S. Wolin in *The New York Review of Books*, May 7, 1970, may be cited, the authors describing the chief executive's conduct of his office as "a new art form" in which "a republic whose public space [is to be] filled with silence" is presided over by "a man whose genius is non-leadership."

all but unique in the directness of its concentration on this function; only dance and mime, of the nonverbal arts, act on consciousness in a strictly comparable way.

It is worth pointing out that no particular choice of formal genre or expressive technique follows categorically from these criteria. They can apply as fruitfully to popular as to high literature, to the practice of lyrical or incantatory forms or on the other hand of purposeful journalism as well as to dramatized fictions. The compelling task is to find a right mode and style of action, which is to say, for writers, a right way of participating, of forming fresh sequences of original address and appeal, in any of literature's consensual occasions.* At the same time it is fearfully apparent that public circumstances will have their effect, making the address to this task at times all but impossible. The seismic process of history cracks open, threatening the common structures of custom and use that have supported every established mode of discourse, unexpectedly creating openings for what appear to be barbarous antitypes, and in general exposing the whole business of validation to an oppressively immediate trial of common acceptance. In these terms we can well imagine why in our own profoundly unsettled era the great "classic" forms seem again to have lost their authority; why instead there has been a rush, or retreat, to modes like confessional writing, where the countersigns of authenticity are more forthrightly secured, being less dependent on wider fictions of social harmony, but where also they are easier to counterfeit and get accepted, an occasion for duplicity that may be inseparable from the creative life.

Our rising distrust, in any case, of received cultural forms and value systems reflects a primary distrust of the whole re-

---

* In his stimulating book *On Modernism: the Prospects for Literature and Freedom* (1967), Louis Kampf comments at length on how the same compulsion has overtaken what he takes to be the cardinal practice of contemporary philosophy. The Anglo-American colloquialism, "doing philosophy," points up the fact that in the era of Wittgenstein this ancient discipline of disciplines has once again turned off from system-building, the constitution of *principia,* and become an open-ended, necessarily unfinishable activity or procedure in which the continuous establishing and reestablishing of "a more or less permanent dialogue" becomes its own self-accrediting end.

ceived social and political order. There is no getting around this loss of confidence. All work is affected, exposed in its very foundations as more problematical than anyone suspected. Legitimately earned prerogatives are put in doubt, unfairly, it will seem; reasoned programs of reform and reconstruction are tainted by the ethos they rebel against. It is the morally compromising consciousness of our own inescapable participation in this wider order, or disorder, that betrays before the fact our ambition to do good work within it, or in spite of it, or even against it. The problem is not philosophical but social, though at the heart of both philosophical and social behavior are the imperatives of self-conception, the operational pictures or fables we make of the meaning of our activities to support us in getting through them. In a stable society, or one lulled into disregard of the symptoms of disequilibrium, we may act in our roles and stations according to received standards, assuming that the virtue in what we do, its power to precipitate effects that are useful and benign (alchemical metaphors seem proper here), will hold firm within the prevailing mix. But in a society deprived of self-assurance, every act may find itself called upon to demonstrate its claim to support, its fundamental legitimacy. This is the test of reality that under conditions of historical crisis books and writers not less than political parties and aspirants to civil power are compelled to meet head on, and the consequences are seldom respectful of chartered privileges or standing patents of approbation.

Not unexpectedly, received forms lose credit most completely among those who may have tried most seriously and honestly to maintain them. It is precisely the kind of book idealized by the older cultural humanism that Doris Lessing's heroine, struggling against the fragmentation of contemporary life and consciousness, finds wholly impossible to write, although it remains the only kind of book that interests her: "a book powered with an intellectual and moral passion strong enough to create order, to create a new way of looking at life." But, we may say, haven't new forms sprung up, possessing elements of just this passion and power, which are freshly, responsively engaged with contemporary realities? If a certain pessimism about present and future prospects has somehow

taken charge of this whole inquiry, isn't it perhaps contra-
dicted by a great deal of what just now can regularly be heard
and seen and (given the least will to do so) participated in,
beyond the deadening reach of academic solicitude? Paul
Goodman, probing open-mindedly for "counterforces" to what
in some recent Canadian Broadcasting Corporation lectures on
the state of the American republic he glumly identifies as "the
empty society," only speaks to a common sense of present times
in listing the irrepressible symptoms of energy and renewal on
the contemporary scene.* Civil resistance movements gain in
sophistication and force, whatever their day-by-day tally of
successes and failures. The churches, so long submissive, have
come back to life as communal agents, in conscience and pastoral leadership. The Federal courts and a scattering of executive commissions and boards have acted with a fair show of
principled independence, giving authoritative support to a
certain erratic loosening into humaneness all across the spectrum of common behavior. A rule of candor and tolerance
spreads among young people, unevenly and not at all without
vexation and needless pain, yet with surprising persistence, a
reserve of inner purpose not yet fathomed.

And by any measure of common effectiveness and assent
the arts, too, in their way, have a share in this confused stirring
and shaking. "There is an odd explosion in the arts," Goodman writes, "of a kind of urban folk art in all genres. It is
entirely inauthentic in style"—that is, with regard to traditional conceptions of performative craftsmanship—"yet it is
authentic to the actual urban confusion." We know what he
has in mind, and what enthusiasm of participation and commitment can be generated by the improvised freemasonry of
these popular modes. Where now except in free-for-all theoriz-
ing about movies, rock groups, performative happenings, does
the missionary spirit of the "New Criticism" still gather student converts? Yet we may regret that it all seems limited to
deliberately ephemeral forms of entertainment, to diversions
and freak shows too provisional and unstructured ever to con-

---

* *Like a Conquered Province*, chap. ii, "Counter-Forces for a Decent
Society."

solidate in full reality the "new way of looking at life" Doris
Lessing speaks of, let alone a new cultural order.

Or is it that art itself, like every other mode of behavior in
a mass technological society, is undergoing some fundamental
change of character, so that it no longer abides by any of our
masterpiece-oriented habits of making claims for it? Is it to
find its future not as a purifier and ennobler of our inmost
value-shaping spirit, according to neo-humanist fictions of
discipline and edification still being used to justify its formal
study, but as an adjunct to mass subservience or mass resistance, whichever is morally, civilly, in the ascendant? The
sense that some such transformation may be upon us is not at
all a new one, and it will not necessarily make us despair.

Looking ahead to the future from the Popular Front per-
spectives of the late 1930's, the young Stephen Spender pre-
dicted, with an eager interest, much of what constitutes the
present scene in literature and the arts, though the new classless society he imagined as the conditioning circumstance has
begun to emerge more through technological than political
revolution. There will be, he guessed, "a great mass of documentary literature"—diaries, propaganda exercises, a fiction
focused on outward events ("realism and adventure") rather
than on the refinements of special sensibility—"in which
writers record the changes taking place in their society, their
effect on the group or the individual"; and there will be "an
art and literature of jokes, free association, dream imagery—
all the accidents of wit and beauty, childhood and death,
which strike us suddenly when we are in the street," a fantastic
art "as classless as birth, death, or our dreams" (*Forward from
Liberalism,* p. 194). With every other young writer now
launching his career with an autobiographical narrative of
his latest adventures, with productions of *Hair* sweeping the
world and finding an audience within a popular subculture as
strong in its freshly conventionalized attractions as any pantheon of past glories, who can deny the force and acuity of this
prediction?

Such an art, documentary or fantastic (or both at once),
is well equipped in its working conventions and procedures
to satisfy the threefold critical measure proposed above. Like

any significant human undertaking it only needs conviction, nerve, and the common luck of talent and psychic freedom. But it will not in itself effect that revolution, or counterrevolution, in the whole structure of civil life which more and more takes shape as this age's dominating task. How, then, will it meet the special crisis-test of reality that presses on it when revolution achieved or failed, desired or feared, becomes the focus of consciousness? How indeed? for that test is one that artists and writers will not be alone in having to face; it is the prospect confronting us all. For the present, I think, it is enough to say that an art and literature of the kind described will neither oppose that revolution nor seek to tranquilize it when it comes, and that the truly humane revolutionary will recognize the generosity, the faithfulness, the reality, of such an art's peculiar kind of assistance. He may himself be too preoccupied to give much time or attention to it, but he will at least have the wit to leave it alone, free to go about its humanizing work as best it can.

Modern Literature
and the Condition of Exile

One must learn to live anywhere, beginning now.
—François Truffaut, *Jules and Jim*

In the present age the critical study of literature, now concentrated almost entirely within the university, has increasingly undertaken to be as systematic in method as other organized disciplines of learning. This, we think, is as it should be, for it is agreed that knowledge should be exact and its extension orderly and empirically verifiable. But this development has had one odd consequence, one which is perhaps characteristic of academic study in general, and that is a certain complacency about the primary matter under scrutiny, which is the fact of literary creation and the mysteriously perpetuated existence of authors—persons who compose poems, novels, histories, plays—as a human type or species.

The creative premise, so to speak, is taken for granted. Men and women capable of becoming authors somehow get born and arrive at the post to begin their careers, whereupon literature eternally advances, according to the more or less of talent, or "genius," rationed out to each generation. The true memorial of this advance is the historical anthology, arranged as a sequence of eminent names and schools and suitably annotated; the chief purpose of the systematic study of literature being, as John Crowe Ransom once put it, to "maintain the anthology." Conditions of work will change immensely, of course; moods of exhilaration and confident experiment alternate with periods of retrenchment and despair; individual motives run a gamut from revolutionary prophecy to Grub Street accommodation; it is understood that Shelleyan legislators-for-mankind are not precisely identical with what have come to be called poets-in-residence. But the essential business of literary creation is accepted as constant, and the thing itself, we suppose, must continue to materialize and to find its place in the reviews, book shops, courses, and reading lists of the future.

But in an epoch of profound and convulsive cultural change—change that overleaps the working lifetime not just of certain unfortunately exposed classes of people but of everyone alive; and what is the present time if not such an epoch? —all that is taken for granted in the ordinary conduct of affairs is itself mercilessly brought into question. What precisely, students of literature (and plain observers) are forced to ask afresh, is the character of the writer's existence, the imaginable trajectory of his behavior? How does his singular vocation overtake him and how is he to maintain himself within it? What life and fortune come to him in pursuing it? And what further place, if any, is this vocation likely to have in a system of society governed by forces and tendencies, in particular by systems of communication, so radically different from anything human beings have lived under before that the freely written and printed word itself seems now, to some, a kind of anachronism? Nothing is more characteristic of the present moment in literary history than the sense that the very continuance of creative literature as we have known and commemorated it has become problematical, and that the writer, the free man of letters, has become—like any other victim of modern technological and electronic civilization—a displaced person.

I assume this sentiment of displacement to be at present a first fact about the high literary calling, or about the idea of that calling as it has come down to us. The writer devoted to anything resembling classic goals—to the business of giving fresh, cogent, harmonious expression to great human truths; to the creation of masterpieces—has learned, if we take him at his word, to think of himself as a being in exile. Wherever we find a fully accountable inquiry into the writer's vocation and the relation it bears to life in general, this note is sounded. A good deal more is meant by it than simply geographical displacement, social and political expatriation. Yet that familiar circumstance of modern history provides an appropriate metaphor, and model, for the writer's life. Declarations that this is the case are not hard to produce. They are one of our age's principal legacies from the era of literary Romanticism, when spiritual exile and the figure of the disaffected wanderer became major secular tropes.

But perhaps an understated prose comment will serve better as a first example of the grip this metaphor has on modern conceptions of the writer's destiny. At the end of his autobiographical memoir, *A Cab at the Door*, V. S. Pritchett, a man of letters born with the present century and sharing his time's commitment to the overthrow of sentimental hyperbole, describes the distaste for the outward circumstances of his early life—home, social system, cultural habit—that overtook him just when his ambition to make his way as a writer was taking definite shape. The freedom this ambition allowed him, specifically the freedom to go and live where he pleased, was intoxicating, and he turned his back on England and took himself to the Continent, to France and Spain, for seven years. If the singularly unarticled profession of literature enabled him to do this, what further inducement would he (at twenty) require?

For Pritchett it was a decision never, apparently, regretted. Yet looking back, he eventually saw that these first steps he had taken did not represent a free choice at all but something closer to a categorical imperative, symbolically enacted. "For myself," he concludes in his book's closing sentence, "that is what a writer is—a man living on the other side of a frontier."

An odd instance of the currency in modern literature of the metaphor of exile is provided by the American literary renaissance of the 1920's. For most of the gifted young American writers of this period, the ritual of expatriation became a prescribed way of life, determinedly undertaken. Critical of what seemed the cultural barbarism of their own country (in which respect they followed the thinking of numerous American predecessors back to Emerson and Fenimore Cooper a century earlier) and freshly disillusioned by the First World War and the failure of literate and right-minded men, from President Wilson down, to temper that enormous catastrophe or even to show that they had learned anything from it, these writers accepted the description of themselves as a "lost generation," in Gertrude Stein's famous phrase. When a first history of their decade-long emergence came to be written by one of their number, the poet and critic Malcolm Cowley, it was cast from start to finish as a saga of exile and alienation.

Or would have been so cast if the damped fires of New World hopefulness and civic idealism had not unexpectedly revived in the telling. The full title of Cowley's book was *Exile's Return,* and the emphasis of the second word, though not prominent in the main story (which ends, fittingly, with a suicide) and though open to ironic extension, nevertheless indicates at least the possibility of happier endings. Cowley was writing personal as well as collective history, and he was writing not in 1929 but in 1933 and 1934, when his youthful projection of himself as a disenchanted and self-displaced novice of literature had given way to what seemed the more responsible picture of a supporter of revolutionary Communism, partisan of a heroic countereffort to change the immediate historical world rather than withdraw from it in scorn and despair. Cowley admitted long after, when reissuing his book in 1951, that there were gaps and contradictions in the original version. His new political hopes had "intruded into the narrative," so that "the whole conclusion" (in which he had come out strongly in the old evangelical-didactic way for the "humanizing function of art") was "out of scale with the beginning." But for all this it is the first word of the title that sets the narrative scheme, which shows how a whole rising generation of writers, finding no other tolerable course open to them, deliberately undertook "to live in exile."

Cowley acknowledged that there was an element of play-acting in this undertaking. The American generation he wrote about was more in hostage to common circumstance than it knew: to a peculiar spiritual inheritance, to economic privilege, to its own youthful ignorance. It had swallowed whole the case against the historic blight of "Puritanism" that H. L.

Mencken's exuberant jibes and Van Wyck Brooks's subtler diagnosis had made familiar (the word stood for everything repressive and hypocritical in American life, from the prohibition of drink to the irrepressible gentility of the literary establishment), but in the idea this generation used to justify going abroad—the idea of "salvation by exile"— it simply reasserted a new version of the naïve perfectionism and promised-land complex that came to it from that Puritan and millennial "spirit of religion" which Tocqueville identified, in *Democracy in America,* as basic to the formation of American life. Cowley himself profited from the persistence of this spirit in secular philanthropy; his own literary pilgrimage to Europe was paid for by a fellowship from the Quaker-directed American Field Service. Moreover, the sentiment that there was a great good place somewhere else where one's creative soul might be saved had a convenient economic justification. In the depressed Europe of the 1920's, American dollars went a long way; the exile's life could be very comfortable. Also, the brief experience of Europe that had come to many of these young writers during the war—Cowley's had been with the American Ambulance Service in France—had given them "a taste for travel and excitement," and a practical familiarity with the Continent as the place to indulge it. Brief stopovers in the American Bohemia of Greenwich Village, or in some metropolitan newspaper office in the agreeably ungenteel company of police reporters and city editors, had intensified this taste. "They do things better in Europe; let's go there." That, Cowley wrote, was the notion that brought these young men to the French Line Pier in 1920 and 1921. Being free to go, they mostly went.

There were of course limits to their willingness, or need, to change their lives. They mostly meant to return to America sooner or later, and while they were in Europe they remained American to the core. With their money and their freedom of movement they formed little American enclaves or, in Paris, joined English-speaking subdivisions of that floating international community of artists, writers, patrons, and serious dilettantes which had come into being during the nineteenth century with the establishment of certain basic services— steam transportation, telegraph remittances, a reliable mail system. In fact their going abroad, Cowley recognized, was in some respects no break at all in their ongoing careers. It simply extended "a long process of deracination" that had begun for them in midadolescence and that was part and parcel of the general experience of "the American educated classes" in their time, an experience of being "uprooted, schooled away . . . from their attachment to any locality or local tradition." The cultural dilemmas they dramatized by sailing off to Europe survived their return home. Back in New York they still felt themselves aliens to the money-grabbing style of life officially sanctioned by the times, and moved out in large numbers to a second low-budget exile in the surrounding countryside, where economically depressed villages a short train ride from Manhattan made it possible for young writers and their wives to camp out in relative comfort. They now considered, Cowley wrote, that "their real exile was from society itself, from any society to which they could honestly contribute and from which they could draw the strength that lies in shared convictions."

Cowley admitted that he and his friends had at the time a very limited vision of the historical civilization (and, one may add, of its regular custom of career-making) in which they acted out the myth of "exile." Thinking of themselves as a new breed engaged in a wholly novel experience, they showed a notable ignorance of precedents. Yet what else were they doing but playing in the free-and-easy American style a legendary part—the novice from the provinces determined to test to the limit his time's opportunities—which the nineteenth century had made very nearly mandatory for underadvantaged young men seeking fame and preferment? In transplanting themselves to Europe for a time, they were continuing that practical education into modern realities which the middle-class households and provincial colleges that so far had constituted their experience of life had left embarrassingly incomplete.

They were moving, that is, in a grooved track. For these young Americans, "exile" was only crisis language, though freshly legitimated, for the familiar custom of the European *lehrjahre*. For a century, since the first delegation of conscientious young New Englanders had gone to Germany for exposure to a practice of high scholarship the very idea of which, the philologist George Ticknor said, was unknown in the United States, Europe had offered itself as the natural place for young Americans to overcome the provincial inadequacy of their preparation. So it had seemed to the father of William and Henry James, a man who in other moods was effusively patriotic, when he transplanted his brood of children to Europe in the 1850's for a richer exposure to high civilization than was possible at home; and so it seemed to Henry James himself, emigrating to Paris at the outset of a career that still stands as the great American case of literary expatriation and artistic longevity. Closer to Cowley's time were the two most notable literary men of the American generation just preceding his own, T. S. Eliot and Ezra Pound. Their power to produce poems in which, Cowley wrote, "we could not find a line that betrayed immaturity, awkwardness, provincialism or platitude" could not be dissociated from their decision to settle abroad. The old picture of the United States as a country which, in achieving exemplary political virtue, had sacrificed a corresponding growth in the arts and amenities still passed current, at home as in Europe. So in literature, if an American did somehow break through by his own home-based effort to a mastery of his art, he would still probably need to look abroad for serious recognition. The case of Robert Frost, who had had to live in England for three years to establish credentials as a poet, lay outside Cowley's tale but would have confirmed its logic.

But in comparison with these predecessors, the American "exiles" of the 1920's were in fact singularly favored. As Cowley pointed out, they found their way in remarkably short order to various satisfactory fulfillments of their ambitions: prompt publication, serious critical acceptance, an "honorable relatedness" (Glenway Wescott's phrase) with their famous elders, even (as for Hemingway) the rewards and privileges of best-seller status. They were the first full inheritors of the great modernist renaissance in European art and literature—of which, in 1920, Paris was the capital city—as well as of its native American counterpart, the culturally enlightened "progressivism" of 1890–1920. Both developments had prepared for their work the possibility of a generous and yet discriminating welcome among their peers. All this more than compensated for the Philistinism that continued to resist them in the public at large.

They had, to boot, the pleasure of each other's company (such as that may be among rival authors) and the convenient support, during the crucial first stages of their careers, of a bull market in free-lance publishing and literary publicity. As practicing writers Cowley's "exiles" proved to be a quickly "found" generation, well provided for staying the course; in due time they won all the prizes and captured the anthologies. More important, they did what no American generation before them had been able to do. In ten years, as Cowley observed, they pretty well removed the old burden of American inferiority in the arts, and in the process helped to make New York a cultural capital increasingly deferred to, after 1930, by younger writers in an increasingly demoralized Europe.

Malcolm Cowley's saga of modern literary career-making concentrated on a single American generation. But his narrative was not indifferent to wider historical contexts. Like other diagnosticians of American culture, from Tocqueville on, Cowley was struck by resemblances in position and outlook, vis-à-vis Europe, between Russia and America, and under the heading "Historical Parallel" he devoted one section of *Exile's Return* to an account of Dostoevsky's "exile" into western Europe in the 1860's. This episode provided not only a complementary case of the exposure of a provincial writer to the rich stimulus of the European heartland but also a dramatic theoretical confrontation of a kind lacking in his American materials: the angry private quarrel between Dostoevsky and Turgenev as to whether a Russian author should or should not Europeanize himself. It was as though Van Wyck Brooks's Mark Twain had had it out with Van Wyck Brooks's Henry James.

But the differences between Dostoevsky and Turgenev in relation to the pull of Europe were less extreme than this quarrel might suggest. As much as Turgenev, Dostoevsky used the experience of expatriation to forge his final character as a writer. He had never been ignorant of the West. He knew its literary classics; Balzac, Dickens, E. T. A. Hoffmann had influenced his early work; and he had shared in the passionate absorption of German philosophic thought by the Russian intelligentsia during his youth. Firsthand experience of Europe, however, seems to have intensified his growing Slavism and that rejection of abstract liberal values which his extraordinary mind had distilled from his own decade-long ordeal of prison and Siberian exile. Certainly it can be said that the richer vision and, so to speak, the historical as well as psychological authority of understanding in *Crime and Punishment* and *The Devils* are fully present in the remarkable European travel book of 1863, *Winter Notes on Summer Impressions.* Dostoevsky's nightmare descriptions of Paris and London—the Saturday night mobs of "white negroes" joylessly swarming and brawling under the brilliant gas jets, past the mansions of wealth and power—and his essay exposing the heartlessness of the Western bourgeoisie have a prophetic intensity matched at that date only in Baudelaire's "Tableaux Parisiens."

The point to make here is not only that Turgenev's and Dostoevsky's different experiences of Europe both derived from Russia's cultural provincialism. It is also that their opposed responses as writers were both made possible by the same governing condition, and that is the actual internationalization of Western literary culture, despite strict linguistic divisions. Literature may well be, as John Wain remarks, "more national than the other arts" in that the writer's basic instrument of language has been forged by the discrete historical nation he was born to. Yet it is hard to find a time in Western literary history when the formative experience of major writers has not been international, multicultural. The fundamental literary unity of Europe: that is the historical constant that an examination of literary exile reveals. It is what makes the life of exile possible for Western writers. Even after the decline of literary Latin and the maturing of the vernaculars, and even with the breakup of that pan-European "literary public" that Erich Auerbach has described in its ascendancy,* this unity has persisted. For writers the republic of literature has always been a country without boundaries, a transportable fatherland. It then becomes difficult to determine in any given case—at

---

* *Literary Language and Its Public in Late Latin Antiquity and in the Middle Ages,* translated by Ralph Manheim (1968).

least the grounds for making the distinction are likely to be
extra-literary—whether a writer has gone into exile or is
entering upon a pilgrimage (from province to capital, from
capital to some remote and exempt sanctuary) to nurture his
growth and advance his career. Even if his transplantation
becomes permanent, he may only be verifying to himself the
singular freemasonry of his calling.

The historical attraction of American and Russian writers
to Europe falls, then, into a distinctive pattern: the attraction
of young men from the literary provinces to the more brilliant
and famous custom of the established capitals. So in classical
times Roman authors had gone to Greece, Sicily, Alexandria
(such travels, Ovid wrote, were among "the rites common to
poets"), and so in the Renaissance northerners such as the
grammarian Ascham or the poet Milton traveled into Italy;
so, too, the young Pasternak, reared in the increasingly cosmopolitan literary environment of late-Tsarist Russia, came west
to Marburg and to Venice.

But for one broad class of modern "provincial" writers,
expatriation may necessarily become permanent. This is the
class of writers from small countries lacking a secure literary
community or tradition of their own. For such men exile may
be a calculated maneuver aimed at reaching an audience equal
to their ambition, or at gaining the professional companionship
and the critical hearing their talent needs in order to have
its proper growth. French, Anglo-American, Italian, Spanish
writers can live out of their homeland for years yet remain members of the national literary community. It is more likely to be
a Polish, Welsh, Flemish, or Rumanian writer who not only
abandons his home province but chooses another language
and thus a wholly different audience to establish his career.

The motives governing these decisions are not uniform.
A master such as Ibsen may be confident of his power to capture
eventually an audience larger than he could ever hope for in
his own country, and a wider fame.* Less imperial talents,

---

* But drama is a special case. As a literary form it has always crossed
national and linguistic frontiers relatively easily. Poetry, too, has its
generic freedoms, particularly in a period dominated by a style like
Symbolism which is at once international in provenance and, usually, too
esoteric in content to reach any broad national public. The modern

like the Rumanians Ionesco and E. M. Cioran or the Pole
Witold Gombrowicz, may on the other hand find in emigration
the means to a literary identity and reputation that otherwise
might not have accrued to them. The case of Gombrowicz
offers typical ambiguities. "What motives," writes the Paris
critic Maurice Nadeau, "drove this descendant of an ancient
landed aristocracy to go into exile in Argentina, several months
before the war [in 1939]? Probably the fear of becoming a
'Polish' writer and of making for himself a place in the literary
history of his own country, between this author and that. . . ."
Perhaps so—whereas writing from the Argentine, though still in
Polish, he would be identified as "European" and "modern,"
a prime candidate for discovery by Paris criticism. Or did he
perhaps go into exile for just the opposite reason: to become
the Polish writer of his time, the one who in a world of great-
power literary imperialism had mastered the provincial di-
lemma by acquiring irresistible foreign allies—for what are
Ferdydurke and *Pornografia* but fantasies of systematic treach-
ery and domination? In either case his winning in due course
the International Prize for Literature is the more appropriate,
if not strictly inevitable.

A particularly interesting twentieth-century case of literary
displacement, most frequently though not invariably involving
a career in exile, is offered by writers from those colonial
provinces of Europe where a European literary language
became the educated norm. This case is limited *de facto* to
English and French writing, but for the literature of these
languages it is a case that may have increasing importance in
the future. Older men of letters like the Martiniquais Aimé
Césaire or the poet-president of Senegal, Léopold Senghor,
could develop their work within the literary establishment of
metropolitan France, where the poet-statesman is familiar
and honored, and receptivity to non-European nuances of
style is traditional. The theme, as with the Guianese poet

Greek masters Constantine Cavafy and George Seferis lived and worked
mostly out of Greece but did so quite in the natural course of things:
Cavafy in Alexandria where he was born, Seferis all around Europe and
the Middle East in the conduct of a distinguished diplomatic career,
having in the first place been separated from his Ionian homeland by the
Greek-Turkish catastrophe of 1922.

Léon Damas, may be exile and deprivation, but the expressive norm is Surrealist-Parisian. But for younger writers, those coming to maturity in the new era of national independence and that ethos of *négritude* that Césaire himself was first to name, the choice of circumstance and above all of language has become more difficult. The gifted Nigerian novelist Chinua Achebe is almost defiant about continuing to write in English: "I have been given this language, and I intend to use it." It is the English-speaking community's good fortune that he and others like him have made this choice, even though it must confirm the separation from the mass of their own people, largely illiterate, brought about by their European education. For the English idiom they work in is English with a difference; it is literary English forced to become the vessel for a whole new range of social and imaginative experience, English refreshed by fraternization with the very different rhythms and syntax of non-European dialects. Such is the case, too, with the work in fiction of writers as richly at ease with London or *New Yorker* English as the East Indian novelist R. K. Narayan or the Trinidadian V. S. Naipaul.*

All of these writers know at firsthand the modern experience of cultural dislocation, which has other forms besides geographical exile. They are writers from the historical crossroads, or battleground, of European and non-European civilization; for them the choice to take a position on one side or the other of a cultural frontier, or to try somehow to occupy both sides at once, is not elected but historically required. There are European equivalents to these circumstantial, geopolitical exiles; borderlanders whose home province has been the pawn of nationalistic wars and *Kulturkämpfe*. Is it wholly coincidental

---

* The case of postcolonial literature where the imported language is also the language of the general population, itself migratory in origin—the literature of Australia, white South Africa, Canada—is fundamentally different. Writers in these countries reputedly are inhibited by the problem of finding an identity in relation to the historical homeland. But the reasons why English-language writers in South Africa have regularly emigrated to England and found a ready public there, while Australians have less commonly done so, seem to be primarily political, and geographical. Also, a high proportion of the gifted contingent of contemporary South African writers is Jewish and has presumably inherited a certain familiarity with cultural repression and the consciousness of exile.

that the boldest representation in fiction of the Hitler calamity has come from a Danzig and Kashubian writer, Günter Grass? —just as, earlier, the self-destructive sickness of bourgeois Europe was diagnosed with special clarity by the Rhinelanders Marx and Nietzsche, by Franz Kafka, a Czech Jew writing in German, and by the Austro-Italian Triestino who published under the name of "Italo Svevo."

Without these writers literature in the twentieth century would be much the poorer. Literary history itself would have taken a different course. Such writers can bring a saving infusion of fresh energy and insight to a literary culture going stale at the capitals—as did the French-speaking Pole, Joseph Conrad, who became for a time the foremost stylist and craftsman in the English novel; or the poets of the Flemish borderland who took the lead in establishing *symbolisme* as European poetry's ruling fashion; or the Italo-Polish avantgardist Apollinaire, impresario of its overthrow. Perhaps because they never overcome a certain interior distance from the literary modes they adopt, they handle these modes with freedom and a necessary disrespect; that is, when they are strong enough not to be enslaved to them. Jean-Paul Sartre has suggested, from the example of Aimé Césaire's appropriation of the method of Symbolism, how a colonial writer may take hold of European traditions with such strange liberty and violence that he not only adds something exotic to them but stretches and perhaps the more rapidly exhausts their inner possibilities, hurrying them on to some definitive termination. The singular case of the Irish-Parisian novelist and playwright Samuel Beckett may also be cited. If "modernism" itself has come to a dead end, as some believe, this perversely creative (or "decreative") disciple of Joyce and Proust, inexorably closing in on silence and motionlessness, may prove to have been its last original master.

When we think of the cultural disorder of modern Europe, we usually exempt the English, whose institutions are a byword elsewhere for stability. Yet something like the structural view projected here of modern literary history, and specifically of the function of exile and displacement in nourishing individual talents, has in fact been the case for the literature of the British Isles throughout the present century. Especially in poetry and drama the several Celtic provinces have been disproportionately productive of fresh voices, new styles, innovations in form. We have only to list names: Yeats, Synge, Joyce, O'Casey, Dylan Thomas, David Jones, Hugh McDiarmid, Edwin Muir, Robert Graves.*

More generally, if we add expatriates from America like James, Eliot, and Pound, and an expatriate *to* America and other regions like W. H. Auden, it can be argued that the major history of modern English literature has been shaped and staffed by outlanders—plus one Nottinghamshire miner's son (and of D. H. Lawrence it may be said that his working-class, scholarship-boy origins were good preparation in the English literary community of his day for the life of exile). The situation in the 1950's and 1960's is not altogether different, though the social tensions at work upon a figure like Lawrence seem to have relaxed. When the freshest talents in English fiction, to many, are an Anglo-Irishwoman, Iris Murdoch (an admirer, moreover, of Sartre and Raymond Queneau), and an Edinburgher, Muriel Spark, and when many of the most promising younger poets have put themselves systematically to school with American masters like William Carlos Williams and Yvor Winters, these modern patterns of displacement and cross-fertilization appear to be holding firm.

A literalist may object, however, that such patterns have always given direction to the cycles of European literary history and deserve no special mention, except among sociologists of human creativity in general. Is there not an element of exaggeration in the rubric for this essay? Is "exile" the right word for those who have crossed frontiers or turned to foreign models by their own free choice, without undue discomfort or inconvenience, and in the observance of a long-established occupational custom; who, moreover, are always legally free to return? "Exile" must be enforced; it must bear the stamp of political compulsion.

---

* The analysis can be pushed further back. "We may reflect incidentally on the fact that Ireland produced many of the most serious social critics writing in English after 1688—Congreve, Swift, Berkeley, Goldsmith, Sheridan." (Christopher Hill, *Reformation to Industrial Revolution*, 1968, p. 231.)

But the violence and disorder of political life in an increasingly totalitarian and statist era have indeed been factors in nearly all the examples so far cited. In Conrad's youth, Poland, governed by repressive foreign regimes, was not an encouraging place for a free mind; it seems no accident that the new note of twentieth-century political terror first heard in English in *The Secret Agent* and *Under Western Eyes* was sounded by this Polish *émigré* who as a child had endured exile with his parents into Siberia. The Irish writers mentioned, mostly dramatists, all knew at firsthand that nation's singular brand of theocratic censorship. In postcolonial Africa the imaginative legacy or burden of European political domination is as elemental for writers as the ecological climate or the ambiguity of their relationship with the older tribal cultures. The case of the poet and dramatist Wole Soyinka, in a Nigerian prison during most of the Biafran war, suggests how well independent Africa has learned European methods of government. Even the privileged American expatriates of the 1920's could list specific political grievances—not just the petty tyranny of Prohibition but the general failure, and from within, of American progressivism—and in their writings would make the corruption of the old American dream of a *novus ordo saeclorum* perhaps their greatest imaginative theme.

Around them and beside them, of course, in the years since the First World War, have been the actual political exiles from every major national literature of Europe. By the time Malcolm Cowley's book was published in 1934, the metaphor of his title had been overtaken with a vengeance. Revolutionary dictatorships in Russia, Italy, Germany, and Spain, precisely because the revolution in each case was ideological, instinctively looked on writers as potential enemies of state. Worse yet, they saw literature itself, and human literacy, as fundamentally valueless if not convertible into instruments of state control. In consequence, for more than a quarter of a century much of the important new literature of Europe was produced in exile by political outcasts and refugees, or under the virtual exile of house arrest as with, during the Second World War, Ivo Andrič's Bosnian trilogy.

To be sure, writers in earlier ages also had suffered from the irritable absolutism of political masters. The psychology of exile can be construed from classical cases. The poet Ovid, compelled to live for eight years in a "half-Greek, half-barbarian town" on the Black Sea, sent back to Rome a stream of eloquent complaints and lamentations, among them the verse letters called *Ex Ponto*, a title borrowed by Ivo Andrić for letters written in an Austrian prison during the First World War. Cicero, like Socrates before him, might have chosen the lesser punishment of exile if he had not been an old man for whom separation from his true polis was no longer tolerable.* The *Commedia* of Dante is, among other great things, the poem of an exile interested in expressing political grievances and paying off old scores. But such authors—even Ovid, who took the trouble to learn the Getic tongue well enough to compose a poem in it—remained within the literary culture they were reared in and did not conceive of separation from it. For them, as for Victor Hugo at Jersey and Guernsey during the regime of Napoleon III, exile might be a wretched personal inconvenience but it hardly interrupted, on the whole it seems rather to have facilitated, their work.

It is in Hugo's century, however, and the new era of ideological revolution inaugurated in 1789, that the peculiarly disorienting conditions of modern political exile materialize. Using the great case of Alexander Herzen, V. S. Pritchett has defined the special fate overtaking exiles from a regime like the Tsarist tyranny that gradually proves itself too deeply entrenched to be overthrown in their lifetime: it is "to see their lives become slowly irrelevant." Herzen himself analyzed the exile mentality with great acuteness. "Meeting the same men, the same groups, for five or six months, for two or three years—one feels terrified; the same arguments going on, the same personalities and recriminations, only the furrows drawn by poverty and privation are deeper." It takes a mind of extraordinary force and tenacity to surmount this condition, though one that does may in the process have made itself into a uniquely formidable instrument of discourse and persuasion. The case of Karl Marx comes to mind—but Marx was an ideologue more than a man

---

* Both would have understood Pasternak's reply to Khrushchev when invited to emigrate to the West at the time of the *Zhivago* controversy: "To leave my country would be for me the equivalent of death."

of letters; he loved literature, but for himself the act of writing was essentially utilitarian and coercive.

It is not simply the exile's outward life that loses relevance but his fundamental ways of thinking and feeling, too. Worst of all, for the writer, his very language may be taken from him. That is why the Russian cases of literary exile seem the most hazardous. More than the special brutality of Russian ideological oppression, the fact that there is no natural Russian-speaking public outside the mother country has made the choice to go into exile or remain at home under duress (or worse) peculiarly harrowing. It is true that since 1917 works by writers hostile to the Soviet regime or indifferent to its canons of merit have been, when available, very promptly translated and circulated in the West. Also, in an era dominated by international modes like Symbolism, Surrealism, the Theatre of the Absurd, quite obscure private or local literary dialects can gain a sympathetic hearing across national boundaries. But Russian has so little relation to the main literary languages of western Europe and the Americas that the writer who is forced to leave Russia or who must look outside for his audience is in effect deprived of his natural speech. It thus seems fitting that a great Russian poet and novelist should have made the consummate statement of the modernist dogma that the writer's true motherland and generative resource is, at the actual moment of creation, his language. With the approach of what is called inspiration, Pasternak wrote in the great fourteenth chapter of *Doctor Zhivago,*

> the ascendancy is no longer with the artist or the state of mind he is trying to express but with language, his instrument of expression. Language, the home and dwelling of beauty and meaning, itself begins to think and speak for man and turns wholly into music, not in the sense of outward, audible sounds but by virtue of the power and momentum of its inward flow. Then, like the current of a mighty river polishing stones and turning wheels by its very movement, the flow of speech creates in passing, by the force of its own laws, rhyme and rhythm and countless other forms and formations still more important and until now undiscovered, unconsidered, unnamed.

In any event the long-run effect of the Russian Revolution on the lives of writers was tragic and pitiable in the extreme, and events of the 1960's make it clear that this story has not yet ended. Even Gorki, a champion of proletarian life with an exemplary record of socialist protest and imprisonment under the Tsar, spent the critical interval of 1921–1928 out of Russia (ostensibly, and with Lenin's support, for reasons of health) and then, though officially the greatest hero of Soviet literature, fell victim to the purges of the 1930's. Ivan Bunin, a man of more conservative literary fashion and an aristocrat who had already lived much in the West, left with the first flight of *émigrés*. But it was the younger generation whose lives were most violently disrupted. The list of those who eventually killed themselves or who disappeared after arrest includes a figure like Mayakovsky who at perhaps intolerable expense of spirit had become a hero of the regime, others like Esenin and Marina Tsvetayeva who attempted to live in exile and did not survive the desperate act of returning to Russia, and still others like the Georgian poets Yashvili and Tabidze who tried to maintain themselves in remote provinces within the Soviet Union. These in particular (though others, too, are named: Babel, Mandelstam, Bagritsky) are the writers, his friends and contemporaries, whom Pasternak poignantly memorialized in the autobiographical fragment, *I Remember,* saying with terse, clinical eloquence: "all of them suffered beyond description, their suffering reaching the point where the feeling of anguish became a mental illness."

One Russian-born writer of this first revolutionary generation who did eventually construct a new literary personality and a career in exile was Vladimir Nabokov, but his may be the case of linguistic emigration that proves the rule. Writing mostly in Russian during nearly two decades of exile in the West and then transforming himself in middle life into an Anglo-American novelist, Nabokov improvised a stylistic manner of extraordinary verbal ingenuity, having, one feels, all the properties of masterliness except natural fluency and natural resonance. Precisely because his effort was not only to establish a new working medium (and thus a new readership) but to preserve himself as a human being solidly rooted in life, an element of strain and artificiality cemented itself into his work, deadening the active flow of it. V. S. Pritchett again (a specialist in these matters) has defined the case well: "Vocabulary, grammar, syntax and the fashions of epithet" had themselves to take the place of the country and culture Nabokov had lost, and as a result he became "a superb exploiter" of the historical languages he adopted to this end but not, like Joyce, their master. He now writes English, including various odd sorts of jargon and slang, with remarkable virtuosity and inventiveness, but he writes it as if it were about to become a dead language; the texts of his novels are scenarios, awaiting realization.

In Fascist Italy the travail of writers lasted for a full generation, but the consequences were less catastrophic. For some they were unexpectedly profitable. The repressiveness of Mussolini's Italy was never as efficient as that of Stalin's Russia and Hitler's Germany. Older literary humanists like Gaetano Salvemini and G. A. Borgese, university teachers and political activists, sooner or later went into exile but found new homes in English and American universities, as did many of their German counterparts. Among younger writers who were not subservient to the regime, Alberto Moravia was unusual in being allowed to pursue his career without serious interruption—he was in fact abroad through much of the 1930's —and to publish as late as 1940 a satirical work like *The Fancy Dress Party* (withdrawn when the authorities belatedly discovered its metaphoric relevance to Fascist politics). Ignazio Silone, a marked man, fled into Switzerland, but it was precisely during his double exile—from Italy and from a Stalinized Communist party—that he turned to imaginative writing; and with the intensification of anti-Fascism around Europe, his novels, so rich with intimations of the struggle to restore a truly human community, were quickly translated into a dozen other languages. Another uncompromising anti-Fascist, the Torinese Carlo Levi, being sentenced to a term of exile in an impoverished village in Lucania, found in the shock of exposure to that other world of the Italian *mezzogiorno* the material for his most notable book, *Christ Stopped at Eboli*. The Mussolini era bore down most oppressively, perhaps, on even younger writers, those coming of age in the 1930's and early 1940's, who found the path to free expression blocked at the start. But many of them, too, turned their situation to advantage by translating foreign authors—as Pavese translated Melville and Vittorini, D. H. Lawrence—and opening the

Italian literary consciousness to these powerfully liberating influences.

In Germany, though the Nazi regime lasted barely a decade, its savagery was far more devastating to the literary community. Those who suffered first were older and established writers, but neighboring countries like Holland, Switzerland, and the Scandinavian democracies stood open to them where they could continue to work and publish in German. In the 1930's Thomas Mann, Stefan George in his old age, and, after Anschluss, Robert Musil all crossed into Switzerland, where Hermann Hesse had lived since 1919 and where Rilke had spent the last seven years of his life. Nelly Sachs and Bertolt Brecht took refuge in Sweden. At the end of the thirties, Mann and the Austrian Hermann Broch, among others, emigrated to the United States (both were promptly elected to the Academy of Arts and Letters). Brecht, too, came on to the United States and as a man of the theatre was able to continue working, despite frustrations, in Hollywood and New York along with refugee actors and directors.* Of the older generation one who remained in Germany was the Nietzschean poet Gottfried Benn, who supported the new regime when it came to power in 1933 but shortly found himself ordered to stop all literary activity. Having once been an army doctor, Benn, officially in disgrace, volunteered for this service again—"an aristocratic form of emigration," he said—but was systematically humiliated in his assignments and, along with those in exile, continued being reviled in the Nazi press until the end of the war.

But worse for German letters than the exile or silencing of established writers was the virtual obliteration of the next literary generation. The dramatist Peter Weiss, who survived because his family had gone to Sweden when emigration was still possible, has expressed with great force the plight of this generation and of all survivors of the Nazi terror, in the auto-

---

* The circumstance of exile in the prime of life during a great world upheaval surely contributed to the particular masterpieces—which have the character at once of circumstantial biographies and universal epics— each of these writers produced in exile: Mann in *Doctor Faustus*, Broch in *The Death of Virgil*, Brecht in *Mother Courage* and *Galileo*.

biographical narratives published in English under the title, *Exile*. From the first, living out of Germany and with his native language being violated day and night by Nazi propaganda, he found "something alien and repellent" coming into all his efforts to write. "I was made to realize that the things I wanted to say could not be said once language ceased being a natural means of exchange." But after 1945 he was still not free. The unimaginable revelation of the death camps intervened. "What do you want then," he calls out to the accusing voice of a vanished friend and comrade. "Must I despair because I was not murdered." Not until two years after the war, in Paris, did he begin to see a way out, by no longer seeing himself as specifically a *German* writer, though he would continue to write in the German language. Then, at last, living in a city where he could talk easily only with waiters, "I saw that it was possible to live and work in the world, and that I could participate in the exchange of ideas that was taking place all around, *bound to no country*." But it is to be noted that this participation came about, for Peter Weiss, in the lingua franca of contemporary theatre.

For French and Spanish literature, the consequences of political oppression and exile in the 1930's and 1940's were in the main less destructive. After the capitulation of June, 1940, most French writers remained in France, whether or not they served in the military and propaganda underground. The German occupation, of course, though lasting but four years, brought about a dislocation comparable to exile. Gide in the south of France, before going on to Tunisia in 1942, spoke of himself in his journal as an interior *émigré,* and it was as such that most writers survived. So it was in occupied France that the classic parable of modern estrangement was published, by a writer, Albert Camus, whose insight into this condition was sharpened by his own exile from the working-class communalism, and the sunlight, of his native Algeria. Of the writers who were out of France between 1940 and 1944, special circumstances govern nearly every case. St.-John Perse, for example, had been born in the West Indies and, as a diplomat and a poet in the Symbolist tradition, was already thoroughly cosmopolitan in outlook; in the United States after 1940 his writing took a fresh start and in 1942 he published his first work in nearly twenty years, the long chant *Exil*.* Supervielle, too, on a visit to his native Uruguay in 1939, simply remained in the New World until the war ended. The cultural ties between France and Latin America were traditionally close, and capitals like Buenos Aires, Havana, and Mexico City (where in 1944 Jules Romains completed *Men of Good Will*) rather than Montreal were the centers of French literature-in-exile. The important journal *Lettres Françaises* was published in Buenos Aires (Supervielle was a prominent contributor); its editor, the *France libre* partisan Roger Caillois. Several authors who were also academicians spent the war years teaching in the United States: Claude Lévi-Strauss at the New School in New York, the critic Étiemble at the University of Chicago.

One particularly interesting case is that of André Breton, who as the doyen of the Surrealists crossed national boundaries as freely as any sixteenth-century humanist. First in Martinique, where he was welcomed by Aimé Césaire and his review, *Tropiques,* then in New York where—among, mostly, painters: Duchamp, Tanguy, Max Ernst, and others—he was active on the Surrealist journal *VVV,* the time of exile for Breton as a writer was hardly more than a stimulating refreshment of his basic faith. It was after the war, when the resistance-hardened younger generation turned to other leaders and doctrines, that Breton found himself to some degree displaced as an active force. So, too, it was after the war that a far more difficult exile began for collaborationists like Céline, specialist in ultimate journeys, who lived in Denmark under police surveillance from 1944 to 1951, or Alphonse de Chateaubriant, who died in seclusion in Austria in 1951, or the respected Drieu la Rochelle, a suicide early in 1945.

For one distinctive reason the situation of the literary exiles from Falangist Spain was unique, and that is the

---

* One of this poem's leading themes anticipates Peter Weiss's discovery; it is the emergence of a new order of consciousness without regard to national divisions and the old historical contingencies. In section V we find this line: "Il n'est d'histoire que de l'âme, il n'est d'aisance que de l'âme." Similarly the last strophe of *Exil* reads: "Et c'est l'heure, ô poète, de décliner ton nom, ta naissance, et ta race."

existence of an immense and diverse Spanish-speaking domain in the New World. Not a few of the creators of modern Spanish literature were themselves American-born—Rubén Darío in Nicaragua (his absorption of Symbolism in Paris in the early 1890's had brought Spanish poetry into the main current of European modernism), Borges in the Argentine, Neruda in Chile, Américo Castro in Brazil—and with the literary "generation of 1898," travel back and forth across the Atlantic, as into northern Europe, had become usual for writers and intellectuals.* For others the enforced discovery of the New World environment, after 1936, came as a fresh revelation, furnishing, as had New York City for García Lorca in 1929, a notable enrichment of resources. The remarkable thing is how many of these writers came to the United States rather than Latin America. These again were chiefly the poets and those with academic credentials, such as Jorge Guillén, Pedro Salinas, or (after an unusual sojourn in Scotland and England) Luis Cernuda. But even Juan Ramón Jiménez, an older man, chose the United States and did not settle permanently in Puerto Rico until 1952. All lived for the day when intellectual and literary freedom would be restored to Spain, but all continued to write with a confidence that where they worked and published would be, for their time, the heartland of Spanish letters.

For many writers political oppression and exile in the twentieth century have had the worst consequences imaginable: an irreversible silencing, utter distraction and hopelessness, the random catastrophe of the firing squad that killed García Lorca in 1936 or of the suicide of Walter Benjamin at the French-Spanish frontier in September of 1940. But not less frequently the experience of exile has led to some unanticipated renewal or expansion of the writer's imaginative will. In some instances it gave new validity to the tarnished ideal of the writer's, the poet's, saving calling within an otherwise brutalized and decadent civilization. In others the raw stimulus of new occasions and new materials acted to rescue some

---

* The tie to Paris was always strong. Among others, Unamuno during the 1920's dictatorship of Primo de Rivera and the poets Antonio Machado and Rafael Alberti in 1939 took refuge in France. Machado, in his sixties, died a month after leaving Spain; Alberti went on to the Argentine.

practiced talent from the circuits of its own previous success. Indeed for many the condition of exile proved a kind of homecoming, to a condition already dreamed of. It provided an objective focus and rationale for an apprehension that had perhaps been gathering within the writer's consciousness with each forward step of his career; an apprehension specifically of his own progressive displacement and alienation as a historical person, in the pursuit of his singular calling.

For—to return to our point of departure—there is an association in modern letters between the writer's elected career and the condition of exile that does not depend on political terror. The logic of this association appears fully established well before the onset of the wars and revolutions of 1914 and after. In English it was given classic expression in Joyce's *Portrait of the Artist as a Young Man*. Everyone remembers Stephen Dedalus' ringing declaration of what common ties the writer must break:

> When the soul of a man is born in this country there are nets flung at it to hold it back from flight. You talk to me of nationality, language, religion. I shall try to fly by those nets.

Joyce added to this declaration, or borrowed from the faded Romantic ethos his own bravura artistry rekindled, a note of aristocratic gallantry concerning the artist's selection of weapons:

> . . . I will try to express myself in some mode of life or art as freely as I can and as wholly as I can, using for my defence the only arms I allow myself to use—silence, exile, and cunning.

Not for nothing was Joyce first among the modernist "saints" whose example was studied and whose virtuous presence, in Paris, eagerly sought out by the self-styled "exiles" of Malcolm Cowley's chronicle.

Like the Americans Pound and Eliot, Joyce, from the perspective of Ireland, could imagine Europe and its literary past as a mythological whole, the totality of which, and nothing less, would be needed to support his creative purpose. The practical result was that once out of Ireland, he could establish working quarters almost anywhere, so long as he remained in reliable communication with Paris. His enactment of the myth of literary exile thus belongs within the pattern, which it magnificently re-creates, of the provincial's escape to the great world of the cultural capitals.* And that in itself is remarkable, a testimony to the conservatism of Joyce's historical sense; for he still believed not only in the Blakean conception of the artist as renewer of generative energy for his species but also in the viability of the old European polis, the family-city of the sensuous and imaginative creature man, within which the artist's cunning work of renewal was to be done.

But at the very moment when Joyce was laboring to complete his last great "European" work, the polylingual *Finnegans Wake,* a writer even more deeply intimate with the central inherited conscience of European Christendom, Georges Bernanos (intimate, one may say, to the point of a certain tremendously expressive incoherence) , was acting out a different judgment of the significance of twentieth-century history. Bernanos was the most distinguished French writer living outside France throughout the Occupation. He had gone into exile, however, not in 1940 but in 1938, when he emigrated to the backlands of Brazil, because, he wrote, truth itself had become sterile, without issue, in Europe.† Catholic by rearing, deeply conservative (like Joyce) as a moralist, a decorated veteran of World War I, a shocked observer of clerical-Falangist repression in Majorca in 1936–1937, Bernanos, writing from Brazil, became a figure of special importance in France during the war years for those younger writers who had begun to remake French literary and philosophical practice. His act of self-exile was a concrete symbol of their own developing conviction that to write consequentially must be to stake one's own life, one's human existence, beyond all the satisfactions of career-making and masterpiece-producing and, for a start,

---

* Joyce's attempt to detach this myth somewhat from the circumstances of his Irishness—in the marriage-tragedy at the dramatic center of his play, *Exiles*—seems the one artistic failure of his magnificent career.
† There is an English analogue, though of less moment historically or symbolically, in Auden's and Isherwood's emigration to the United States several months before the outbreak of World War II. They, too, saw themselves as escaping some spreading incapacity for creative truth in a decadent cultural establishment. But they remained within the English-speaking community of writers, artists, and patrons; they simply felt that its reserves of vitality had moved, if anywhere, to the New World.

to cut one's ties with prize-awarding establishments of any kind.

These crisis-bred existentialists, however, still believed in the value to the entire civil culture of the activity of writing. ("Existentialism," Sartre wrote in 1946, "is a humanism.") Theirs is a specific case of how an abrupt political catastrophe, by providing a mediate rationale for honest work, may forestall for a time the necessity of seeking some more absolute justification. Yet the fact is that a more extreme and absolute pattern of literary exile than any so far mentioned already existed in modern literary history, offering throughout our century a challenge to literary performance that has spurred knowledgeable writers to ever more radical gestures of self-rejection and metamorphic change. This is the pattern Rimbaud in particular created: it is nothing less than the abandonment not simply of an irreversibly decadent Europe (and in the way of his going into Africa, as commercial agent of the rawest kind of imperialism, Rimbaud had taken the worst of the old Europe with him) but of literature itself, as a legitimate undertaking. At first, believing like other Romantic visionaries in the possibility of some transcendent utterance, he had imagined a revolutionary new language; a language "of the soul for the soul," freed from the restrictions of phenomenal existence; a language as different from ordinary tongues as perfect silence. Then by an inexorable logic silence itself became the only tolerable language, as blankness for Mallarmé threatened to become the only tolerable appearance of the printed age. "No more words": such was Rimbaud's legacy to the writers of the future, in whose company he had established his leadership with contemptuous ease.

The idea of the necessary alienation of writers had received categorical expression some years before when Baudelaire wrote (in the journal, "Mon coeur mis à nu," the idea of which had come to him from the rootless American, Poe) that "the man of letters is the enemy of the world." What Rimbaud dramatized was the complex further notion of the writer's or artist's progressive alienation from himself, from that more human and virtuous existence he might otherwise have entered upon. The habit of thinking of the imaginative writer's life as a kind of unnecessary sickness was not original with Rimbaud, nor with his older contemporary Nietzsche, who strenuously popularized it. It has many roots and also many applications within established literary culture. Thus in Thomas Mann's stories of the self-destructive perversity or demonism of the artist-figure, we observe not only the adaptation of Werther and Faust mythology to the modernist phenomenon of an art that is essentially self-preoccupied and self-aggrandizing; we see further the surfacing of the ancient idea of creative inspiration as a possession by demons in which the mind is, literally, beside itself and out of itself. Rimbaud's orginality was moral; it was in finally refusing to see anything heroic or admirable or to find any sort of legitimate compensation in such diseased states of mind, and in proposing instead the life of random action and adventure as morally superior to the parasitic quasi-existence allowed to the writer. In the precocity of his genius, a master at seventeen, and in the disgust he promptly came to feel for the whole ethos of literary creation, he remains a specter at the banquet of all modern literary humanisms.

At this terminal point, where the very continuance of what we call literature is thus challenged, the subject of literary exile properly opens out into the broadest historical, and anthropological, considerations. The crisis in the vocation of literature is inseparable from the collective historical crisis of our revolutionary century. The condition of dislocation and estrangement (including, now, self-estrangement) experienced by modern writers is obviously related to the condition of all workers in a mass technological society and therefore, potentially, of all human beings. Nothing is more characteristic of contemporary society than the emergence within it, in all countries, of a kind of intellectual and literary proletariat, educated within an obsolete system of preferment and insufficiently employed except as skilled personnel in the bureaucratized state, as a permanently disaffected and unstable class or sect.* Contemporary literature, universally self-reflective, has made disaffection of this kind its great theme. A survey of another kind could be written on the primacy of the theme of

---

* One sees what kind of "foreign devil" Mao Tse-tung has been fighting with his "cultural revolution," though one may doubt his success.

cultural exile in twentieth-century fiction—and on how, increasingly, our most compelling narratives are produced by those who have acted out some form of this condition in their lives.

André Malraux would offer an exemplary case: a writer who, adventuring illegally in Asia in his youth in the manner of a Rimbaud, defined "absurdity" itself (that modern philosophical idol) as European; who returned to "Europe" only when it presented him the finite practical causes of defending Republican Spain and reconstituting a shattered France; and whose dramatic heroes have regularly been homeless intellectualized borderlanders, the Schleswiger Perken, the half-caste Kyo, the Alsatian Vincent Berger. Other cases have already been cited, Camus for one; and alongside *The Stranger* we might put in particular the exemplary fables of his collection, *Exile and the Kingdom.** Or, returning to the American milieu, we could trace the fortunes of the literary generation of the Beats and hipsters. Here we would see a striking inversion of the process Malcolm Cowley chronicled. Instead of making apprentice-pilgrimages into "exile" in order to become accredited writers within a noble tradition, the characteristic figures of this generation found their vocation as writers in consequence of having already detached themselves from accepted social roles, inventing instead an anarchic undersociety of their own. They went "on the road" first, they "dragged themselves through the negro streets at dawn," they formed communes in abandoned mountain farms or warehouse lofts in city slums or went halfway around the world to submit themselves to the discipline of Zen masters; then took up writing about it. Or we might speak of an even younger American generation, many of them black, so absorbed in a struggle for survival as free beings that they hardly have time to be anything but confrontation spokesmen and propagandists, or possess the will to tell any story but their own necessarily repetitive and unfinished one.

What such extensions of this inquiry would also reveal is the paradox that among all such symptoms of fundamental disturbance the enterprise of literature was nevertheless main-

---

* One especially, "The Artist at Work," is a paradigm of the modern artist's progressive detachment from belief in his own existence.

taining itself in a certain hopefulness and expectancy. But the new forms that result are hard to fit into traditional anthologies. They seem rather to be competing for recognition within the special domain of popular arts and performances. Much of what is freshest and most "authentic" in contemporary writing seems an adjunct of this world: the world of films, public recitations (including the ritual of public confession and of mock political trials, as in the shapeless plays of Rolf Hochhuth, which exist, as regards performances, without benefit of a stable text) , mock-commercial "advertisements" for the self, electronic displays, street riots, and "happenings" in general. Such goings-on appear to have, just at present, the strong support of a revolutionary upheaval in cultural behavior that has leaped across the traditional boundaries dividing classes, nations, races, and ideologies. Precisely at the moment when *alienation* and *exile* had got fixed as cant terms for the condition of the free man of letters in the old sense, these popular arts and the improvised communities of youth and liberation that nourish their inventiveness have demonstrated an extraordinary power to make themselves at home anywhere in the world.

They are thus asserting at least an embryonic version of that universal new order of consciousness which we noted as a countertheme in St.-John Perse's poem *Exil;* that fresh exchange of living ideas, "bound to no country," envisioned by Peter Weiss. So far the exemplary products of this movement, particularly in literature, have not been original and self-contained art works in the classic mold but the by-products of an emergent way of life—a way of life that finds its principal validation in extraliterary occurrences, the deliberately ephemeral and interchangeable acts and communings of the new worldwide guerrilla-sect of the young and uncommitted. Against such a background, literature as we have known it appears to have gone into exile from itself. Yet literary documents attesting to the reality of this way of life and consciousness do now exist and may possibly contain (or so we must think, from all we know of historical precedent) the durable elements of new artistic tradition. To express despair at the future of literature may only be to complain, rather pointlessly, that the classics of this tradition have not yet appeared.

The Novel in a Time of Troubles

Whether a random levee of novelists and novel-readers, in weekend debate,* can reach agreement on the broad question of what is happening to the novel—what significant fresh turn, if any, it has taken as a literary form, and whether there is any serious virtue in the future we can project for it—I am inclined to doubt. But that is no reason for misgivings. Why *should* a consensus develop among us? On the whole it would be more worrisome if one did. Where everybody is of one opinion, chances are that understanding, insight, intelligent concern have gone to sleep, or else that the subject is no longer worth discussing. But if the hope, transcending mere opinion, that the novel might speak to us once again with the force and authority we imagine it once had—the conscience-organizing force and authority of major art—is a hope we truly share, might not an unreconcilable diversity of impressions and convictions be a first sign of some possible fulfillment? For true art, in Pasternak's words, is always more one-sided than people think. As a species of activity, though necessarily collective in

---

* This essay was the opening paper at the University of Iowa's Second Biennial Conference for Modern Letters, on the subject of "the new fiction," October 19–21, 1967—the weekend, as it happened, of the march to the Pentagon, which, coming to a climax a thousand miles to the east, gave an edge of displaced hysteria to the conference proceedings.

all its contingent materials and occasions, its vocabulary of
elements, it presses by its very nature toward individuality and
distinctiveness, toward self-accomplishment rather than generalized satisfaction. That is its special value to us and the
source of our deepest interest in it. The concrete enterprise
of art will do anything to serve its own gratuitous desire to
come into being, to command our attention on its own uncom-
promised terms. And in order to complete the arc of its emergence, it will if necessary subvert any rule we establish in its
name, or any critical program, however sympathetic and well-
intentioned, we think to lay out for its convenient use. It arrives to distract us and to free our minds, to assist us in freeing
ourselves, from the grip *of* opinion and consensus. This may
or may not be a main part of its own animating purpose, but
it is a main effect by which we recognize its real presence.

Yet, to contradict myself a little, on one central matter
I suspect that there may be a consensus; whether or not this is
so, let it serve as the ruling fiction of my talk. We all know
why we are here. The novel, our meal ticket as writers, critics,
teachers, is in trouble—with regard to its historic function as
an instrument of imaginative freedom, an organizer and re-
fresher of conscience, it has been in trouble for quite a while
—and we have an interest in finding out why and to what end
this is the case. If anything reassuring has recently appeared
on its fever chart, then we would like very much to know
about it. If not, then we want to know the worst, without
wishful evasions. For the novel has a special place in our concern. A mongrel and parasite among literary forms from its
beginnings—we remember that the first modern novel, *Don
Quixote*, began as a parody-critique of another kind of fiction,
and then in its unanticipated sequel turned into a parody-
critique of itself as well as of the bad faith of its imitators—
the novel has always been bound with peculiar intimacy to the
prevailing fictions of common life and opinion. At its best
this intimacy has been critical and subversive, not least of the
novel's own previously agreeable conventions. What important novelist has not put his work before us as in some fundamental way a species of antinovel, a corrective to the suddenly
transparent artifices and accommodations of existing fiction?
Like a Machiavellian family schemer, a secret witness in the

old Gothic manner, the novel exploits our household illusions and anxieties for its own advantage, and yet refreshes the waste of ordinary existence with its privileged masquerade of connectedness and consequentiality in human affairs. This ironic complicity with the evolving consciousness of its readership (ever deluded, ever hopeful) has been central to the continuing life of the novel as a form, and it is why we are sensitive to the question of the novel's well-being; we still expect it to begin reorganizing our apprehension of life, painfully and violently if necessary; we still take its presence or absence in this role as a measure of cultural health.

The child of the modern liberal social order, sharing and reinforcing its dedication to the ethos of individualism and the contracted unitary action (marriage, fortune-making, the career open to talent, the whole aggressive drama of self-promotion and self-esteem), the novel has flourished as that order has flourished, or imagined itself to be flourishing, and is seemingly in decline as our confidence in present historical tendencies has declined. The great age of the novel was the long bourgeois-imperialist peace or civil truce (periodically threatened and interrupted yet never wholly annulled) between Waterloo and the disastrous renewal of European civil war on an unprecedented scale in 1914–1918, that war being the climax-catastrophe that produced after 1915 a last great cycle of masterpieces, written by men of the brilliant prewar era (Mann, Gide, Lawrence, Forster, Svevo, Musil, Broch— and Proust and Joyce, too) who were shocked by the historical convulsion of their time into this further effort of mastery. To be sure, the older nineteenth-century and pre-1914 novels that we prize most were nearly all in rebellion against the social and cultural conditions of that long pseudo-peace, against its covert violence and inward rot. Reading them now, we find them rich in prophecies of confusion and ruin to come. But the kind of high artistic or executive confidence that brought them into being, and that to our eyes is the hardly imaginable quality they have in common, surely derived from the civil and intellectual confidence of that age, a fundamental confidence in the reality of the future and in the human will's effort to shape it to its own deepest preferences which was shared, despite much outward pessimism, by rulers and rebels alike.

We appear not to have that kind of confidence now, that old liberal-humanist presumption. Or if we do, we have it with the insolence of our first coming-of-age and we lose it fast. The conditions of contemporary existence, the wider conditions governing the production and consumption of novels, hardly permit it. What these conditions are, everybody knows; it is enough to say that, foreign or domestic, political or ecological, they are always nowadays at red alert, and that as we have time and energy of mind to spare for reading novels at all, our wish is intensified for some countervailing show of force and intelligence in what we read. These conditions are a burden and distraction for our serious novelists, too, many of whom can hardly bear to think of writing in a way that will not be apocalyptic in its impact and the potential basis for some new ordering of the age's essential spirit, some momentous historical reversal of tendencies that grow worse even as we try to fix our minds on them. The patience necessary for the effort of art (or even of effective polemic) to come to maturity and in any given instance to complete itself seems more and more of a luxury. Readers' patience, too, is in short supply. And this makes a difference, for the novel is, in relation to other literary genres, a mass form; at least it is hard to imagine the novel without its having, again relatively speaking, a mass readership. Poetry can survive, and flourish, without that, and so even can drama, but not the novel. Quite obviously, then, the concern that brings us together is not simply with the novel but with the entire civil crisis, the multiple interlocking crises, of the present historical moment. We cannot detach ourselves from these circumstances. Nobody needs to have it explained why Mr. Norman Mailer calls his new book about a Texas disc jockey and an Alaskan bear hunt *Why Are We in Vietnam?*, though it might just as well be called *Why Is Detroit Burning?* In fact, the perfect, immediately recognizable aptness of both title and subject, the ease with which we assimilate them, may serve to suggest why the book itself, though a genuine tour de force, has in the end no greater authority for our imaginations than any passing wire-service sensation the emblematic significance of which is all too immediately and completely apparent.

These public circumstances, however, are not the only source of the novel's present difficulties. The novel in its higher flights has not had to take second place to any other literary form, not even epic or tragedy, forms it assisted in displacing and pillaged in the process, but it has made its way by keeping contact with its humbler origins in folk gossip and folk curiosity. By definition the novel brings us the news of the day, the unreported news if you will, and entertains us, takes hold of us, with divinations of the way we really live, or might have to live under certain all too conceivable emergent conditions. And it is, in part, in this function of news-delivering entertainment—seeking to hold our attention by transforming the formless data of contemporary circumstance and moral consciousness into a significant narrative progression—that the novel is in trouble. For this part of its traditional service has been preempted by other narrative and expository forms that can get at us more directly: by the movies, with their extraordinary power to imitate not only the minuter gestures and rhythms of human experience but the larger spatial relations and temporal sequences, too, and by a documentary journalism possessing, in an electronic era, surrealistically developed resources for representational intensity.*

The American novel in particular has suffered from such competition. Its own majority commitment to a vivid immediacy of sensation and feeling as a first test of truthfulness, and its mistrust of the indirections of the critical or the architectonic intellect, have if anything increased as our century has advanced. But when I think of fictional sequences that in recent years have moved me with their show of life to a continuing recognition and assent, I think more often of movies than novels—films of Bergman, Truffaut, Godard, Agnes Varda. I might even maliciously throw into the argument the

---

* Resources, we may add, for creating the events it means to record; for the vested interest of electronic journalism in inventing news and processing human affairs into newsworthiness far exceeds any material investment we have in maintaining the art of the novel.

film of *Lolita,* which resolved various doubts about Nabokov's performance into the positive judgment that what he had written was not after all a novel, really, but an exceptionally clever scenario waiting to be filmed. So also, though I loyally submit to the imaginary conspiracies, the intricate combat with fantastic and malevolent institutions, elaborated by Joseph Heller (*Catch-22*), John Barth (*Giles Goat-Boy*), Thomas Pynchon (*The Crying of Lot 49*), Robert Kelly (*The Scorpions*), John A. Williams (*The Man Who Cried I Am*), or by the half-Americanized Andrew Sinclair (*The Project*), how can their ingenuities compete with, say, the bare recital in the *New Republic* last month (September 30, 1967) of what has happened to Robert Williams of Monroe, North Carolina, in his ten-years' grapple with the actual law-bearing institutions of our democracy, or with a straightforward testament like *The Autobiography of Malcolm X*? (The examples may remind us how idealizing the novel is, and ought to be.) As a form for the times, even drama has stolen a march on the novel, turning against its own threadbare mechanisms of representation and in the process stripping down its essential vision of human life to the autonomic combat of actors—isn't that what our postrealistic plays and theatrical happenings are really about?—figures engaged in driving each other up and down the stage or competing for attention with an audience they essentially despise: the perfect formal embodiment of our worst nightmares about common relationships in an affluent, self-liberated society terrorized by its own spreading freedom.

One could go on at length in this vein, defining all the particular distractions that make up the special plight of present-day novelists, whose books flare for a season and, we hope, sell, then disappear without a trace. But suppose our attention was fixed on the situation of the novel elsewhere than in the United States? Contemporary English novelists face the same public conditions (though perhaps not with just the same intensity of shock and guilt; Vietnam at least is not directly theirs) and certainly the same competition from the new expertness of rival media. Yet we find a remarkable number of them moving along in fine fettle, year by year building up a body of work that steadily maintains itself, or

advances, in craft and in popular acceptance. I am not thinking now of purveyors of popular merchandise like C. P. Snow,
not to say Agatha Christie, but of the work of Anthony Powell
and Iris Murdoch, who seem to me the most substantially interesting and accomplished novelists of the post-1945 period,
and, at a lower but thoroughly respectable and engaging level,
Durrell and Golding and Doris Lessing and Muriel Spark
and Anthony Burgess and maybe even Margaret Drabble, who
is still very young; others could be named.

For American readers it is a spectacle that compels attention: a generation of novelists intelligently and energeti-
cally talented, getting their work done, establishing an identifiable corpus of work that is not just the playing out of some
unindividuated early promise, and gradually giving the whole
period much of what is distinctive in its literary character. We
are reminded of certain persisting differences between the
English literary situation and the American. These English
novelists appear to feel, as much as any American or European contemporary, the impulse to show the age something
of its distinctive form and pressure. They can be quite openly
didactic; they are perfectly willing to point a moral and adorn,
speculatively, their tale. But none of them seems to feel
obliged to produce work of Scriptural authority; none is under
a compulsion to aim at revolutionizing contemporary consciousness in order to exist and function as a novelist.

To put the matter another way, they all write as if they
had no special doubt about being read. We detect in the whole
bearing of their work—their willingness to operate within familiar conventions, their steady productivity—this rather astonishing assumption: that a sufficient reading public exists
for their effort as writers of fiction, and that no supraliterary
measures need be resorted to in order to get a hearing from
this public and even make some durable impression on it.
In its own conception of itself and its function, the contemporary English novel at its best still bears a constructive relation
to an imagined national estate as well as to a continuous
earlier tradition of novel writing. At some level these books
are all written as letters to the English and they concern in
one form or another a definable condition-of-England or spirit-
of-England question. In particular they celebrate those low-

pitched, novelistic virtues—subjective honesty, avoidance of cant and pretension, fellow feeling to some other end than personal advantage or the maintenance of special privileges—which we see would be of genuine service to the commonwealth, the whole civil estate.

One may doubt, of course, whether the national experience is as precisely addressable and as uniform in spirit as these novels (and the twenty or so intelligent reviews each has a chance of getting in the British papers and magazines) would imply. There remains, as always, much of real life that goes unrecorded in British fiction, that escapes its trim reckonings. It is nevertheless true that for the English novel certain stable and facilitating conventions, compositional, stylistic, moral and imaginative, remain in force on both sides of the fiction-making transaction; that is, with both authors and readers. This has, I think, two beneficial consequences. First, individual novelists find themselves engaged, technically and imaginatively, in a common task. A certain unspoken consciousness of each other's existence, resulting in a tacit division of labor that allows each one to keep on his own track, stabilizes their workmanship; their differences are, finally, family differences. Second, they can be sure, if they have any talent at all, of a reception and an audience; that is, they can be sure of being intelligently received and discussed in relation to some objective conception (and by objective I simply mean collectively shared) of what their effort might involve and what its uses are.

Now it is quite possible for Americans to be very superior about all this; to detect in it some ultimately crippling compromise and betrayal of the writer's full responsibility; to speak of a mini-literature and of a failure of English literary nerve in settling for it. But for the moment, lacking, I think, a demonstrably superior corpus of prose fiction, we might recognize the virtues of the English situation. Not only does it serve to keep lesser talents usefully in business. It also keeps lines of action open for the potentially major novelist; it allows him to experiment and to develop, if he is going to develop, at his own pace yet with some assurance along the way that he is being listened to, and thus to move on to the creation of a genuine oeuvre. It allows him also to proceed to the creation of a literary character of his own that has effectual weight and moment, a literary character that is more than just an attention-getting device but that may become a causative force in times to come, a creator and enabler of the consciousness, if only the literary consciousness, of the future.

For American novelists does any such situation exist? Has it in fact ever existed?—for the suspicion arises that the distractions of present history have only intensified an occupational estrangement that the serious American writer of fiction has always known. The reading public that is genuinely discriminating and responsive in Great Britain is small, no doubt, and perhaps largely private, a kind of underground; but it appears to exist, it can be felt by writers as a real reciprocal presence. Held more or less firmly in place by the competitive literacy of the weekend papers and certain magazines, and back of that by the persistence of a conversationally literate subculture still fairly independent and secure in taste and judgment, this public is still able to arrive at intelligible opinions (not necessarily correct ones, of course) ; it still exists, as a critical court of appeal, however erratic or Philistine its reactions may be.

What can be found to correspond in the United States? Who actually reads the new novels this conference has in view, *reads* them, that is, beyond dully consuming them as *Valley of the Dolls* is consumed, under the prodding of well-managed merchandising campaigns; reads them, and keeps them in mind?* Who does in fact read Barth, Pynchon, John Hawkes, William Burroughs, Susan Sontag, Kurt Vonnegut, Jr., Stanley Elkin, Brock Brower, the authors of that "new fiction" we have come together to talk about? College students mostly (who read as they should, impurely, for information and private utilitarian purposes, in order to find out what it is they are supposed to know and whom they are to compete with) , and also a few of their teachers, and various with-it people composing an audience more concerned to keep up with the

---

* Some months after this talk was given, an impromptu survey revealed that among readers who had actually bought certain new novels of merit that had also been best sellers—books by Saul Bellow, John Barth, Vladimir Nabokov, John Updike—an embarrassingly small percentage had ever finished them, or got much past the first fifty pages.

growth stocks than to play the reader's true part in the dialectic of literary origination. In the affluent American desert of product consumption where almost anything may suddenly get licensed and acclaimed but nothing is seriously kept in mind for more than a season, there are oases or encouragement, to be sure, and some of these are very lush indeed, but how creative a supporting role can anyone claim for them? *The New Yorker* still gives the odd young writer of promise some valuable initial support, but *The New Yorker* itself is a product more consumed than read; and for a good many years in any case the larger part of its fiction department has been pieced out by English, Irish, *émigré* contributions. We have been better off with *The New York Review of Books* than we were without it, yet nearly everything of value that it carries, in the way of literary reviewing, is written by Englishmen, the same writers we also read in the London papers.* And there are still the academy- and foundation-sponsored quarterlies and writing schools, but do these really give critical direction to contemporary writing? Are they not simply a part of the untraceably erratic system of academic and foundation preferment that has settled like a vast oil slick over our recognized intellectual life?

No, what the American writer confronts is what he has always confronted, and been driven to extraordinary measures to circumvent: measures of cunning, exile, and silence devised, as we know, by Americans like Poe, Hawthorne, Melville, Twain, Cable, James, well before Joyce gave a definitive name to them. He faces not a reading public capable of discrimination and a reciprocating encouragement but a disorganized wilderness of lost souls requiring, first of all, conversion, and indifferent in a week to any less convulsive experience. The first task for each new American writer is to fix into place an audience that does not otherwise exist for him. And the second task, the one that regularly wears him out, is to try to keep this improvised audience from lapsing back into its normal condition of atomized impermeability. He may not relax with

---

* As of 1969–1970 this seems less the case; the balance in *The New York Review* between English and American contributors is now fairly even. Perhaps this is because it has become more a journal of public affairs—and a good one—than a literary review.

it for a moment. He must convert it spiritually, transform its fundamental character by extraordinary exertions of mesmeric authority, and keep it mesmerized without intermission. Otherwise it will suddenly dissolve and vanish, and he himself will cease, as writer, to exist. He must, in a word, create a society of readers; he must do this over and over again; and he must do it among a people, the Americans, who have done everything in their natural power, throughout their history, to resist effective socialization.

Our current literature, poetry and drama as well as fiction, bears the marks of this condition of things, which is, as I have meant to suggest, primarily a social condition, having nothing less than the whole weight of our national history behind it. And it is in terms of certain familiar conditions in our past history, certain phenomena of our social life which are being renewed, not unexpectably, in our disturbed present, that the character of contemporary American writing makes most sense to me. The new novels I read do not convince me that American fiction has taken a significant new turn in technical or imaginative invention, or even in moral outlook. What instead they reveal is that some old habitual forms for expressing popular anxiety and disorientation have moved in on the literary vocation, have, in a democratizing and institutionally demoralized period, fairly taken it over.

The American literary scene, where it is not altogether given over to merchandising, resembles nothing so much as one of the wild, freewheeling sectarian revival movements of a century and a half ago. The symptoms correspond quite remarkably, and it may be to the point to list a few of them. There are, wherever we look, the same public conditions of social and spiritual disorder, of cultural displacement and disaffection, of frustrated millennial ambition. There is the same frantic effort among writers and readers alike to capitalize on this circumstance, the same impatience with anything short of final and catastrophic solutions, without delay. There is the same premium on the naked excitation of raw feeling; the same intense concentration on the immediate ritual of soul-saving, without regard to other standards of liberation and community. There is the same Pyrrhonistic hostility to traditional intellect and traditional languages of exposition: a matter of great importance to the very continuance of a serious and effective literature. There is the same almost exclusive reliance on personal confession and anecdotal testimony and the same distrust of other presentational conventions; the same fierce competition in reciting ever more horrific "evidences" and "cases of conscience" (which hardly have to be searched for); the same trafficking (I quote here the hero of Norman Mailer's *An American Dream*) in "spirits and demons, in devils, warlocks, omens, wizards, and fiends, in incubi and succubi"; and there is, coincidentally, the same downward conversion of individual persons and events into monitory examples and case histories. There are the same radical confusions about sincerity and hypocrisy and everyday "bad faith." There is the same reductive yet momentarily irresistible simplification, through pulpit-prosecutor's parables, of essential issues and themes. There is the same ritual stylization of language into catchwords that will elicit the maximum immediate stock-response, and the same repetitive vocabulary of orgiastic incidents and plot climaxes. And finally there is the same dismaying lack of effect on the larger national drift of social and institutional life; the same ultimate subservience, in the mindlessly exploitative order of modern society, to the major play of political and economic force, a subservience that takes the form of pretending—as in the final vision of the rather likable heroine of Pynchon's *The Crying of Lot 49*—that simply waiting with head down among all the roar of electronic relays, all the monotonous litanies of insult, filth, fantasy, brute repetitive sex, will somehow call into being "the unnameable act, the recognition, the Word," the "magical Other" that will redeem us.

My probably overdrawn point here is simply this: popular revivalism, seemingly derelict in our time as a historical agency, except of course within sections of the black community and a scattering of lesser aggregations of the dispossessed,*

---

* But during the same month in which I was writing this talk, the Draft Resistance movement, in meetings like that at the Arlington Street Church in Boston where Michael Ferber preached the sermon that coincidentally won him an indictment for conspiracy by the United States Attorney General's office and the Clarence Skinner Award of the Unitarian-Universalist Association, was reawakening with fresh effectiveness this ancient instrumentality of communal will and power.

has established a new foothold in literature and the arts, which grow as monotonously orgiastic as the leisure-class voyeurism they find themselves in practical competition with (for isn't it true that contemporary novels are mostly read now as *Playboy* is read—if that is the right word—or as actors are watched undressing and worse in underground and side-street *cinema de vérité* establishments?). I think this is a development of obvious cultural and historical interest. But with respect to the creation of a consequential literature, I also think that it may be essentially sterile. I mean that in aiming at a conversion-inducing immediacy of sensational effects and transforming revelations, our fiction is playing a game it cannot win, unless it falls back on the simple parody of the put-on. This may explain all the overextended jokes that pass for fiction these days, some of them by remarkably ingenious and spirited jokesters like Heller and Barth; novels, as John Barth himself has charmingly confessed, like *The Sot-Weed Factor* and *Giles Goat-Boy*, "which imitate the form of the Novel, by an author who imitates the role of Author".

Or perhaps the novelist simply isn't interested in "winning" the old game of broad cultural persuasion anymore. Following a progression characteristic of the older popular revival movements, writers of fiction, who once thought of themselves as a brotherhood of craftsmen engaged in capturing public attention and perhaps reforming public consciousness, have now "come out" from the common life as an independent and autonomous sect. Our fiction has more and more the aspect of an endless camp meeting. Writing novels, like constructing art objects, acting, playing music, hanging around universities, has become a special insulated way of behaving, a way of escaping unbearable constraints and, to a degree, denying their reality. Francis Fergusson has recently commented on this (*New York Review,* August 3, 1967): "The most advanced cults in the arts, whose pull affects a great many highly gifted artists just now, are as compulsive and allsufficient and unassailable as any other new religion: credo quia absurdum est." It is a development characteristic of the human imagination in a time of troubles, the Toynbeean term that may still be remembered. The common consciousness splinters, grows universally suspicious and derogatory. Every half-reflective mind fabricates its own religion, its own rituals for binding the evidences of things together and exorcizing what it finds unnameable; every writer becomes not just a maker of virtuous objects but an evangelist for his own self-fashioned faith. And all this, we know, perfectly reflects the conditions of behavior, the secular rituals, of a fragmented, immitigably exploitative society; it has, to repeat, the weight and mass of our whole national history behind it.

Of course the broad situation I have been describing is not a new one in our literary or our cultural history. Masterpieces have come out of it, or out of something much like it, in the past, for it was during a comparable period of intense sectarian fragmentation and self-conscious, almost programmatic social disorder that the great mythopoeic fictions of our nineteenth-century American "renaissance" emerged. And it may well be that the masterpieces of our own time are simply out of sight at present or have been temporarily mislaid, just as a hundred years ago *Moby-Dick, Walden, Leaves of Grass* were pretty much out of sight or officially mislaid. On the other hand the last thing you could say about these books of the 1850's, for all their rhetorical pretense of being direct transcriptions of a dedicated personal experience, is that they were composed without full benefit of traditional literary and philosophical resources. Think what kind of structural and imaginative support they could draw on among the ideologies of the transcendentalist era and, back of that, the rich intellectual and argumentative legacy of the Reformation; what support also from the new Romantic ideology of the sovereign eloquence and self-sufficiency of fully accomplished art.

If our time is to have a literature equal to the extraordinary occasions of its own emerging history—equal to them and not merely submissive—I doubt that it will come into being without some comparable thrust of reflective, self-critical, philosophic intelligence; without also some corresponding degree of *artistic* seriousness. But these are what finally seem absent among the borrowed substructures of contemporary writing. Our fiction, we might say, is simply not fictive enough, as our poetry is not sufficiently poetic, that is, sufficiently involved in the *making* of new forms. A spasmodic subjective truthfulness, a fidelity to immediate sensation, cannot do the job by themselves. Truth to immediate experience, sensual, emotional, moral, and economic, must surely remain a first test of virtue in literature. But, to borrow a formulation of R. P. Blackmur's for the achievement of modernist literature in general, sensibility (and sensuousness) must be made into "a substance of thought" if we are to have a literature that can break out of the condition of mere subservience to the present moment and the appalling drift of present history.

Whether any such happy development is actually possible for American writing and specifically the novel, I have rather strong doubts just now. The current evidence is not altogether encouraging. But it's hard to imagine a doubt, a cultural prognostication, that one would rather have proved wrong. Popular songwriting has immensely surprised us in the last few years with its fresh inventiveness, its critical and interpretive freedom, and its rather extraordinary relevance, as have, over a longer period, our painting and sculpture, too; these may be the best of omens for what concerns us. Why shouldn't the novel, with its solid formal roots in popular consciousness, be the next creative genre to follow suit? But it will take some doing, and one may fear that the casualty rate among those attempting it will, as always, be high.

AFTERWORD (1970)

The account given above of the situation for the English novelist as opposed to the American idealizes it, of course, perhaps to the point of absurdity. It may set members of the class in question laughing up their sleeves. Yet I think I am describing conditions and differences that really exist.

For a test we might compare two accomplished younger novelists, Joyce Carol Oates (American) and Margaret Drabble (English), as they appear to us in representative recent books—*Expensive People* (1968) and *The Waterfall* (1969) — not dissimilar in theme. How much more adroitly the American writer goes about the business of mingling and opposing "fiction" and "truth"; how easily she improvises a whole series of mechanisms for parodistic undercutting—writing dismissive reviews of her own book from one prejudiced angle or another; interrupting the narrative with ironic digressions on technique ("How to Write a Memoir Like This"); offering alternate titles, stories within (and contributing to) the main story, antitruths of ordinary duplicity within the larger antitruth of "good" fiction. By contrast Margaret Drabble plugs along with no more of a departure from old-fashioned circumstantial realism than an alternation between first-person and third-person narration and without the virtuosity of style, really, to make even this technique sharply effective.

But as to cumulative force and a final impression of truthfulness, which keeps its hold? For myself I find that it is the English writer's story that stays more steadfastly in mind, and that—by some technically understated power to fix itself nearer the center of common feeling and apprehension—compels a more central attention. Beyond doubt, expert technique intensifies the process by which a piece of writing gains authority with us, but it cannot by itself repair failures or deficiencies in primary conception, the writer's moral grasp on the figures of his invention. C. Day Lewis has spoken well to this point. "Technique," he wrote, with special regard to poetry, "is not only the conscious ordering of words and rhythms. It includes the discipline of creative meditation, and the patience which will not broach memories and ideas until they are matured. These, too, are part of the composing of a poem . . ." (*Notable Images of Virtue*, pp. 48–49). My point is simply that such discipline and patience, to the degree they are collectively determined, seem at present less difficult to come by for the English novelist than the American.

Fortunes of the Novel:
Muriel Spark and Iris Murdoch

In our present low-pressure literary climate, new novels by
Muriel Spark and Iris Murdoch are events of particular interest. Who better exemplify the creative fortunes of the past
ten or fifteen years in English writing? The two most admired English novelists to come forward since the early 1950's
(neither has suffered the lapse of critical interest overtaking
gifted contemporaries like William Golding and Kingsley
Amis), they have also been very nearly the most productive:
The Mandelbaum Gate (1965) is Muriel Spark's seventh
novel since *The Comforters* (1957), and she has also written
stories and plays, while *The Red and the Green* (1965) is Iris
Murdoch's eighth since her notably self-possessed and free-
handed maiden venture, *Under the Net* (1954). And each has
done more than publish a string of well-regarded books. Each
has created a substantial fictional world, reasoned in design
and fresh and provocative in detail, a world of gesture and
occasion that, growing recognizable from one novel to the
next, has become ground and cause of its own further acceptance; each, in so doing, has acted to keep the novel itself
alive as a creative form and open to serious use.

Reprinted from *The Massachusetts Review*, Spring, 1967, and Summer,
1967.

Neither, to be sure, is yet a novelist to put beside the Anglo-American masters of the earlier part of our century: James, Lawrence, Joyce, Faulkner. In plain truth neither seems to possess this kind of power and originality; neither will transform the novel or alter consciousness in the same imperial way. In a word, neither is likely to produce a masterpiece. They belong, it appears, to the rank of those who work within received forms and conventions and aim (both are unembarrassedly didactic) at some intermediate correction, perhaps improvement, of common understanding. Their work and the approval it has received can in fact be seen as part of a twenty-year rebellion against the very idea of masterpieces, which may be a foreign idea in any case in a land whose writers have not in the main felt obliged to produce The Great English Novel or to "maintain the sublime in the old sense."

More precisely this rebellion has been against a certain conception of the writer's task, a conception derived from the whole intense ethos of European modernism and last expressed with much confidence by an English writer in the opening sentence of Cyril Connolly's epoch-haunted word-cycle of 1945, *The Unquiet Grave:* "The more books we read, the sooner we perceive that the true function of a writer is to produce a masterpiece and that no other task is of any consequence." The virulent anti-Cyrillism of English letters since the late forties hardly seems accidental, nor does Connolly's own withdrawal. And the rebellion I am speaking of involves something more than willful insularity, the new sincerity-haunted little-Englandism of settling rather than rising expectations and a diminished world position, though that state of mind has flourished since 1945, not unproductively. The best part of it is not the negative contempt for masterpieces as such that it sometimes results in. Rather it is a dissent, at once practical and philosophical, from the premature consignment of the writer's "true function" to so paralyzingly remote and exalted an end. It also has in view a scaly new generation of academic censors whose variously orthodox reconstructions of the English literature syllabus so often seem to require rejecting all contemporary authors as unworthy. It declares, "allow us, please, to get on with the job, and let immortality (or any other great tradition) take care of itself."

That one of our two novelists turned at the beginning of her career to a very different model and definition of the writer's true function—as Iris Murdoch turned to Sartre, the subject of her first book (1953), and, less programmatically, to the excellent Raymond Queneau, to whom she dedicated *Under the Net*—is, again, symptomatic. The Sartrean picture of the writer as one far too occupied with survival as a temporal agent to be concerned with the immortality of masterpieces, throwing out work after work simply to resist the sickness unto death of contemporary life: this has both shaped her conception of her own activity and perhaps justified a certain pellmell profusion and slipshoddiness in her performance.

"It is the function of the writer to write the best book he knows how to write," Iris Murdoch has said.* Not the strict point of this formulation so much as its tone and angle mark it off from Connolly's high-handed pronouncement. In its studied casualness it carries the implication that the problem of the writer's function is simply one of practical morale and that it may be prejudicial to the very existence of literature to expect individual works to be, under scrutiny, any less imperfect and unstable than contemporary behavior in general. Iris Murdoch's speculative emphasis is on the writer's persistence in his work rather than on the finished product and the competition of masterpieces. Following Sartre, she has spoken pointedly of the making of works of art as not only "a struggle for freedom" but as "a task which does not come to an end." Against the bourgeois idolatry of masterpieces and

---

* "Against Dryness: A Polemical Sketch," *Encounter*, January, 1961. A series of philosophical essays by Iris Murdoch is indispensable to anyone concerned with her work or, for that matter, with contemporary English writing. The most important are: a paper in the symposium, "Thinking and Language," *Aristotelian Society Supplementary Volume XXV* (1951); "Nostalgia for the Particular," *Proceedings of the Aristotelian Society*, LII (1951–1952); "Vision and Choice in Morality," *Aristotelian Society Supplementary Volume XXX* (1956); "The Sublime and the Good," *Chicago Review*, Autumn, 1959; "The Sublime and the Beautiful Revisited," *Yale Review*, Winter, 1959–1960; "The Idea of Perfection," *Yale Review*, Spring, 1964. Their bearing on her novels is considered in A. S. Byatt, *Degrees of Freedom: The Novels of Iris Murdoch* (1965), and Peter Wolfe, *The Disciplined Heart: Iris Murdoch and Her Novels* (1966).

their creators (an attitude which she has called "Romantic"),
she advances an image of endless marginal struggle with, at
best, only limited and provisional success. "Art, too," she has
asserted, "lives in a region where all endeavor is failure."
Hence it "must not be too much afraid of incompleteness."
Her solutions as a novelist ratify her speculative pronounce-
ments, and in their conjunction she has become a writer whom
anyone concerned with the immediate future of literature
must come to terms with; she stands at present for as effectively reasoned a program of creative renewal as exists in the
English-speaking world.

Muriel Spark has not declared her purposes and point of
view so fully, but where we do find her speaking about writing,
it has been with the same period-blend of diffidence and laconic counterstatement. Her writing is simply what she has
found it possible to do. She once characterized the artist as "a
minor public servant"—"If he starts thinking of himself as a
public master, he's in trouble"—and though she is as willing
as any modernist defender of the autonomy of art to "read anyone with a good style," her explanation of "the whole secret
of style" is notably unheroic, unFlaubertian: "It's simply not
caring too much, it's caring only a little."* Yet she cannot be
called unambitious, and with *The Mandelbaum Gate*—elaborate in design, brazenly artful in execution—she has staked out
a bold claim to major critical recognition.

In a sense this is her first proper novel. All her earlier
books were held down to novella length and regularly fell into
the subordinate forms of parable, extended anecdote, morality
play; one was presented as a "ballad," while the title of another, *Memento Mori*, indicates its limitations in form and
desired effect as well as its theme. These books also have been
short on narrative elaboration, though complicated in plot,
and long, relatively, on commentary, authorial glosses, talis-
manic refrains. But *The Mandelbaum Gate* is a larger affair.
In scale it is as different as, say, *Les Faux-monnayeurs* from
Gide's earlier recitals and "symphonies" and appears to represent a comparable expansion of purpose.

---

* "My Conversion," *The Twentieth Century*, Autumn, 1961.

Consider the setting. Muriel Spark's Jerusalem is as active in the scheme of the book as the India of E. M. Forster's most ambitious novel; the care and detail with which she has worked it up as a ground for action and judgment surpass anything she has previously attempted.* There are in fact conspicuous resemblances to the scheme of *A Passage to India.* We have the same three-way contrast, within a context of chronic political violence, between transient English and two separate communities of natives: the one group absurdly alien to the life around them and, in their own view, safely immunized from it—"a free travelling Englishwoman," the thirty-seven-year-old heroine, Barbara Vaughan, pilgrim, tourist, undercover fiancée, reassuringly calls herself in one moment of crisis—and the other two, Arabs and Israelis, locked together in mutual hatred, "biologically unable" to pronounce each other's racial name across the fortified boundary that divides the Holy Land into two armed camps. As if Muriel Spark's usual contempt for official English good manners and English Pharisaism was not sufficient—an attitude keyed to a fine feminine pitch of Scottish flyting throughout her earlier work—she has this time set her English characters down in a place where their infatuate concern to establish a "delightful English atmosphere" or "small island of mutual Englishness" and their persistence in the spontaneous English smile and the collective English giggle seem doubly idiotic. The setting abounds in threats of violence, physical and spiritual, to the security of her English sojourners. The very climate menaces them. "We English have to keep in the shade," her second protagonist, Freddy Hamilton, a minor consular official and to Barbara Vaughan's first glance a scandal of tepidness, tells his Arabic tutor; presently, doing just the opposite in a wholly unaccustomed plunge into the risk and passion of life, he suffers physical breakdown and loss of memory. Attributed officially to sunstroke, Freddy's amnesia becomes a central agency in the

---

* Yet—if a reservation may be offered without intent to detract—is this really more of an achievement, in terms of formal invention, than the visionary London of *Under the Net,* a setting also resonant, though more casually, with ancient heraldic names and pungently moralized contrasts of landscape and decor? Past one's first dazzlement there is a temptation to say that Muriel Spark has now reached the point in composing novels where Iris Murdoch began.

complicated plot of the novel, for much of which "Mad Dogs and Englishmen" would seem an appropriate subtitle.

And there are of course the holy places. Their presence in the book intensifies all its accents. The fact that Barbara Vaughan is, among other errands, on pilgrimage is allowed to justify her in exacting complicity from everybody she meets. A Catholic convert, she is determined to see every listed shrine, whatever the difficulties—"You have such trouble for your religion," remarks an Arab friend who has put her own precarious status in peril to help Barbara—but she is also half Jewish by birth and despite British citizenship is in constant personal danger once she has crossed over, against advice, to the Jordan side. But go she must; though the novel sharply questions many other attitudes, it doesn't seem to question this. The heroine is afflicted, the author tells us bluntly, "with the beautiful and dangerous gift of faith," so that her reasons are no ordinary reasons. "I feel a terrible need to do something positive," she says, in reply to warnings, "and if I'm going on a pilgrimage, I'm going on a pilgrimage, that's all." ("I understand," the reply comes—rather too acquiescently.) In any event, before the trouble her journey causes is finally overcome, one after another of the sacred Gospel place-names has been orchestrated into the narrative and, inevitably, held in ironic judgment over all actions and motives. The workmanship of *The Mandelbaum Gate* in this respect is quite dazzling.

Thus, in both its ancient and modern aspects—as, first, the place, Barbara Vaughan somewhat too cozily reflects, where it all "really began," i.e., the endlessly disturbing mission of Jesus in the world, and, second, as the center of a Hitchcockian intrigue of petty informers, rival sects and faiths, confused pilgrims, espionage agents, blackmailers, passport manufacturers, curio merchants with back rooms where the real business is done (this last character is in fact very attractively realized), not to mention an important understratum of the young, the rising generation, who in the freemasonry of their indifference to all this immense self-perpetuating "System," as they call it, will do anything to maintain a measure of freedom—in both rich aspects the Holy Land makes a bountiful setting for Muriel Spark's development of her themes. These, too, are elaborately orchestrated: falsehood and truth, passion and faith, responsibility and self-responsibility, betrayal and self-betrayal, spiritual sickness and spiritual health. Over all, in the image of the pilgrim's faith, is the ideal of a transforming freedom and purity of behavior taking the forms of an ultimate acceptance (the "It would suffice us" of the Seder is sounded early in the book) and a rather aggressive submission to destiny (the "waves"—mysteriously supporting—"of what was to be").

Muriel Spark's novel does not foolishly pretend that such faith can avoid the corruptions of ordinary life. As in Pilate's day, truth, elusive anywhere, is wholly unfathomable in Jerusalem; deception and betrayal are the norm. "It's difficult to separate the apocryphal from the true in this part of the world. It always has been," Barbara Vaughan observes. True enough. Not much in *The Mandelbaum Gate* is what it pretends to be, a condition that is at once a source of practical danger and the occasion for scenes of strenuous comic confusion that, again, bring to mind *A Passage to India*, if not *Scoop* and *Black Mischief*. The invincible deceitfulness of human behavior is second nature to Muriel Spark. One can mention only a few instances among the many she has adroitly worked into the novel's progression. Thus, the Middle East Visitors' Union Life Trust insurance company and travel agency, offering security and friendly assistance to all, is in fact an espionage and blackmail enterprise, preying impartially on everybody. A monk's sanctuary in the Potter's Field is a well-equipped way station for smugglers and border jumpers, and in its dim interior (a nice example of the book's incidental workmanship) an old chair gleams, in Barbara Vaughan's troubled sight, like a menacing rifle barrel. A smooth couple in the English diplomatic corps turn out to be spies serving "Nasser's post office," an information channel to Egypt; they are Communists, too, introducing, in the author's view, another kind of absurd personal commitment. And in the background looms no less an event than the Eichmann trial—the year is 1961—but Barbara Vaughan, adding this scene to her pilgrim's itinerary, cannot connect its dreamlike rigmarole of statistics and abbreviations to its actual horrors and sees in its central figure merely "a character from the

pages of a long *anti-roman.*" Her attention is drawn instead
to the faces of Eichmann's judges, wearing "the recognizable
scars of the western intellectual"—and a few pages later we
hear that in another part of the city Martin Buber is being
held incommunicado for having spoken compassionately of
the Arab enemy.

Nothing here is what it pretends to be, and in this tangle
of deception and intrigue very little turns out as it was designed. We see that the author means us to understand these
conditions as fundamental to the soul's pilgrimage in the
world, not just as details in some colorful un-English muddle
characteristic of the Middle East. In the widening light of such
ironies, it is hardly surprising that doubt is eventually cast on
the religious shrines, the holy places of Jerusalem. Not all are
authentic—so at least we are told by an English priest preaching at the Church of the Holy Sepulchre, to the farcical annoyance of the bigoted friars who keep the place and supervise its
crammed schedule of pilgrims' masses. Some of the shrines
"are sheer fake, others are doubtful." But such considerations,
the priest continues, do not really matter. It is enough that
pilgrims have always visited them; it is enough that "the great
Dead," worshiping here, have themselves "sanctified" them;
"it is enough"—now—"that we are here." "It's always the right
place if you pray there." Like the English wild flowers spot-
ting the landscape, with their charmingly displaced vernacular names, planted in the Holy Land from seeds smuggled in
by generations of freeborn English travelers, the beautiful seed
of faith is constantly being resown, sometimes in very irregular
ways.

This sermon, which opens the long last chapter, is clearly
choric to the book as a whole, and in it we seem to approach
some significant resolution of themes, though it is always well
with Muriel Spark to keep track of the perky narrative ironies
such declarations are guarded with. She has learned very well
the art of detaching argument and point of view from particular characters and episodes and confiding them instead to the
whole elaborate crisscross of her story. It would be like her
to temper any key declaration with a full display of the trouble stirred up in attempting to live by it. Or to show that
ignorance of what one is doing—Freddy Hamilton's amnesia

is the extreme case—is a regular concomitant of virtuous action. Life, in this writer's novels, moves in ways every bit as mysterious as those attributed to the Creator, and the novelist's best contrivances can hardly hope to imitate these mysteries completely; some sort of manipulation is always necessary. But there are contrivances and contrivances—they can intensify the fictive illusion; they can also be used to dodge the narrative responsibilities peculiar to that illusion once established—and it is just when Muriel Spark settles down in *The Mandelbaum Gate* to rounding out her ingenious story and resolving her themes that dissatisfaction arises.

Story first: at a certain point bald plot management takes over from the ironic counterpointing of character and situation, theme and governing circumstance, inward motive and outward manifestation, that has charmed us into imaginative complicity. We are asked to believe in too many merely arbitrary and convenient new developments. The completeness of Freddy's amnesia, essential to the plot, strains credence but can be tolerated within the familiar Jamesian character-fable he is controlled by: the belated coming-of-age trauma of the free, privileged *bien pensant* of liberal tradition. But other important matters begin to be thrust on us without this kind of formal backing: the offstage murder of Freddy's mother back in England; the farce of the arch-Protestant-English Miss Rickwood's instant conversion from mannish bluestocking to Middle Eastern houri, "unflowered and nearly killed" by a caricature Arab sensualist and paterfamilias; the melodramatic treason of the English diplomatic couple—a key plot agency which, plausible in conception, becomes steadily less so the closer we come to its actual workings. Each of these story-arrangements can of course be fitted into the book's complex of themes. Each makes its contribution, ideally, to the design of the whole, since each shows a different kind of deception and unpredictability in human affairs and the violent overturning of a different kind of maladjustment to life. But each also is incredible according to the rules of evidence the novel has been following—it's not that we think, "This couldn't happen," but rather, "This belongs in some other kind of book"—and the refrain of "quite absurd," delivered in

one pivotal situation after another, is not enough to overcome disbelief.

At these moments Muriel Spark's own concern begins to
resemble what elsewhere she satirizes as the English habit of
looking in any contingency for "the funny aspect," "the joke,"
that every human event, distanced in the mind until safely
weightless, can be reduced to. I am not scorning the technical
adroitness that brings the story forward to these flashy resolutions. One's pleasure in keeping up with so much sheer narrative cleverness is real pleasure, and one can admire the virtuosity that brings it all through to a composed end, just as
Muriel Spark herself years ago wrote admiringly of John Masefield for winding up a fantasy-novel, *The Midnight Folk,* "in
the celebrated manner of telling, in one rapid flourish, what
happens to everyone and everything."* But I find it significant
that Muriel Spark's novels have been praised most fulsomely
by other writers of fiction, including critical system-builders,
who, one suspects, have been free to relish the machinery of
her inventiveness, perhaps to borrow from it, because they
have known that on the deeper ground of imaginative truthfulness and completeness, where each writer must guard and
nourish his own vision, it offers no serious competition, it
preempts no vital inner space.

This view is not simply impressionistic; there is, in *The
Mandelbaum Gate,* a real specifiable emptiness at the narrative
center. The novel has a weighty case to make: about faith as
a human undertaking, and about the passion of acceptance
and commitment that alone gives direction and harmony to
individual life, though day by day it may only "make trouble"
for everyone concerned (the notion of "trouble" echoing
about this novel recalls the notion of "muddle" as the basic
circumstance of the life of feeling and choice that we remember from Forster and Virginia Woolf). Yet it must be said that

---

* *John Masefield,* 1953, p. 174. The long passage she quotes is worth
looking up. It reads like nothing so much as the bravura finish to one of
her own books. Her interest in Masefield is worth prospecting; so, too,
her interest in Mary Shelley, on whom she published a critical study. I
suspect that Muriel Spark is nearer to certain English traditions of genteel
popular entertainment than has yet been recognized by her more enthusiastic admirers.

the faiths that ring true in the book are those provisional, time-locked faiths operating along the narrative's rich margins: not Barbara's convert's and pilgrim's faith nor diplomatic Freddy's brief interval of unconstrained commitment to "life" but the passionate Arab-Israeli hate-faith that divides Jerusalem—"a blood feud between Semites, that's all," one of the English says of it, unconscious of having identified its profounder fatality—and also the absurd and touching faith of the young Arabs, Abdul and Suzi, in their own free future and in each other. What indeed these last two seem to have discovered is the practical truth that *all* mere faith is "bad faith," the meaningless residue of a history and a "System" which, taken seriously, are only plots to rob new lives of their portion of freedom. One notices admiringly how convincing and attractive this younger pair of non-English characters is, how the book warms to their company. It is as if the response to life that lies deepest in their creator's imagination is not the one defined by her main story; it is something altogether more egocentric and unconsidering.

By putting Abdul and Suzi Ramdez beside Barbara Vaughan, the blank at the center can be identified more precisely. *The Mandelbaum Gate* is, after all, a love story—quite fittingly in terms of its wider themes, for love is commitment and faith, spiritual agency and spiritual patience, and the "trouble" it causes is, in the absurd and treacherous muddle of worldly life, comparably homeopathic. The love between Abdul and Suzi, brother and sister, is strongly realized in the narrative, and the book gains much from this imaginative feat, since their casual trust and affection, their confident delight (when it occurs to them) in each other's being, their "pact of personal anarchism," prove fundamental to the story told, providing the practical means both for Barbara's safe passage and Freddy's short happy "life." That "life is love" is the burden of Freddy's discoveries, too, during his turn in the sun. It is rather Barbara's love for her fiancé, Harry Clegg, and, more important, her concrete presence as a woman in love, that remain blank. Yet this is the central datum of the story. More even than the fact of her conversion it is what has changed her life as we know it in the novel, and what has drawn her to Jerusalem. There are of course good compositional reasons for not bringing Barbara and Harry Clegg together in the main action except at long-distance. But Barbara must be felt as a woman in love if the other responses claimed for her, and the whole fictional argument about faith and the "sufficing" of human beings, are to be more than presumptuous gestures. On this I can only report a finding that the motion of love is premised but not substantiated, and, further, that to come late in the book upon Barbara's brief meditation on sexual love as "child's play, unself-conscious and so full of fun and therefore of peace," is to lose one's inclination to take this character seriously on any level (yet immediately after these thoughts of hers the author tells us straight out that Barbara has gone into "one of her religious turns, and was truly given to the love of God"; weighty theological declarations follow).

This heroine seems to me most conceivable in her slack and graceless moods, when she is febrile, negligent, without consideration; when her "emotions are exhausted" and she grabs at the willful satisfactions of acting on impulse and letting others, friends, the "System," God, pick up the pieces. The moment of being sufficed becomes, with her, so far as the narrative shows us, only this trough of personal exhaustion. One feels that there is simply no place for the action of love in the world of free-traveling Englishmen and women that Muriel Spark clings to as a novelist, for all her sharpness about it. Or is it that love is the great occasion that her books reach out toward but that she cannot find the way to write about directly, circumstantially? Despite the larger, fuller design of *The Mandelbaum Gate* we fall back once more onto the simplifying ground of stacked parable and trumped-up morality play where everything is preconceived and self-illustrating and the risky options of actual life, the life of passion and change which, wherever we meet it, commands our sympathy, are never really entered into—though the necessity of such initiation is a stated theme. At the center, instead of a graspable action of love, faith, participation in destiny, Muriel Spark gives us her sharp, definite ideas about these things and about the effect they have on individual men and women. The very shrewdness of her explanations, the hard insistence with which she develops her case, seem in the end hindrances to completed understanding. She knows all about her main characters, and that too perfect knowingness may be why her account of them gradually dies out of our sympathetic interest—though ordinary curiosity keeps us reading on to the end, to verify the plot resolutions and the moral wages this abundantly entertaining novel is keeping in store for them.

Muriel Spark's endings are usually surprising as well as brisk and pointed, but invariably they are presented as being *satisfactory*. Knowing all about her characters, she arranges something appropriate for each. All are satisfied, within the course plotted for them; all get their due and are provided for. And this, I think, is what she writes about—the satisfying of men and women, in the double sense of their being paid off squarely and their being inwardly appeased and neutralized. The controlling substance of her vision and witness is not love but the satisfactions of love, the thing itself remaining unexamined; not faith but the satisfactions of faith; and not the real progressive mystery of conscious, recollective being but the self-exempting satisfaction of having possession of the right thoughts to face life with, such as the assuaging thought that "with God all things are possible and nothing is inevitable." No wonder then that the action of love at the center of *The Mandelbaum Gate* must be idealized and set apart, screened off from the fine confusion of will, crossed purpose, and blinkered self-assertion that drives the novel forward; for the intense economy of love has little to do with satisfaction, a touching and forgivable need in human beings but, by the measure of love, an inferior affair, without consequence.

About Iris Murdoch's novels a first point to make is that the subject which, by this reckoning, is evaded in *The Mandelbaum Gate* has more and more preempted their center. If I were asked to fix these two writers in a phrase, I would say: Muriel Spark writes about satisfaction, Iris Murdoch writes about love. To be sure, she does so tentatively, awkwardly, even coarsely. The sensibility behind *The Red and the Green* is not on any page distinguishably finer nor the craftsmanship greater; an effect of fabrication and contrivance is, if anything, *more* conspicuous in Murdoch's recent work than in Spark's. The very choice of love as her subject smacks of doctrinaire calculation, and so do her means of developing it. In fact, Iris Murdoch's work has now so openly taken on the appearance of a program—the more so when set beside the work in criticism of her husband, John Bayley,* that it is possible to feel that both she and her admirers have got trapped inside, accepting certain forced narrative arrangements and stratagems merely because they fit.

It is a program at once for the novel and for life. Iris Murdoch accepts as axiomatic Sartre's maxim that, whatever the obvious differences between literature and morality (and in her English way she pays even less attention to these asserted differences than does Sartre), "at the heart of the aesthetic imperative we discern the moral imperative." Her interest, as a university philosopher and a participant in postwar symposia of the Aristotelian Society, in the much-debated "other minds" problem, embracing both epistemology and morals; her deepening concern for the more truthful conceptualizing of those actual "forms of life" which she has followed Wittgenstein in identifying as what "is given" and "has to be accepted" by philosophy; and her preoccupation with bringing the conduct of both life and literature down "under the net" (i.e., the net of ideas and social usages human beings employ to contain naked situational experience—again, the figure is taken from Wittgenstein), have all led her to concentrate on the volatile domain of love as that sphere of action in which the real dynamics of human behavior may be apprehended most directly.

These concerns have led her also to the instrument of the novel, which in her book on Sartre she defined—"the novel proper"— as being simply "about people's treatment of each

---

* Studies will be done of this interesting, possibly systematic collaboration. There are sentences in Iris Murdoch's recent writings parallel in vocabulary and logic to sentences in Bayley's *The Characters of Love,* and both have made much of Henry James's remark about Balzac, that "it was by loving [his characters] that he knew them; it was not by knowing them that he loved."

other." She became a novelist in order to deal freshly with matters on which the intellectual tradition she was reared in had, it seemed, reached a dead end. The problem of knowing "other minds" (a kind of philosophic counterpart to the durable English obsession with "personal relationships") having proved insoluble as raised, through the analysis and classification of linguistic propositions—thus producing another of "those exasperating moments in philosophy when one is relentlessly prevented from saying something which one is irresistibly compelled to say" ("The Idea of Perfection") — she turned to making up complicated stories about actual encounters between such minds and about the natural existence of such primary moral phenomena as intention, love, individuality, sincerity, and choice, conceiving of the successful novelist as a prime model of man at grips with the job of responding truthfully to the turmoil of actual experience.

Her concerns as a writer have shown a severe consistency. They have hardly progressed, but she has refined and concentrated them. From the first her novels have been composed as if to illustrate one of her own later declarations, that the novelist's fundamental job is to create "real characters," i.e., personages who will be "more than conventional puppets" and at the same time "other than oneself." Her strategy for accomplishing this job has been to make use of the very problem of knowledge that it chiefly involves; for it is precisely through their conceptions (always more or less "wrong") of themselves and, by extension, of each other and of the world in general that she identifies her characters to us, and it is through an extended succession of crises in which these wrong conceptions are acted on, shattered, then revised under fire and perilously re-formed, that she tells their story. At this stage it hardly matters what the story is, only that it follow this rhythm, this succession.

The method is one that, as she works it, balks at tidy resolutions. There is a sense in which her stories do not end and her books, and even the episodes that make them up, go uncompleted. These features of her work seem to be licensed philosophically—as by her proposition that "to understand other people" (the vocation that, in her view as in John Bayley's, joins an author to the personages of his story and both to mankind, and is synonymous finally with "love") "is a task that never ends."* She sometimes gives in a little to the temptation to suggest, sentimentally, that her characters have progressed to a new stage, have learned something that will transform them, have grown "more mature," but the moral truth of this is only that, realistically enough, they are older and tireder and so more inclined to be circumspect in acting upon the solipsistic pictures of reality they currently entertain. At the heart of her vision there are no such false consolations. She sees men and women as beings afflicted from first to last by the impulse of *self-conception*—but therefore, through this same treacherous but endlessly generative impulse, as beings also capable of *love* and of *freedom,* and consequently (and in this respect *The Red and the Green* marks an interesting new departure) of *history.* The unexpected inner strength of her work derives in no small part, I think, from her success in linking these key terms of contemporary moral philosophy in a related series.

The much advertised peculiarities of her practice of fiction are liberally displayed in *The Red and the Green.* Once again we are given a big cast of characters who dance out an intricate sequence of private relationships. Her reshuffling of these relationships and her staging of scenes in which radical shifts and reversals take place have become famous. Eaves-

---

* Her first broad statement of the novelist's special problem of truth, opening the last chapter of *Under the Net,* is hardly distinguishable from Virginia Woolf's thinking thirty years before:

> Events stream past us like these crowds, and the face of each is seen only for a minute. What is urgent is not urgent forever but only ephemerally. All work and all love, the search for wealth and fame, the search for truth, life itself, are made up of moments which pass and become nothing. Yet through this shaft of nothings we drive onwards with that miraculous vitality that creates our precarious habitations in the past and the future. So we live—a spirit that broods and hovers over the continual death of time, the lost meaning, the unrecaptured moment, the unremembered face, until the final chop-chop that ends all our moments and plunges that spirit back into the void from which it came.

Later formulations have been more austerely philosophical and better focused:

> But since reality is incomplete art must not be too much afraid of incompleteness. Literature must always represent a battle between real people and images; and what it requires now is a much stronger and more complex conception of the former. ("Against Dryness.")

dropping, improvised symbolic linkages, a multiplication of chance meetings that beggars Hardy, are now quite ordinary in her work; if you read her, you simply have to get used to them. You have to learn not automatically to be put off when additional characters required to be present at the ironic climax of some intense private interview simply pop out from behind the door or loom up through an attic window; and if four male characters are in love in their several ways with one woman, as is the case in *The Red and the Green,* you are not wholly surprised when all four arrive at her house in succession in the middle of the night, for decisive assignations.

Virginia Woolf once wrote that she had spent a morning trying to get a character out of a room. Iris Murdoch, it appears, has become indifferent to such niceties and scarcely bothers to mask the contrivances her stories advance by. The knotted calculus of misconception and revision that organizes her characters' lives and relationships absorbs her and determines other measures. An increasing preference for tight family combinations—brothers and sisters, parents and children, uncles, nieces, aunts, nephews, in-laws, cousins-german, the children of deceased wives' sisters: she uses them all—is symptomatic and deserves comment, for in *The Red and the Green* it engrosses the whole scheme. Nearly all her novels have a dramatic core of blood ties, at least as important as marriages or ordinary volitional love affairs. Incest is a primary condition —a condition, we may recall, far too frequent in Western fiction (that product of self-terrified bourgeois freedom) to be written off as merely perverse or sensational. For incest is preeminent among those fatally fixed blood relationships loved by Gothic novelists and their remarkably numerous heirs (and symbolized in the use of isolated houses, secretly linked rooms, dark connecting corridors, and night visitations—all features of Iris Murdoch's storytelling), as opposed to the essentially contractual relations of the more realistic novel of society.

The strain of reasoned Gothic fantasy in Iris Murdoch's novels is thus not necessarily a sign of weakness, of imaginative failure. Conceivably it represents an intelligent choice among accessible traditions. At the least it can remind us of the historical uses and virtues of the Gothic mode in fiction, a mode that flourished almost without check during the manifold revolutions of the late eighteenth and early nineteenth centuries; that helped to recover for the basically realistic form of the novel some of the imaginative freedom of allegory and romance; that is a formative element in the whole explosive advance of Western fiction from Scott and Balzac to Poe, Dickens, Lermontov, the Brontës, Hawthorne and Melville, Gogol and Dostoevsky; and that was from the first, with its more serious English-speaking practitioners (Ann Radcliffe, Godwin, Brockden Brown, Mary Shelley, Hogg, Peacock), a wonderfully congenial instrument for psychological analysis and free speculative inquiry. In its oddly stylized way it both asserted and criticized that liberal individualism, that image of man as a free rational unit of being, which remains the dominating concern of all of Iris Murdoch's effort as a writer, if not of most of modern literature.

The family network in *The Red and the Green,* comprising three generations and twenty identifiable characters, is too complicated for summary. A lot of rather flat narrative explanation is required simply to get it all out into view and to prepare for the main encounters and reversals of the story. After a few chapters I found that I had to keep a chart. Leading characters, for example, may have been married to two others, or are considering second marriages, and will be in love of some kind with a third, fourth, and fifth, all within a tangle of kinship that does not become simpler. But, to repeat, the particulars hardly matter, except that they exist. It is the tangle itself, and its effects, that controls the "meaning" of the novel. What is thus confirmed, dramatically, is a certain quality of life—more precisely, a *medium* in which life takes place—that the whole texture of the book persistently insinuates and that represents Iris Murdoch's most direct borrowing from Sartre: a medium best defined in the Sartrean metaphor of *viscosity*. It is the insoluble viscosity of reality, down "under the net" of conventional understanding, that makes knowledge of reality so fallible and truth so elusive, though we must descend there if we are to live at all. It is the impenetrable viscosity of the individual human spirit that makes other people *opaque* to us (Sartre's word again) and understanding them, or ourselves, so nearly impossible.

These concerns emerge early in her fiction and steadily

expand. Beginning with the night swim in the murky Thames in her first novel (a fine tendentious scene) and continuing through the business of miring a car (property of an elfin girl named "Rain") in the mud and then in a river in *The Sandcastle,* and through the muck-choked lake of *The Bell* and the fucoid salmon-pool of *The Unicorn* (places of suicides and other consummations), a remarkable number of important episodes in Iris Murdoch take place under water, or in some other setting embodying her vision of the dense germinous matrix of actual life that mocks and humbles the brittle efforts of understanding to regulate its behavior. There is nothing so flashy in *The Red and the Green* as the thick vegetable-spermatic dream-jungle that provides the scene of action for *The Italian Girl,* nothing so patly symbolic as the experimental rose-farm in *An Unofficial Rose.* But there are various contrasting gardens, one with a sludgy fish-pool in which a provocatively dropped earring must be ritually groped for; an extraneous country bog ("the consistency of sticky fudge") glistens along the path of one troubled soul moving through his ordeal of change, and "black air" stifling as a fall of soot besets another; a vision is recurrent of the huge ocean sucking and churning at "senselessly jagged" rocks, among "holes and crevasses, ugly slits and irregular gashes"; while the River Liffey, "viscous" with a "more than usual opacity," its "gluey water . . . foaming a little like stout" under a sky that looks "like thin wet paper down which highly diluted blue paint is almost imperceptibly running," serves in one spiritual crisis to mirror its observer's abject confusion. (Such descriptions can seem, however, the most labored and unproductive part of Iris Murdoch's storytelling.)

The title itself points to a similar contrast of framing elements. Red England is all politic reason, good manners, tea and stucco villas, war- and career-making, short-run tactical compromises, infantilism and "muddle"—and worldly success. Against it is green Ireland, the "dark wet island," the buildings of its beautiful capital "all glued together by a jelly of filth to form a uniform organic surface rather like a fish," its old country houses settled into a "formidable sinister stillness," its religion something "primitive and dark," a "half-potty second-rate provincial dump . . . with its stupid clergy and its stupid poor," nevertheless capable of a blazing free release of spirit and an "inconceivable" hopeless bravery that transfigure momentarily their inevitable defeat—for the time is 1916 and the climax of the book is the Easter Rising. Two characters, one from each side, are killed in the open clash of these two elements, and in a brief "Epilogue" we hear of the violent death of others in the years following; we are reminded also of the petering out of "all that nineteen-sixteen nonsense" in the shabby anticlimaxes of old age and subsequent Irish history.

The use of the Easter Rising is particularly interesting. Surely it represents, for Iris Murdoch, something more than a lapse into the fatuities of historical romance, as some reviewers have charged. Her purpose seems to me wholly serious and consistent. It is to strengthen, perhaps also to test, the truth and force of her fictional apprehension of life by extending it into a further range of actual experience. She has been criticized for dealing only with private lives and so selling short her wider philosophic purposes. Her first two novels—*Under the Net,* with its London setting of job-crawling and street-corner agitation, and *The Flight from the Enchanter,* in using the displacements of contemporary east European history— did have a foothold in the public world where solipsistic fantasies would seem harder to maintain. But since then she has retreated into an, as it seems, methodically isolated and closed sphere of private intrigue. In the terms of a famous description, in her book on Sartre, of the differences between the "worlds" of Oxford analytic philosophy and continental existentialism—the one a world "in which people play cricket, cook cakes, make simple decisions, remember their childhood and go to the circus," the other a world "in which they commit sins, fall in love, say prayers or join the Communist party"— we can see how resolutely she has forced her way as a novelist into the first three divisions of this second, more momentous and humane world. But we are bound to notice also the relative absence up to now of the fourth division, the political, that sphere of ideological passion and collective spirit-mutilation into which so much of the life of our convulsive century has been sucked up.

This is not a sphere that the novelist can occupy at will.

Since 1945 *Dr. Zhivago* is the supreme exception; elsewhere, against the brilliant but fragmentary success of a Günter Grass, we have to put the silence of André Malraux; we see that *La Peste* fails where *L'Étranger* and *La Chute* succeed, that Silone has withdrawn into rewriting his great work-in-exile of the 1930's, that *1984* increasingly seems a casualty of its own despairing diagnosis of the simplifications of Newspeak, and that the one English-speaking novelist, Anthony Powell, who to my mind has effectively used the cycles of public and national life as a context within which his absurdly short-sighted characters maneuver their unchangeable ego-fixations has done so only by means of an extraordinary comic obliquity.

Thus it is no reproach to Iris Murdoch to say that in *The Red and the Green* the gain from this expansion into the collective and historical is limited. The virtue of it lies in her understanding that a historical event, as it overtakes individual persons, represents to consciousness simply an intensification or reinforcement of ordinary experience. It only augments the opacity (to reason) of self-conceiving human life and, perhaps, accelerates its incalculable transformations. The Easter Rising figures in *The Red and the Green* as an additional medium or environment of personal experience—like sex, art, religion, certain romanticizable types of business (the theatre, wine-importing, rose-farming), or the endless human quest after spiritual enchantment and submission: the familiar materials of her earlier books. Furthermore, with all its multiplied chances for fanaticism and melodramatic surprise, this legendary event, and clearly Yeats's great poems about it are assumed, has the advantage of having actually occurred and so seeming normal and inevitable. For once it allows Iris Murdoch to tell her story without recourse to the interceding witch-girls and central-European enchanters who were getting to be a kind of necessary bad habit with her. The vivid sense we get of the Rising as a palpable historical tide advancing to engulf all her characters, invading their private schemes, arrangements, visions of the future—typically it is not really believed in as a possibility, even by those closest to it, until it actually spills over—is a main source of imaginative strength in *The Red and the Green*. "History" (the word is used openly) is reestablished as a name of utmost resonance for that life which men and women themselves willfully, blindly create and which then requires of them nothing less, as we Americans are supposed to know, than their lives, fortunes, and sacred honor.

But this novel is not meant as an interpretation of history. The Rising itself comes to us by refraction, through a cloud of casual rumor and of private ardors and despondencies. The outcome being foreknown, there is no need to present it in comprehensive narrative succession, and the book advances instead through an interrupted series of twenty-six short chapters, each one focused through the single point of view of one or another of the half-dozen main characters. Political passions are efficiently absorbed into the more usual calculus of behavior Iris Murdoch erects for her people. So, to take a leading case, the young rebel Pat Dumay is acted on not only by Irish patriotism but by (1) a degrading male rivalry with his English army-officer cousin (one more of the author's life-fearing Englishmen with double names) ; (2) the failure of his relationship with his bumbling stepfather, Barney Drumm; (3) an incestuously protective love for his young brother; (4) a tormenting attraction-repulsion for his provocative Aunt Millie, who recognizes in him the nearest counterpart to her own reckless craving to act out an absolute freedom of spirit; and (5) a ravaging self-despite, a fear of his own body and the touch of others and above all of women (symbols, "muddled and unclean," of the "frailty and incompleteness of human life"), a lust finally for some perfect triumph of retributive justice and purified self-assertion.

One observes, incidentally, that the stuff of a psychoanalytic explanation of history is here in some abundance, in the manner of Sartre's "L'Enfance d'un chef," and is laid out with a certain bluff expertness. But not only is this not Iris Murdoch's purpose, it is the very opposite of her purpose. Like her other more recent novels *The Red and the Green* embodies instead a concern she made powerfully explicit in her essay, "The Idea of Perfection," where one of the argumentative tasks she set herself was precisely the proper separation of *moral* questions from the sophisticated behaviorism of psychoanalysis. "What is at stake," she wrote there, "is the liberation of morality, and of philosophy as a study of human nature, from the domination of science; or rather from the domination of inexact ideas of science which haunt philosophers and other thinkers." Like other closed conceptualizations of the totality of human conduct, conventional psychoanalysis, she argues, carries within itself the consequences of its own historical emergence, an effort to neutralize the historical and individual character of experience and to supplant not only all other moralities but morality itself, in a timeless stasis of fixed and perfectly comprehended motivation.

In any case, although the Rising determines the overall progress of the story, the two most fully realized characters, Millie and Barney, have only a gratuitous and absurd kind of involvement in it—Millie, theatrical to the end, yet a woman of real force, tying bandages in an obscure back room and then, we hear in the "Epilogue," taking comfort in an embarrassingly dotty old age from a satisfying whiskey-image of herself as the angel of the martyred cause; Barney, a kind of clown-saint of invincible muddledom and self-immolation, choosing to join the fight almost absentmindedly from an abyss of private despair, then accidentally shooting himself in the foot and having to be left behind. But neither can be pinned down to any textbook analysis of psychological malfunctions. In the fullness of middle life their abundant peculiarities of temperament have been transfigured, so to speak, into the lengthening and irreversible occasions of their moral histories. They change less, yet are more open to life, than anyone else in the book. They are as good characters as Iris Murdoch has yet devised; and in the degree that it is their book, I would risk suggesting that *The Red and the Green* will stand higher in the canon of her work than critical comment on it has yet imagined.

Every thread of relationship and change ties through Millie's part. Radiantly pretty, elegant, kindhearted, vulnerable, self-indulgent, both studied and impulsive with her favors, vulgar and noisy, humorous, unresentful, ruthless at times but not cruel, invariably playacting but never tiresome (except to the envious) or mean, at once generous and severe with her four men (according to her sense, not foolish, of each's special need), romantically suicidal and romantically courageous, she is on the side of life—"unrealistic, comfort-loving, imperial Millie," her recognized lover calls her—and she pays for it, and makes others pay for it. Iris Murdoch is not sentimental about the consequences. "She respects no one. She does not see where another person begins." This is said, to be sure, by her disapproving sister-in-law, Kathleen, her moral opposite and, moreover, Barney's wife in a still unconsummated second marriage; yet something of the accusation sticks. In the conceptual world of Iris Murdoch's writing, we recognize it as the worst accusation imaginable. Nevertheless the moral balance sheet, I think we are meant to see, is in Millie's favor. The love she offers is real love, the courage real courage; that is why she acts, as she does, catalytically upon every occasion she enters, including the Rising itself. She gives more than she takes; she claims no consideration she does not earn; and the judgments of her two older lovers—that her "wickedness" is irresistibly "pure-hearted" and her faults are "touched by romance into gaiety and by charity into innocence"—are not, I think, meant to be dismissed as infatuation.

Fine as Millie is, Barney Drumm is in some ways an even finer creation, his story drawn to a tighter, more efficient line. In him the vocation of *self-conception* has become paralyzingly complete.* The excitement and distress of observing himself and adding up his accounts, moral and spiritual, corrupt

---

* In working out Barney's part (and more than a third of the book is given over to him between his first and last appearance) Iris Murdoch revives a device she used in *Under the Net:* a manuscript journal in which her protagonist, writing in normal bad faith, nevertheless distills from his self-excusing reflections a certain equivocal truth. Jake Donoghue's journal in *Under the Net* begins as a record of the conversation of a proteanly gifted friend who has Jake under his spell. Though fearful of Hugo's finding him out, Jake allows himself to circulate the journal-manuscript among other friends and then allows them to persuade him to publish it; in so doing—and in giving his book the nicely ironic title of *The Silencer,* for it is of course his own submissiveness he is exorcising—he begins the process of freeing himself from Hugo's quite-unsought-for domination. Coming across a copy of his book later on—naturally he hasn't kept one himself—Jake feels curiously separate from it and independent of its dialogue-arguments, which in any case prove to be less dominated by Hugo's views than he had thought, largely because he has caricatured them. Yet it is in the brief passage quoted to us from *The Silencer* that we find the explanation of the title, *Under the Net*—and it comes in the Hugo voice! The same passage also contains the philosophic key to the title of *The Flight from the Enchanter.*

everything he undertakes. Failed priest, failed scholar, failed husband and stepfather, he bumbles about his life in a fog of blasphemy and ineffectual penitence. He is always temptable and always gives in to his temptations, not least of which is his craving for absolution and his self-pitying condemnation of others for not providing it. So it is that when the thought at last comes to him "that possibly he ought simply to act rightly and expect no one even to notice it," it is indeed a "terrible thought." It is his fate to pass beyond consolations, even the greatest. It abruptly occurs to him, on the morning of the Rising, that the real truth of Easter is the emptiness of Christ's tomb, His absence from His followers' seeking, and no longer the all-too-dramatic and punitive events of Good Friday, and he begins to see that what is required of him is "something which lay quite outside the deeply worked pattern of suffering, the plain possibility of change without drama and even without punishment." As if a burden had been lifted (I am following the author's own language), Barney resolves on a new straight-forwardness, and, nice detail, discovers himself praying, for once in his life quite unself-consciously. But in the next moment, given a chance to act on this resolve, he bungles, as usual. In a last frenzy of self-pity and guilt, he sees that he will not be believed, that he is not to "get credit for anything with anybody"; numb with despair and hardly caring, he makes plans to take part in the oncoming fight; now at last, surveying the wreck of his life's affairs, he feels truly "frightened" and "cornered," yet feels this "in a way that was not entirely disagreeable," as if "a life beyond his own had taken charge of him." It is a fine, oblique culmination, and it seems to me altogether persuasive and not at all imperiled—quite the contrary—by the anticlimaxes that follow.

Or is all this too mechanical and diagrammatic, a rigged geometry of token events and straw characterizations? The case for the importance of Iris Murdoch sooner or later has to deal with a simple but fundamental objection: that precisely on her chosen ground she does not write well enough, and that for the kind of diagnostic exposition of changing states of mind she uses to fill out her narratives certain standards of precision and intensity have been set in the development of the novel that, having become in the best sense conventional in the understanding of sympathetic readers, cannot simply be abandoned. Here is a chapter opening halfway through *The Red and the Green:*

> Pat was giddy with impatience. It was still only Thursday morning. Sunday rose up in front of him like a black cliff. The mountain must open to admit him, how he knew not. He could foresee nothing except that he would be fighting. This time next week he would have been fighting. Perhaps he would be dead. His first startled fear was diffused now into an aching desire for action, and his body was weary of the interim. In the two days since he had been told he had grimly lived the reality of it into himself. To the mystery of Sunday he was dedicated and resigned, becoming in every cell of his being a taut extension of that violent future.

Anybody can see how choppy this is, how flat in its detail. The point of view shifts loosely from inside to outside, neither substantiating the emotion claimed nor fixing a sharp observational perspective. The passage does, it is true, announce with a certain clumsy thoroughness a complex of crossed motives and feelings that, if the reader is willing, will yield results before the chapter ends. Indeed, to restore to this first paragraph the four additional sentences that complete it in the text—sentences written in the same signboard vocabulary and toneless conceptual style—would show this style capable of as much pathos and suspense as are needed. But step by step it seems a slack and careless kind of narrative scoring, as if too preoccupied with laying out the ruling equation to uncover the natural life within.

This considerable reservation touches Muriel Spark's writing, too. As much as anything it is what divides these novelists not only from the prose craftsmanship of Forster and Virginia Woolf but from that of a much nearer predecessor like Angus Wilson, whose postwar epistles to the English rise out of much the same common judgment of contemporary life. Both Murdoch and Spark show a kind of airy disregard for that refinement of interior observation and description that typifies the major tradition of the novel through the later nineteenth and early twentieth centuries. Neither is sensuously persuasive, though both assert sensuousness as a moral idea, a psychological force. Neither commands much visual or kinesthetic power;

their landscapes, though often painstakingly detailed, are cardboard landscapes, like the camera directions in a movie scenario, and the dramatic resolutions they devise depend regularly on a puppet-show crudeness of physical gesture. Neither has any notable gift for mimicry (almost essential, one would think, for basically naturalistic narration), except for that one anonymous and dispiriting voice, the evasive sentence-stammer of the well-behaved, which any clever Englishman can produce in his sleep. Their manner in prose is expository and assertive—and the risk they run as novelists is that precisely at the narrative climaxes the reader will feel not that he has been privy to a truthful rehearsal of discovered human experience but that he has been lectured at; that the people whose histories he has been asked to consider are not real people at all but a demonstrator's specimens. Both, in a word, strike one as deficient in imagination, the name we give that abundant free power of, at once, divination and projection whereby the dry bones of anecdote and case history are restored to life, recovering that power life itself holds in reserve to abolish the distance we are trained to keep between ourselves and other beings.

My own sense of the matter is that they have each decided that this risk must be taken, this kind of deficiency endured, if they are to exist as writers of any kind. They seem to me very nearly the first serious English novelists who have not only broken with the exalted ethos of modernism, the supreme commitment to "writing well," but are no longer in any way haunted by it. With Muriel Spark this interesting departure strikes one as a kind of personal accident. She writes as, since her conversion and within the unstable climate of contemporary moral feeling, the way opens to her. With gusto she tells us all she knows; my point has been merely that in her first full-scale novel we come to see that this will not be enough. But her claim that she has learned to speak "with my own voice as a writer now" is nevertheless a true claim, and "some kind of truth" does emerge from her very readable books, though less than she supposes.

Iris Murdoch, too, has possessed from the first a distinct literary personality: an indispensable source of interest. With her humor and moral generosity it is a very attractive personality as well. Her further distinction is that she has put this virtue at the disposal of a reasoned conception of the uses of literature. She has something of importance to demonstrate, something that imposes itself on her working consciousness as important, and this double weight is communicated in all she writes. Anyone can see the flimsiness of composition in much of her work and, more damagingly, the incompleteness of imaginative absorption. She leaves a lot to the reader—so much in fact that one begins to suspect that her negligence is itself programmatic. She seems to have taken literally Sartre's eloquent description in *What Is Literature?* (her book on Sartre dwells on the passage) of writing as above all else a collaboration of author and reader in an act of freedom; a collaboration, continually to be renewed, wherein the willful misdemeanor of mere literature finds its one incontrovertible justification. She keeps herself free as a writer from the "consoling dream necessity" ("Against Dryness") of purified craftsmanship and absolute artistic fulfillment; she counts on the reader to fill out what she has left blank, and to give life and truth to all that despite an honest effort remains glib or sentimental or merely adverted to in the exposition. To use the language of existentialism, she is not afraid of "bad faith," knowing that acting in bad faith is at least to have acted, and consequentially; it is at least a serious beginning.

Just here we find her special importance in contemporary English writing: she has found a way out of silence and the dead end of a crippling obsession, crippling to philosophy and literature alike, with perfect truth and unimpeachable sincerity. She knows that it is not artistic incompetence that afflicts English letters but a deeper, more organic malady. E. M. Forster diagnosed this malady nearly half a century ago in a famous essay, "Notes on the English Character" (1920), that still provides the shrewdest of glosses on English fiction in this century (and earlier, for it fits Meredith's and Thackeray's work as well, and—with adjustments—Jane Austen's and Fielding's). Forster called it the "undeveloped heart" and continued to make it the monitory subject of his novels until, arriving at the point of recognizing himself as one of its notable victims, he could not in good conscience continue his career. Lawrence, too, recognized it as the *mal anglais* and raged against it; Elizabeth Bowen wrote her best novel about it. Its source, so we learn from the English themselves, who do nothing so artfully as expose and burlesque it, lies in the whole geologically blocked system of English ineducation, coded, manipulative, methodically and conscientiously warping: ineducation not only—for those put through the mill of respectable English schooling and domestic rearing—in the life of the senses and emotions but in the commonest knowledge of one another as persons.* How else can one explain why the plea, "only connect," carries so much weight in Forster's fiction, and why it resounds there so forlornly?

The silence of E. M. Forster . . . along with the death of Lawrence it has hung over the English novel for nearly forty years, and we have all somehow known that nothing else in the period since was quite so important. Iris Murdoch's first novel confronted this specter directly. In the passage already cited from *The Silencer,* her hero's published journal, we find this declaration:

> I know that nothing consoles and nothing justifies except a story—but that doesn't stop all stories from being lies. Only the greatest men can speak and still be truthful. . . . For most of us, for almost all of us, truth can be attained, if at all, only in silence. It is in silence that the human spirit touches the divine.

But this is spoken, we notice, by the Hugo-voice, the voice of Jake's enchanter, and the rest of *Under the Net* describes Jake's progressive disregard of it.

The "undeveloped heart," from which the only sure escape is into silence and inanition, is the regular affliction of Iris Murdoch's leading characters, as love and its shocks and failures are her constant subject. In this respect her work takes its place in a classic line of moralistic English fiction. But what particularly marks her off from her nearest predecessors, the stricken generation of Graham Greene and Angus Wilson, perhaps even from a contemporary like Amis, is that she is

---

* In this regard, of obvious importance for novelists (whose whole function, in Iris Murdoch's words, is to write "about people's treatment of each other"), an observation of Gissing's in his book on Dickens still applies: "one may remark in passing that the English people is distinguished among nationalities by the profound mutual ignorance which separates its social ranks."

no longer weighed down by guilt about this condition, or by a parochial craving to kick at those who commonly profit by it. She does not, so to speak, hold herself responsible for it (as a woman, and an Irishwoman at that, she has less reason to). If she is to survive as a writer, she knows that it must be with the help of others, of her readers. Her very abruptness, arbitrariness, imaginative cursoriness have for the reader the force of a direct appeal. "Go along with me," her books say; "as to winning our struggle out of prejudice, division, self-enclosedness, the deformations of fantasy, the virus of nonlife, of course one can't be sure—but you'll have a fairer chance in company like mine than out of it." It is because she sees her work as constituting, like the moral life itself, "a task which does not come to an end" that she has shouldered her way to the center of her time's effort in literature. Like Sartre she seems to work too hastily, yet my own finding is that she draws one after her. No doubt I will read Muriel Spark's next novel, sooner or later, out of ordinary inquisitiveness—what will this ingenious talent do next? But I will read Iris Murdoch's as an act of participation, of honest complicity however marginal, in the central disquietudes of present life and history, these being, after all, the life and history that are ours to endure.

* * *

"But the good and evil that we dream of," Iris Murdoch writes in a recent essay, "may be more incarnate than we realize in the world within which we choose. This too is why deliberation at the moment of choice often seems ineffectual."* Here is as good a rubric as any for the narrative scheme of her latest novel, *The Time of the Angels* (1966), in which the monstrous religious mania of a Nietzsche-transcending Anglican priest has turned a stranded rectory in a bomb-ruined winter wasteland of central London into a troll-cavern where freedom and sanity are systematically violated and the enemy of the Good (one key character, the priest's estranged brother, is trying to write a book called *Morality in a World Without God*) is an immensely plausible and natural mechanism of fantasy that

---

* "The Darkness of Practical Reason," *Encounter*, July, 1966.

can speak in a voice at times indistinguishable from that of the free, reality-seeking human imagination in its grandest flights.

With a living writer one must remind oneself to resist the progressivist or growth-rate fallacy. *The Time of the Angels* is an absorbingly interesting book by, I think, the most consequentially entertaining of contemporary English novelists. Is it Iris Murdoch's best novel? I think not. Returning to the Gothic mannerisms of *The Unicorn* and *The Italian Girl,* it is also flawed in rather the same way; plot rigging is flagrant, and main narrative resolutions are blatantly forced, though by now a certain kind of boisterous melodrama might as well be recognized as one of this author's stable and generally effective defenses "against dryness." Being her latest book, *should* this be her best, biggest, most perfect? Certainly not. It is enough to say that *Angels* is as serious and vivacious, as secure in its diversely compassionate characterizations, as touching and forgiving in its pictures of the spiritual ordeal of human life, as the most admired of its predecessors. What more at present can one say than that a season without its new Murdoch would seem a dry season indeed?

Of course the possibility remains—this book renews it—of thinking that Iris Murdoch is mistaken in her calling and is no novelist. Mr. Denis Donoghue took this line in reviewing *The Time of the Angels* in *The New York Review of Books,* appealing to the standard of the novel proper, the work that deals, like Tolstoy's, like James's, with "morality, society, family, palpable relationships" as these exist in life and not simply in some willful interior vision. But having said so, one might reasonably go on to ask: where *are* the proper novelists of our day? If Iris Murdoch does not touch our consciousness of real life and move us with her projections of familiar experience, who in our literature does? Who *has* avoided her lapses into abstraction, contrivance, sensationalist overmanagement? Who *can* write—or see—like Tolstoy, or who work the Jamesian apparatus? Or is it equally possible that new uses and mutations of the still open form of the novel remain to be created and secured, and that the clear facts in the case of Iris Murdoch—her executive energy, the self-amplification and self-assurance of her fictional world, the promptness and persistence of her reception—are as good evidence as may be had for thinking that some part of major literary history (at once a history of forms and a history of consciousness and sensibility) is moving through the channel of her performance? On whom, in this case, is the critical *onus probandi?*

The flaws in her new novel are the more conspicuous, I think, because of its basic strength. As sometimes before, particularly in *The Flight from the Enchanter* and *The Unicorn,* there is a dimness at the dramatic center. Carel Fisher—"troll King" of "the dark unvisited cavern-like environment" of the rectory, who asserts that "the death of God has set the angels free" to terrorize human beings, and that "the truth" may be "just a black pit, or like birds huddled in the dust in a dark cupboard"—is better realized as a dramatic agent than was Mischa Fox, the enchanter.* But we must believe not only in the idea of Father Carel's madness, his subjection to fantasies of a special contemporary authority and destructiveness, but also in the idea of his absolute power over others, particularly over Pattie, the mulatto orphan-servant whom Carel makes his "black goddess," and over Elizabeth, the incestuously bound sleeping princess of this fog-shrouded death house. The conception of Elizabeth in particular, despite its casual brilliance of outline, is a blank and a point of weakness in the mechanism of the story. It is notable that the stagiest happening in the novel is the means of fixing Elizabeth and Carel in their decisive relation. I can accept everything postulated about Elizabeth as a character, yet the nightmare of the "captive mind" remains as implausible morally and domestically, and as counsel-darkening, as it is politically, though of course it is what we most fear—and *The Time of the Angels* has at least the strength of the reality of that fear.

It can be seen that Iris Murdoch has constructed a kind of novel-machine—*A Severed Head* was its first dazzling free

---

* Is there an echo in this of that fine-tempered novel of the twenties, David Garnett's *Go She Must,* with its benignly mad rector, whose house has been made into a swallow's nest—"Angels," says the Reverend Mr. Dunnock, "they are angels"—and his self-imprisoned daughter?

In Iris Murdoch's first novel, starlings flying about and befouling an empty flat are an emblem of the seething chaos of existence lying "under the net" of our adjustments and defenses against it.

flight—which moves, at once, her characters and her ideas through a dialectical series of confrontations and reversals that convey her understanding of the moral life as it rises from the obscure dynamics of our interlocking yet self-enclosed personal histories. Sometimes this machine seems to run on unattended, at the expense of the uses it was designed for. More frequently it justifies itself by highlighting and giving precise configuration to the strong moral and psychological truths fed into it.

It seems capable, this time, of new and attractive ironies. The austerity of Iris Murdoch's conception of the Good as a function of our incessant collective ordeal of feeling and consciousness is such that any simpleminded or dogmatic solution to the problems of life becomes almost automatically a target for satire and contempt. "Do-gooders" in particular offer themselves as the self-elected fools of her vision of things —men and women operating from privileged sanctuaries who would set others' lives straight with right thinking and plain dealing—and the dream of solving the dilemmas of existence by making a profession of serving others is a delusion particularly blinding. Yet a charming feature of *The Time of the Angels* is that the official "do-gooders" really do help to save some of the others from entire catastrophe. So Norah Shadox-Brown, the busybody ex-headmistress who is one of those "whose only troubles are the troubles of others" (and who has the familiar divided name of so many of Iris Murdoch's moral fools), turns out to be, within limits, a real guardian and benefactor. The politic intervention of a theologically up-to-date bishop is similarly double-edged. On the other hand formulations that we recognize as drawn from the author's own profoundest understanding are sometimes put into the mouths of characters, such as Carel himself, who stand to gain a sinister personal advantage by imposing this understanding, this vision, on others. The novel's imaginative freedom in redistributing its own governing conceptions is exemplary.

In fact, at various points one may feel that this imaginative freedom overflows the all too efficient design of the book. As has happened before with Iris Murdoch, the narrative sequence follows the scheme for a closed preceptive fable but is alive with intimations, and many details, of some larger, freer fictional venture. Behind the adroit philosophical fabulist, a natural novelist may still be groping for position, a writer whose creative imagination is still seeking access on its own terms to the high ground of the wholly substantiated and self-authenticating novel of full-scale comic or tragic development. If, once again, her artistic cursoriness is sometimes annoying, it is because the fringes of her story and the unfilled further outlines indicate the possibility of something richer and ampler. I do not in any way mean that she ought to sever relations with the philosophic issues she regularly addresses. For the great service of philosophic ideas in Iris Murdoch's fiction has not been in establishing theme or narrative design but in objectifying her own lively and equitable sense of the shape of common experience, and in confirming, by this other means, a natural generosity of apprehension that seems to me her decisive resource as a novelist.

In any case her ideas are ingeniously absorbed into the sequence of events. They also infuse the casual presentation, the writing. A phenomenological assessment would show, I think, the special kind of unity and coherence this novel approaches. *Motion* of various kinds—going or drifting "away," acts of parting, getting out or breaking out, ordering others to "get out" as a way of resolving difficulties, being "on the move," and in particular the motion that ends in touching and being touched—is fundamental. It is by "the complex language of movement" that the unspoken secrets of the moral life are betrayed; "goodness" itself is defined as residing "in a movement"; and highest approval is reserved for "that free impetuous movement toward another, that human gesture which makes each one of us most wholly himself." The opposite of motion is quiescence: silence, sleep, immobility, apathy, a face (Carel's) "too much in repose," a self-satisfaction grown "monstrous" in its passivity, the inertness of the chrysalis, the condition of becoming "untouchable" (his *"Noli me tangere"* marks a climax in Carel's descent), a vision of the whole world metamorphosed "into something small and sleepy and enclosed, the interior of an egg." The book's sinister imagery of fog, cold, caves, darkness, and its dramatic apparatus of sleeping pills, demon music, and false dreams, support this

second pattern. And the vocabulary of motion finds its anti-
type in the characteristic violence of surprise, reversal, and
inward shock and change that have become Iris Murdoch's
narrative signature.

By these continuous means a medium is established in
which the key elements in the story's progress come to be
known, a medium that derives from the very atmosphere of
the mind, for it borrows the mind's surrealistic coloring and
its rhythm of excitation and protective resistance. The effect
is, apparently, deliberate: we notice how the realization of
this fictional medium matches her recent description of the
mind's natural life ("the constant quiet work of attention
and imagination") as "a sort of seeping of colour, or the
setting up of a magnetic field" ("The Darkness of Practical
Reason"). Whatever one thinks of her effort as a whole, one
has at least to recognize these strong correspondences of form
and theme. "Those with whom the angels communicate are
lost": that is Father Carel's black revelation—but the truth
the book reveals at each crisis is that "the angels" have their
terrible power over us only through our knowledge, our
fantasies. Here again the recent *Encounter* essay gives us the
appropriate gloss: "I would see the enemy of freedom as
fantasy, the bad use of imagination: something relentlessly
natural to human beings. . . ." Other imaginable glosses come
to mind. "We had fed the heart on fantasies,/ The heart's
grown brutal from the fare," or, "Whatever flames upon the
night/ Man's own resinous heart has fed." The concerns Iris
Murdoch works by can hardly be accused of preciosity.

AFTERWORD (1970)

Since *The Time of the Angels* Iris Murdoch has published
three more novels, at a rate of one each year; by the time this
note is in print there may well be another. Such old-fashioned
fecundity is a kind of embarrassment to critics and annals-
keepers, whose habit of mind prefers a greater stability in the
order of evidence. *The Nice and the Good* (1968) and *Bruno's
Dream* (1969) have their share of the virtues and idio-
syncrasies described above. The former, starting with its

title, strikes me as a little too baldly controlled by the philosophic argument, though it is furnished with a fine amplitude of dramatic, and comic, detail. Perhaps, too, the category of the "nice" is not metaphysically equal to the task of balancing or setting off the category of the "good"; for once the conception rather than the execution seems flawed. *Bruno's Dream* returns to Gothic liberties of treatment, but this is in keeping with its main narrative occasions; it has at the center a strong, lucid rendering of the pain and spiritual panic of old age and of the sad house it must keep.

Miss Murdoch's latest novel, *A Fairly Honourable Defeat* (1970), seems to me one of her two or three best, and a book, in the end, of harrowing force. A first reading tempts me to think that it is the work in which the philosophical fabulist and the natural novelist have finally coalesced. In designing her novels Iris Murdoch has all along been responsive not only to the pressure of her own acutely interesting moral ideas but equally to the special agony of this age's insoluble arguments with itself as to what is required of human beings, and what is permitted to them, in the face of unprecedented historical evil—of which the "final solution," racist and colonialist terrorism, the totalitarian repression of entire peoples, the monstrous aberration of Vietnam, are the consubstantial symbols. One of the hardest truths that we have had to learn, and evidently must go on learning, is that the evil generated by these undertakings (all of which have had, at some point, their right-thinking apologists) does not end with their blunting or reversal by opposing forces; it enters history and cannot be removed from history's sequences; it spreads and spreads, and in—to conscience—the most troubling cases of all, it inhabits its own most pitiable victims.

The argument has been powerfully advanced that evil on this scale has transformed the moral and civil universe; that as a consequence certain things which used to be thought of as the supreme distillation of civilized values can perhaps no longer be tolerated in any form. "After Auschwitz, no poetry": Adorno's peremptory cry touches some real nerve of guilt and terror. But we see that the cry is itself terroristic, a forced surrender to the thing it would bear witness against. We have only to change it (as it has the form of a command) to, "After Auschwitz, no poets," to see what intolerable civil measures it must result in. Ours is, of course, not the first age to know something like this threat of an absolute transformation of moral laws. "If there is no God, no rule for life except that which human beings are able to impose on each other and make customary and familiar, then *all is permitted*" —that is the theorem which tempts and ravages Dostoevsky's thoughtful heroes, and which returns to haunt the present with nightmares of irreversible self-damage. It is the nightmare specifically faced in *A Fairly Honourable Defeat,* precisely how, it may be left for readers to see for themselves; comment on a novel still too new to be widely known should not give away functional secrets.

The book does, in any case, take the overform of a parable, and it means this: In our time, in the West, something uniquely terrible rages loose in the common life, entering the conscious behavior of decent men and women and constraining and warping everything that is done. And it *must* be paid for, it *will* take its toll. Because it has existed, it will continue to exist, the common life pressing to experiment further with what has been discovered to be possible. Thus the supervention we most fear becomes the analogy we find ourselves living by; it gives its shape to what *we* see and do, so that we cannot merely say, *"they* did it, those others, though we warned and warned them." Against this all too plausible terror, the fresh power of life that we call, ultimately, *love* may or may not provide effective resistance; may itself survive only through undeserved accidents of good luck. But it is the one power of resistance that is equally natural to us, and equally common—and of Iris Murdoch's latest novel I am saying only that it seems to me to light up this particular conflict of forces, dominating our time, as brilliantly as any English or American novel of the past thirty years.

American Literature:
Traditions and Talents

A main point of interest now concerning T. S. Eliot's celebrated essay, "Tradition and the Individual Talent," is its
bearing on his choice to settle in London and make his career
there. That choice, like Henry James's before it, appears emblematic in our literary history. In several respects it mani-
fests itself as a characteristically "American" undertaking. We
sense an air of purposefulness and portentous consideration
about it, a freedom and efficiency in its execution, and not
least the hint of some large prescriptive judgment upon the
abandoned home province. Not less "American," in a broad
view, was the essay itself. In its high practical seriousness,
its technician's concern for the making of works of art, its
zeal for a professional "extinction of personality," its quasi-
scientific reasoning, it was as fine-drawn as a theoretical disquisition by Edgar Allan Poe. Written half a century ago, it
remains as provocative, and as nearly presumptuous, as it
ever was. It truly marks an epoch in Anglo-American literature—but we tend to believe that only an American would
have thought to write it, would have stated his position in
just these terms.

For though addressed to a British audience, the essay
goes at once to the bottom of certain distinctively American

First published by Press of the Times, Oberlin, 1960.

critical issues then current. Specifically, it outflanks the rising preoccupation with what Van Wyck Brooks was calling at the time a "usable past," and the whole anxious inquiry as to whether creative imagination in the United States might at last be "coming of age" and by what kind of effort. Its effect was to expose argument as informed and sincere as Brooks's as being rather too visionary and declamatory, not closely enough concerned with the writer's immediate practical task of delivering himself of good work. Yet it is every bit as full of the high expectancy of that lively moment in our literary history, and of something else, too, which may be called ambition: a severe, professional, calculated ambition to compete with the known masters of European letters at their own most exacting level.

The argument of the present essay is not as hopeful concerning the future of American writing as it seems possible to have been in 1915 or 1917. For one thing it is not advanced from the standpoint of the creative writer; any bold new talent capable not only of promise and piecemeal inventiveness but of finished performance can brush its inferential logic aside. If that happens, no one will be gladder than its propounder. But I must assume, while the present creative drought continues, with no more than scattered local relief in sight, that a vital literature is not something we have a right, as it were, to expect to have produced for us. It may have become something that in a civil way we are cleverly learning to do without, another among the items of traditional culture spectacularly absent (as in Henry James's famous bill of particulars) from American life. And what is literature anyhow but, to borrow a phrase of Eliot's, a "superior form of amusement"? Who can prove it necessary to the good life, to the survival of civilization? More and more it becomes a matter of leisure-class entertainment; more and more it takes its prevailing character from the character of the great diversion-hungry middle rank of cultivated society upon whose sufferance it has been dependent for some two hundred years or more. The broad diffusion of polite interest in it and taste for it is no small factor in the cultural conformity, the rule of publicity and information, that we all complain about. The day-by-day practice of it generates at least as much petty human viciousness as the rare best of it has ever had power to "purge." Nevertheless it does persist as a conceivable vocation. Its peculiar appeal to the absolutism and excitability of the young, the undetermined, the spiritually dissatisfied, seems undiminished. No matter what sorry state the practice of literature is in, it continues to transmit the motives that call people to its dubious service. And though at any given moment it is a pushover for the time-serving and career-making, it remains by the same token a perfectly open system. Great individual talents may enter it at their hard pleasure—though not simply at will. Its problematical and contingent nature does not make its product less worth prizing. Among the forms of amusement by which we seek to make life a little more than just endurable, literature offers itself as indeed a superior one; and there is always some use in thinking about the conditions in which it has been made, and may yet be made again.

Eliot's position was that without a devoted apprenticeship to "tradition," the most gifted individual talent would not mature properly, would not get its work out live and whole. He was not the first American writer afflicted with this sense of the hazards of his occupation. Before him a notable succession of our novelists had testified to the exceptional difficulties of practicing their craft in the United States. According to Fenimore Cooper, however, the great problem was a "poverty of materials," and Hawthorne, too, complained chiefly of the discouraging lack, for novelists, of variety, depth, and romantic mystery in American social life.

It remained for Henry James to turn this sense of practical difficulty inward and get to the bottom of the problem. Not poverty of materials betrayed the American novelist; James could be witty enough on that score, but much of his own best work shows that he instinctively subscribed to the optimistic Emersonian view that the American materials are "incomparable" in their singularity and freshness, requiring only a corresponding boldness of treatment. Betrayal came rather from the absence of challenge and discipline in the critical atmosphere, from the poverty of stimulus to finished performance. James felt early on that "the face of nature and civilization" in the United States was "a very sufficient literary field," as he wrote Charles Eliot Norton in 1870. "But it will yield its secrets," he continued, "only to a really *grasping* imagination"—and he stayed abroad, in the Paris of Flaubert, Turgenev, the Goncourts, the Théâtre Français, and the *Revue des Deux Mondes,* then in the London of Gosse, Stevenson, the Reform Club, Lord Houghton's breakfasts, and the *Fortnightly* and *Cornhill,* in order to encourage and make habitual in his work just that energy, just that pertinacity, of practical imagination.

A tradition of grasping hard enough and long enough (as well as tactfully and seriously enough), a tradition of unstinted performance—that is what was missing. To judge from what passes nowadays for creativity in our literature, it is what is still missing, for all our new critical sophistication.* There is indeed an American literature, sometimes of remarkable vivacity and originality, but there is not a continuous and viable American literary tradition. The chief feature of our literary history is its brokenness and disconnectedness. There is no continuous major line of descent or development; the practice of the significant individual writers or generations of writers does not positively inform the practice of their successors, who are successors in time only, and by the contrivance of anthologies and academic reading-lists. Each new practitioner does not, to borrow Eliot's extravagant way of putting it, write "with a feeling that the whole of the literature of his own country has a simultaneous existence and composes a simultaneous order." What Harold Rosenberg has said of American painting is true in the large of American literature: "its best examples consist of individual inventions which do not carry over into the future" (*The Tradition of the New,* chap. 1). We may say in general that the literary traditions which have mattered most in the United States have been English and European; and the succession of major talents in American writing, as in Irish, is not intelligible except in relation to those traditions, being dependent on their

---

* The few exceptions that force themselves upon our attention seem at best still largely promissory, though just now, at the beginning of the 1960's, I should be inclined to bet on Robert Lowell still and John Updike, and on the Saul Bellow of *Seize the Day.*

continuity and "progress" and scarcely conceivable apart from them.

The situation is plainly paradoxical, since for a century and a half most of the significant American writers have been partisans, doctrinaire or consenting, of an idea of American literary independence. A survey of major works, moreover, would show no small number of uniformities, and most strikingly the persistence of a relatively narrow range of formal practices—storytelling in the first person and the idealized (or allegorized) adventure-chronicle, for example, or various forms of prophetic confession and private witness-bearing. But something more is meant by "tradition" in literature than the mere recurrence, however artful, of particular devices and effects. Almost the commonest observation about American writing is that it has made a specialty of starting all over again. It has done this on principle and with self-satisfaction. It has proceeded as though the past and its models were most useful when disregarded. It has been peculiarly uncomfortable with established precedents. It has been willing to work alone and in the dark, suspicious of other ways of proceeding even when it knows all about them, as nervously and erratically it does usually make a point of doing. Yet the result, technically, is repetition; as if by self-scruple, American writing has been condemned to repeating its own discoveries. Above all else it has been inhibited by fears of some catastrophic loss of personal integrity. As a result its triumphs in art appear as personal triumphs, of principally a personal—and circumstantial—interest. It is out of touch, and prefers to be. It is, in a word, provincial. And it is in good part provincial by choice, by self-determination, at the least by acquiescence. The need to come to terms with this provinciality has been, at least since Cooper and Emerson, the generic lot of the American writer. It is what he has had instead of "tradition."

The distinction here may seem, on the face of it, rather a quibble. But provinciality is precisely not a feature of *literary* tradition; it is a feature of cultural and historical tradition. And its effect on literary tradition, on the development of a transmitted discipline of accomplished performance, has been to inhibit, to frustrate. American literature, I have been saying, has lacked such a tradition; to a peculiar degree its history is hit-and-miss, a sequence of accidents. When renewal has come, through the stimulus of European example, it has always been constrained by the presence of certain persisting conditions of American cultural life, certain historically continuous modes of thought and feeling, of moral habituation, of social organization. To discuss the more important of these conditions, and some of their effects, is what is proposed for the remainder of this essay; for they are the conditions in which our literature has found its occasions, its themes, its very voice and forms. But only in a handful of masterpieces has it cut loose, so to speak, from the historical straitjacket and gained the freedom and generative power of self-governing art; and these rare triumphs have signally failed to breed healthy successors. The reasons for this, I think, lie "outside" literature; at least they cannot be explained by an examination of the literary record alone.

The best and fullest account of the American provinciality is Emerson's, and runs the length of his extraordinary journal. As might be expected of the moral biographer of the "American scholar," Emerson anticipated the finding Ernest Hemingway was to set down a century later, that "something happens to our good writers at a certain age." In his journal of April, 1841 (he had been reading Tocqueville's *Democracy in America*), Emerson drew this sketch of "our present literary and philosophical crisis":

> . . . for the most part there is great monotony in the history of our young men. . . . We are a puny and fickle folk. Hesitation and following are our diseases. . . . America is the country of small adventures, of short plans, of daring risks, not of patience, not of great combinations, not of long, persistent, close-woven schemes, demanding the utmost fortitude, temper, faith, and poverty. Our books are tents, not pyramids; our reformers are slight and wearisome talkers, not man-subduing, immutable, all-attracting; discharging their own task and so "charming the eye with dread," and persuading without knowing that they do so. There are no Duke Wellingtons, no George Washingtons, no Miltons . . . among our rapid and dashing race; but abundance of Murats, of Rienzis, of Wallers, and that slight race who put their whole stake on the first die they cast.

"Who put their whole stake on the first die." It is the special mark, and burden, of the provincial that he is never sure of his chances, even when acting with what may be sublime appropriateness. He is haunted by the revolutionary's or comeouter's great question, "What is to be done?"—and so disturbed by the fear of having *nothing* to do that he cannot bide his time, or so fascinated by the dreadful possibility of doing the wrong thing that he rushes to fulfill it, to execute his distinguishing gaucherie. He is not sure what may be taken for granted. He must explain and justify, particularly himself. He cannot trust traditional modes; there is no established manner for him to work in or against ("No article so rare in New England as Tone," Emerson remarked). He cannot even be sure of an audience; cannot, that is, count on steady employment, especially if he is seriously ambitious. "I know," Emerson wrote, "three, four, five, six, seven, or eight persons, who look at nature and existence with no unworthy eye, but they are players, and rather melancholy players in the world, for want of work." Want of work means want of development, as Emerson's London monitor, Carlyle, kept preaching. But the poor provincial cannot assume that the work he needs will be forthcoming. He cannot see how his talent is to be encouraged to grow and mature unless he devotes his own main energies to the job; and he has only his own overtaxed judgment to keep this job of self-encouragement from becoming full-time and exhausting. He must do it all himself. The risk he takes is obvious. For when you have only inner checks to serve you, the question becomes, who, if anyone, shall be master?

We may take our cue again from Emerson's journal, a rich source of conjecture in these matters precisely as one of its governing motives, and that one in particular which seems to me to hold together the famous inconsistencies and to make Emerson more accessible at present than he has been for a hundred years, is a steady practical concern for the mind's *morale,* the "scholar's" equivalent of some enabling state of grace. It was during the troubled, stock-taking period of his late thirties, after his first successes as a writer and lecturer, that he made the following entry:

It seems to me sometimes that we get our education ended a little too quick in this country. As soon as we have learned to read and write and cipher, we are dismissed from school and we set up for ourselves. We are writers and leaders of opinion and we write away without check of any kind, play whatsoever mad prank, indulge whatever spleen, or oddity, or obstinacy, comes into our dear head, and even feed our complacency thereon, and thus fine wits come to nothing, as good horses spoil themselves by running away and straining themselves.

"We set up for ourselves"; to a special degree the provincial's education must be self-education, and his culture self-culture. This is not just for want of the official apparatus of instruction; he quite suspects what it may cost him, but what else is he to trust? how else can he prove his sincerity (preeminently the provincial virtue)?

Of course his predicament has, for compensation, its potential advantages ("we play the game with immense advantage," Emerson could reply to Carlyle's strictures on America). The provincial's circumstances also give him his characteristic freedoms. They give him nerve to feel, as a matter of common possibility, that "one should be able to see that things are hopeless and yet be determined to make them otherwise"—Scott Fitzgerald's remark. Or to be merely exhilarated, like the narrator of Edmund Wilson's *I Thought of Daisy,* by the notion that "Americans might turn into anything." They permit him to rush at sudden openings, in the confidence that someone else is on the job at the center—in case there still is a center. But his freedom is more likely to be his undoing than to make him greatly original. His worst burden is distrust of his own opportunity; it is that fear of freedom which is distressing enough in the bound-over but peculiarly poignant in the already free. He will use up his capacity for growth and fruition in studying the laws of growth and fruition—and how to submit himself to them. "Nature herself was in a hurry with these hasters and never finished one," Emerson wrote; "you shall not find one good, sound, well-developed apple on the tree."

In desperation, then, the free provincial retreats to his alternatives. He will fall back upon preaching old lessons, in the delusion that they are new gospel, and in the process reduce himself to the stature of a "village explainer" (Gertrude Stein's epithet for Ezra Pound), though he may also prove a perfect Lord Root-of-the-Matter (Churchill's epithet for Harry Hopkins). Whether he is the Sweet Singer of Michigan or "Walt Whitman a kosmos," he will make a show of writing as though no one had ever written to any purpose before. The result may be original enough. But such originality by itself is no guarantee of weight and moment, nor of salubrity:

> I do not like the Plain Speaker so well as the Edinburgh Review [Emerson observed]. The spirit of the last may be conventional and artificial, but that of the first is coarse, sour, indigent, dwells in a cellar kitchen, and goes to make suicides.

Acutely mistrustful of convention and artifice, the provincial may simply shut himself off from what is legitimately available to him. He is a man self-dispossessed of his privileges, and he is liable never to get down to the proper business of his trade. His unfamiliarity with the letter pledges him prematurely to the spirit. Unacquainted or uncomfortable with the full range of properties in the things that concern him, he lunges precipitately after their distilled essence. His instinct is, in a word, *antinomian*—as is his legacy ("Beware of antinomianism," Emerson wrote in self-admonishment). He is the natural sectary, than who, we may say, no one more needs an Establishment in view.

Thus he not only lacks tradition but is hostile to the very idea of it. He must speak out, like a Hemingway character, against the "big words," the received expression of the common experience of things. Similarly he must bear ritual witness against the very vocation he has got himself into. Though as a writer he may be preternaturally self-conscious (especially of the problem of intellectual morale, Emerson's great subject), though he may be a dedicated experimentalist or apostle of craftsmanship, he may nonetheless, like Frost, like Faulkner, prefer to call himself a farmer; if he accepts the role of man of letters, it is because he has had an unbalancing taste of the libertine priestliness it allows him to put on. His need to insist that "books are for the scholar's idle times" alerts us to his special Scylla-Charybdis: on the one quarter an exaggerated spontaneity, on the other an exaggerated bookishness. (We observe their risky conjunction in Whitman and Melville, in Cummings and Faulkner, and decadently in Henry Miller and the current rash of Kerouacs and Ferlinghettis) .

In either case, exaggeration. The provincial must exaggerate to exist ("I trust you realize what an exaggerator I am," Thoreau wrote; "I lay myself out to exaggeration"). He knows no *mesure* but in the personal wrestling with personal tensions ("Deliver us," said Emerson, "from that intensity of character which makes all its crows swans"). He lives between extremes and has no means of getting a foothold except personal ones; poverty of means drives him back all the more on himself; and the steady, radical drain on personal resources that must result proves exhausting, debilitating. Small comfort then to be told, as Emerson told himself, that "exaggeration is the law of nature." What follows is the quintessential American disillusionment, so often coming with the unraveling force of a betrayal—it is the discovery of life without "prospects," in the midst of still "incomparable" natural advantages; it is the revelation that what has been lying in wait for us all our unconscious arriving years is an inward impoverishment which proves to be the form of our accomplished life, turning its unique promise of beauty and advantage (as with our New World landscape) to waste and ashes.

It is, as James said, a complex fate. I think it marks most conspicuously the generation of the "American renaissance," whose ambitious and richly talented members were the first to experience the full scope and persistence of it. We call them provincial without derogation—we see that we are in the same fix, and that we do not respond half so resourcefully. The various competing systems of understanding brought forward in our own time to fill the gap, the critical humanisms and reconciling new orthodoxies, seem at the core mere wishful and evasive rationalizations, expressions of nostalgia for a tidy order that is no more and probably never was; in the meantime sectarianism, specialization, dead-letter clerkery, a terrible inward division of labor, tighten their leasehold over our actual culture. But the values of an imagined center still haunt us, and it is rightly by them that we judge ourselves and our works.

In such circumstances the impulse to self-judgment, though part and parcel of the provincial insecurity, can have its creative uses. It is not itself the cause of the trouble it finds. With a writer concerned, as Eliot explicitly was, to try out his personal impressions in the form of objective laws, it may lead to as provocative and serviceable a manifesto as "Tradition and the Individual Talent" has been. The studied and constricting refinement for which New England literacy especially is notorious, and toward which Eliot early recognized his own destructive bias, is only a perversion of this impulse, though a cautionary one; but without its nervous guardianship the vitality of many of our classic books might well have been squandered in mere self-assertion. This impulse is itself one of the oldest of "American" traditions, and from the beginning one of the strongest.

For "America," we know, was an idea before it took form, if it ever has, as a "civilization." It was invented by Europeans almost before it was discovered. It was, it still is, a state of mind, a set of expectations (increasingly of violated expectations), not simply a territory for settlement and enterprise. And it is one of Europe's most magnificent and original inventions, though like most modern inventions there is something arbitrary about it, suggesting a closing off of other possibilities. Historically it is the outgrowth of certain energies that were abroad in Europe in the sixteenth and seventeenth centuries—and first of all of the rational and humanistic apprehension that the order of human life might well be what men choose to make it, and that it can be made better (more prosperous, more comfortable, more splendid, more just, more happy) if adventurous men would only apply themselves systematically to the job.

What, under pressure of such a conception, was "America" to be? It was to be the place where Europe would fulfill herself; where civilized life could be organized anew from the foundations, and human society (and its creeds and churches) would be perfected at last. It was to be a province of Europe, but also a climax of European history. Here what was vital and worthy in the Old World might be lodged in the common order of things, and what was vicious and inert might be cast off. Christianity itself would have a new beginning, the Golden Age would be restored. "America" would be something new on earth, a "new order of the ages," and what was "American" would in a fundamental way be different from what it had sprung from. Most presumptuously, it would be something better.

It is hardly surprising that so lofty a conception should have put a grave burden of idealism and aspiration, and correspondingly of self-consciousness and self-criticism, on American imaginations. However comfortable life is made, however blessed with victory and crowned with good, the doubt remains: are we meeting the standard we once set ourselves? are we true to our own ideals? are we, as Thoreau asked, conducting our lives "sincerely" or have we fallen into a "division of labor" which is "mean and sneaking," a self-betrayal? Scarcely an important book in our literature is not in some way concerned to pose such questions or intimate such judgments, and so to submit the actuality of American life to the test of its own inward measure. This well-known American idealism can take very perverse forms, as we know. It makes a habit of rushing in where angelic doctors would be diffident, and laying down lynch law on matters it has just discovered its interest in. It is too often a function not of civil aspiration but of a regressive separatism. At the same time it is a fact of our lives and understandings, and indivisible from such virtue as we properly attribute to the way of life, the laws, the institutions—and the literature—we call "American."

As a topic for speculation this national idealism is admittedly abstract. But as a historical phenomenon it hardly needs demonstrating. It has infused our behavior as a people from the beginning. It has activated, and been invoked to justify, new deals, programs of four or fourteen points, wars for independence, innumerable reform movements, "crusades" for union or democracy or social justice or houndstooth political purity, liberal and illiberal trade and immigration policies, leagues for liberty, leagues against the saloon, imperialisms and anti-imperialisms, all manner of "great debate," and right, left, and center (not to mention top, middle, and bottom) of nearly every public controversy. "Americans are eminently prophets," Santayana commented in 1920; "they apply morals to public affairs; they are impatient and enthusiastic."

They even, he might have added, impatiently and enthusi-
astically attack their own idealism with a curiously idealized
and question-begging doctrine of self-interest which is advanced in the name of "pragmatism," or of "toughness"—as
sometimes, for example, when Mr. Acheson or Mr. Kennan
lectures us on the principles of foreign policy. The historical
truth is that this habit of mind is centrally installed in three
broad conditions of the American settlement which are bone
and tissue of the American manner of life—as they are the
source, I want now to suggest, of such continuity and consistency as may be found in the enduring literature of the
North American province.

   In the first place, American society, compared with what
it came out from, is democratic, or has irresistibly become so
(always excepting the terrible anomaly of Negro slavery),
and its literature is a democratic literature. By this I mean
simply that the imaginative writing which interests us as such
has been done, not much of it before 1830, by men who have
lived in an increasingly equalitarian as well as free society,
and have breathed its special atmosphere. Moreover, they
have at bottom accepted this kind of society, even when they
have been most strenuously critical or contemptuous of it;
they have not seriously imagined living in any other.* Further, they have in their fashion championed the ideal of
democratic society (or some reductive "populist" version of
it), have been inspired by it and on occasion praised it as
the best imaginable; and they have accepted as a matter of
course, sometimes of religious faith, the preeminent interest
of the ordinary, democratized man, man alone and "without
qualities," representing nothing but his own nature and history. (As writers they have been familiar enough with all the
ordinary queerness of this nature and history to be as sensational as the traffic permits.) And it is largely as they document this shift of interest that American writers have fas-

---

* The only real exceptions, like Pound and certain Southerners, have been
so bizarre in their opinions as on the whole to reinforce the sense of the
dominant norm. So, in the public sphere, glaring contradictions and
violations of the democratic order are in the long run recognized as such,
and are seldom otherwise than outlandishly defended.

cinated European readers. For what in the European view *is* democratic America but a prophecy, for good or bad, of the universal future? This was its interest to Tocqueville, its wisest interpreter, who saw in the United States a version of the way of life that lay ahead for parent Europe, in the new era of technology and the democratic masses. America had simply got into it first, there having existed in the New World no entrenched forms and endowed institutions able to restrain the revolutionary energies creating the modern social order.

"Revolutionary" seems an altogether just epithet here; for the second and third of the historical conditions chiefly determining the manner of American life and imposing on American literature the equivalent of a formative tradition were indeed revolutionary conditions. Their transforming power is what up to the present has settled the prevailing character of this open and volatile new "civilization." Two great gatherings of social energy in the Europe of the late Renaissance are in question here. The first is what we speak of as capitalism, the instrument of that economic revolution through which certain Western nations have created the modern era and half-Europeanized the rest of the world. The second is what we know as the Reformation, and the militant sectarianism which it released into the mainstream of Western history.

The importance for our national history of these two forces—revolutionary capitalism and revolutionary protestantism—can scarcely be overstressed. Both were committed, as if by definition, to overthrowing the traditional order of feudal and Catholic society, and both were at a first climax of vitality during the out-populating of North America. Both, too, were well adapted, or found it impossible not to become so, to exploit the opportunity of an empty, physically rich continent. In this respect the two forces had much in common. Often they coexisted in the same communities and in the same people, the characteristic "new men" of the modern era. When Max Weber wanted an exemplary case of the conjunction of the "Protestant ethic" with the "spirit of capitalism," he chose the arch-American Franklin, whose chronicle of his own life and contacts encompasses half the themes of our meager national folklore. From this conjunction, in the open New World circumstance, the American character (if one can be identified) has developed, and from it American literature (such as we find it) has emerged. Thus, inquiry into the characteristic ethos of either force may bring into view certain distinguishing qualities of our imaginative writing.

Designations like "capitalist" and "bourgeois" have so long been overlaid by innuendos of propaganda that it may be useful to recall what they properly refer to—in this case, the character of a class of men personally detached from landed or communal status and occupied, singly or in combination, with investment and speculation in an essentially accidental market. Lacking other capital, such men were able in America to invest themselves, speculating profitably on their own futures. This class is now identified with the dominant privileged order of Western life. But in the late Renaissance it stood forth in a different role; it was the bearer of social revolution and political liberation. And in the emptiness of the New World its rise to authority was contested only by its own pragmatical lawlessness and the stimulating obstinacy of physical nature. Its accession to power was absolute. As a result its values and ideals were installed in the United States more rapidly and thoroughly than anywhere in the world.

To name some of these values and ideals is in effect to describe the moral atmosphere in which our literature has been made. The foremost perhaps was personal liberty, the liberty of each man to shape his life as its chances might allow. ("Masterlessness" was D. H. Lawrence's name for it, a fundamental "American" characteristic.) Capitalist society values energy, independence, hard work, doing for oneself, and the proofs of success; it also pretends to value, whatever it practices, honesty, sincerity, truthfulness, sobriety, frugality, tolerance, self-discipline—all those virtues itemized by Franklin which allow business and affairs to run smoothly and profitably. And whenever we find an American writer celebrating these virtues—even when like Thoreau he is attacking capitalist society in the interest of a higher "economy"—we find him registering the vital presence of the liberal capitalist mentality in American life. If this mentality should clot, wither, and disappear, "American culture" as a distinguishable entity may also be found to have disappeared, a price, perhaps, of that world order which for better or worse, whether as an alternative to disaster or as a result of it, we are slowly and blindly sliding toward; a price, too, which in some parts of the world may not be unwillingly exacted.

But of course there is another, darker face to this mentality, equally distinctive. As liberal capitalist society acts to free the enterprising individual, it acts also to isolate him, to cut him off from human ties. As it develops the custom of freedom and self-interest, it also encourages, at least it fails to check, the contagion of irresponsibility. As it permits men to rise spectacularly in status, it also leaves them free to degenerate and go to pieces, as picturesquely as they like. It cuts them off from nature, too; it makes them provincial, so to speak, with respect to the whole imaginable domain, the full economy, of life on earth. When only an exploitative, stock-holding relation to nature and humankind is encouraged, the other possible relations must go begging; and those whose imaginations are most distressed by this drift of things are compelled into single-handed gestures of compensation.

Consider in this regard the lack of natural sensuousness in most of our literature (a subject Mr. Leslie Fiedler has treated provocatively), and the shyness of the fundamental relationships of the continuing human family in our classic fiction. Then consider the corresponding stresses and exaggerations, sometimes, of course, wonderfully creative—as in Whitman on "standing at ease in nature" or the "manly love of comrades"; in Thoreau on "friendship" or Wallace Stevens on the *idea* of reality; in Hemingway's unbalancing effort after honesty and immediacy of feeling; or in the stranglehold of private confessionism and epithetical description on our unventuresome current poetry. The very instinct of idealism withers and hardens, becomes a negative passion for technical efficiency, in art as in business. The abstracted ideal view is taken not by considered and principled choice but through disappearance of the capacity to imagine any other.

Is it surprising then that themes of loneliness and rootlessness, of isolation, of personal deprivation, of fanaticism and madness, run so powerfully through American writing? Have we not identified here a clear source of the persistent vision, in our literature, of the special violence that overtakes human beings as pathetically or heroically they attempt to fix their lives into some sustaining relation? American writers have told us what American life has demonstrated, that to be free is to be alone, and that such loneliness is a way to madness. Our fiction is populated with lonely men on the edges of madness, in postures of comic lunacy or tragic insanity. Isolatoes, Melville called them, and with Ahab, and then Bartleby, drew two of the most affecting portraits of the type in our literature. They are the "man of the crowd" of Poe's story, or men guilty, through pride of their own being, of "unpardonable" sins against their fellowmen, like Hawthorne's Ethan Brand. They are such as are described in Hawthorne's story, "Egotism," who find their "pleasure—perhaps the greatest of which the sufferer is susceptible—in displaying the wasted or ulcerated limb, or the cancer in the breast . . . for it is that cancer, or that crime, which constitutes their respective individuality." They are the "grotesque" of *Winesburg, Ohio,* turned in like "twisted apples" upon the accidents of their personal existence; the damned of Nathanael West's vision in *Miss Lonelyhearts,* who "have no outer life, only an inner one, and that of necessity." Their very speech has become nervously histrionic; they express themselves in watchful declamation or defensive mimicry, or in the ingenious spinning out of hallucinatory tales, as if seeking to call into existence, by tricks of spellbinding, that audience which they know is not there for them except as they manage to create it and which will disintegrate the moment they stop.

But it is apparent, as we review these themes and mannerisms, that most of them may be attributed in equal measure to the third of these basic conditions of the American settlement, the evangelical and sectarian legacy of the Reformation. The fixation upon loneliness and moral isolation derives, it seems clear, from this source, too, from the radical protestant stress on the individual conscience. The main effects of the protestant temper on our literate culture are familiar enough and may simply be listed—the ethical severity and high-mindedness; the violent alternations of spirit between intense assurance and intense despair; the preoccupation with depravity in human nature and corruption in human works, and the general predisposition to deal unmediatedly with ultimate issues of the soul's or society's destiny, in terms of drastic moral absolutes and "without tarrying for any"; the excessive value put upon spontaneous personal testimony and private anecdote; the implicit spiritual democracy of the gathered churches and the congregational order, the Baptist and Pentecostal communions and Friends' meetings, and by extension the vision of a "holy community" or fraternity of the chosen that declares itself, sometimes fantastically, in writers like Whitman, Hart Crane, Sherwood Anderson, the Cummings of *The Enormous Room,* Eugene O'Neill and Allen Ginsberg; finally, the zeal for crusading and converting which catches up authors not less than preachers (some) and politicians (a few) and free-lancing, lance-breaking journalists of the old school, and which proceeds stylistically from passionate fact-finding to equally passionate prophecy.*

One effect of the protestant inheritance, however, needs fuller description here, not only because it is less immediately evident than these I have listed, but because it may be, for the making of books and the constituting of "tradition," the profoundest effect of all. This is the habitual antinomianism of our literature, by which I mean again that intellectual antinomianism Emerson warned himself against. As with the religious heresy it has widened out from, it is the disposition to rely, sometimes exclusively, on the excited individual sensibility and on the immediate data of particular experience, in minds bred to a distrust of settled forms and established ways of speaking (and reinforced in this distrust with each new surge of aroused inward consciousness). It is a suspicion, in short, of this world's names. It is different from philosophical skepticism, however. It puts its trust in intuitive assent at the expense of rational method, and it will give up every sort of formal or objective sanction to preserve the feeling of integrity of spirit.

---

* These characteristics are not limited to writers reared in the ethos of the Protestant churches. The same "American" temper has appeared more recently in writers whose inheritances are Catholic or Jewish.

Historically it appears as the underside of quite another component of the protestant mentality, that elaborate intellectual discipline and deference to authority which Calvin, especially, salvaged from the disintegration of medieval Christianity. That is what the antinomian disposition "comes out" from and against; yet it is in its own way equally dogmatic, finding its greatest champions in Luther and Paul; it is the chief ideological agency of the continuing protest of Protestantism. It takes the form of anti-institutionalism, anti-intellectualism, anti-traditionalism—and so constitutes, we see, one of our most tenacious national modes of thought and judgment. And in literature, in expression, it further exaggerates the American need to "make it new"; it stiffens the refusal merely to do a good job through proven conventions. It distrusts even the improvised conventions of its own making. It prefers not to finish its projects, fearing that the life may go out of them, that they will not be "sincere" ("what I write to fill the gaps of a chapter," Emerson said, "is hard and cold, is grammar and logic; there is no magic in it; I do not wish to see it again"). The antinomian instinct accepts, perhaps even chooses, the risk of parochialism, of ignorance and inadvertence; it turns its back on classical ideals of completeness and continuity, in the organization of society as well as in the practice of literature—except with regard to the life of the individual temperament, which, if only by default, it makes sovereign. Small wonder that Eliot, defining his purposes as he did, decided to go into other parts—or that the remarkable authority of his example, so overbearing for one generation, should so abruptly diminish in the next, the latest.*

---

* "Antinomian" is not the most convenient term imaginable, but it has the considerable merit of suiting certain major facts in our literary history. It helps, for example, to explain the passionate conviction with which a succession of significant talents has insisted that American writing should be, above all, original and new—or that it should reflect, more particularly, a Hart Crane's persuasion that here in America "are destined to be discovered certain as yet undefined spiritual quantities, perhaps a new hierarchy of faith not to be developed so completely elsewhere." This habit of mind has given special urgency, I think, to the long debate between two classic schools of American literary controversy: that which has argued that because our society is new and traditionless its practice of art should defer

Provinciality, disconnectedness, watchful self-consciousness, an extreme civil and sectarian idealism, democratic anonymity, an uneasy measure of parish vanity or of populist spleen, capitalist libertarianism, Puritan conscientiousness, Utopian anticipation—and, we should add, a continental rootlessness and a continental affluence and security—these are the large circumstances within which, in lieu of a "tradition," American literature has so far been created. But what about the future? Can we expect some decisive new turn for the literary life in the United States? Is there any prospect of the crystallization here of what James and Eliot went to London in search of, a sustaining and enabling tradition of performance? Or will there be any more "literature" at all which is worthy of the name? And will it bear any vital relation to what has gone before?

For the fact is that the special and privileged conditions of the American settlement, more or less binding through most of our history, seem now to be changing rapidly and fundamentally. Clearly our provinciality is lessening by the moment in relation to the Europe it was born from. That in considerable part is because Europe itself and the "West" now begin to appear more than a little provincial, as power and influence even out across the world. The divisions and contentions in the wake of the Reformation seem more than ever intramural; the capitalist ethos finds itself challenged, perhaps displaced, as the chief agent of historical change; liberal democracy is no longer the sure model of the universal future; sectarian idealisms are swallowed up in concern for the survival of the race as a whole and the protection of each new generation's chance at life.

Yet these changes call first of all for readjustments in politics, in the public sector of consciousness. What they do not require is the preliminary liquidation of "provincial" differences. Indeed, if art is to continue in the world, and not

---

to matured precedents, and that which has argued that for exactly the same reason its practice of art ought to put all precedents aside.

These are extreme positions, and no good writer has gone all the way into either. So Eliot's essay on tradition stops to acknowledge that "novelty" in art must be preferred to "repetition"; while Emerson's scholar, though his books are for his idle times, proves on acquaintance to have been a great reader—"antinomian" is not necessarily "uninformed."

art only but the degree of rooted amenity and civility that makes life worthy and art possible, these differences—these distinguishing local observances and motives, and the languages or styles in which they are declared and in turn preserved— will be found to have maintained themselves, in each province according to its separate luck and custom. Eventually they may well give way before the emergence of some unitary world culture, as yet unimaginable in its precise forms. But if they are willfully, impatiently uprooted by force or fiat, however right-mindedly, the anticivilization of sophisticated barbarism will follow. There will be men of letters, book clubs, careers and grants-in-aid, birthday celebrations and laurel crowns, but there will be no literature.

So if any writing of permanent value is still forthcoming in the United States, it will not, I think, be a product of the boundaryless classicism Eliot had in view in 1917; it will not be written by men whose principal effort has been to get the feeling of the whole order of past literature in their bones as they write.* Rather, it will be the work of men of more circumscribed and practical, though not less serious and intense, expectation; and we will know them as writers in good part by their omissions and refusals as well as by their deliberated allegiances. We shall find them, I think, speaking in the recognizable manner of their province, but we shall also find that their impulse to speak (whatever its personal resources) will prove the most phenomenally responsive to the constituted nature of their province's distinguishing conditions. What they write will thus continue to be different in outlook and manner from the classic literature of humanist Europe. It need not, however, be the less artful or magnanimous. It will show a rich and unembarrassed experience, though more or less accidentally acquired, of our democratic, technological, dissociative culture; and it will show not only familiarity but a good deal of unexpected sympathy with this culture's local forms of behavior. To get at the life of its subjects it will risk

---

* Nor will it be by writers wholly preoccupied with the political and social reformation that has become the special burden of our era, in a world tangibly threatened with self-annihilation. Literary courage and innovation always hearten us, but it will take political and civil courage to rescue us from further disasters (1970).

sentimentality and extravagance, in ways that may at first be distasteful to sophisticated judgments. And it will display a style which, by conspicuous artifice, will appear freshly intimate and colloquial, yet capable of rhetorical heightening, of fervency and idealization. It will, in short, be recognizably "American."

Yet its makers, who will not be legion, will probably turn for practical inspiration almost anywhere except to the work of their American predecessors. Probably the experience of the two high periods of creative accomplishment in our literature (1835–1860 and 1910–1935) will be repeated, in that some general European inspiration will be the decisive agent, however homegrown the energies to put it to use. If there is another American "renaissance," it will be even more closely connected with a European one. It may even supply some of the prime impetus, though in the observable present state of our writing, one does not quite imagine how.

What such new talents *will* find by way of encouragement, in the literature of their own province, is a series of personal examples and case histories. They will see that the American circumstance has indeed managed to yield its originating masters—those few writers (we know them by their works) who at some point have had the imagination and stamina, the boldness, resolution, and patience, to turn to objective account the whole character of the life they have found themselves committed to, the whole conceivable nature of their unfolding experience. Such writers have done more than document, however quickeningly, their personal condition. Taking forthright hold of the actual dispositions of American life, they have been, of all our writers, the surest realists; yet probing deepest into the potential or ideal nature of American life (as delivered to them out of their province's peculiar history), they have also been the most profoundly imaginative. Their careers continue to show that even in America the high creative impulse may for a time be fulfilled, however melancholy the usual aftermath.

To give their names is really beyond the compass of this essay, which is only an effort at putting in order some sufficiently common judgments and preferences. But if pressed,

I should have my own choices ready. I should speak at once of Melville, of Whitman, and of Emerson, who remain, in their several ways, the freshest of our writers, as well as the most provocatively intelligent; their wit, so to speak, is still the liveliest potential cause of wit in others. Then I should argue, perhaps obstinately, for Hart Crane and for Henry Adams, the first for the precocious authority with which he pursued the artist's classic objectives of "analysis and discovery," and coincidentally redefined them for his age; the second for his definition (uniquely comprehensive, among American writers) of the public and historical circumstance regulating the making of American lives. Correspondingly, I should be puzzled how exactly to rate Hawthorne, Poe, James, and Eliot. No intelligible scheme of evaluation can dodge the rare professionalism of their careers or the extraordinary virtuosity and intelligence of their best work; yet with none of them can one feel wholly satisfied that their achievement was not purchased at too dear a price, too radical a sacrifice of our common residual knowledge of experience, too severe a dismissal of the known world's illimitable possibility. On the other hand I should keep room for certain fine mimetic humorists and honest entertainers, without whose efficient marginal work this common knowledge would be much the poorer. And if I should close then with a series of individual titles—*Huckleberry Finn* and "Old Times on the Mississippi," *Winesburg* and *The Country of the Pointed Firs, Jennie Gerhardt* and *In Our Time,* "Flammonde" and "Hugh Selwyn Mauberley" and *Transport to Summer, Walden* and *The Enormous Room, The Great Gatsby* and whichever of three or four of Faulkner's engrossing novels I had most recently got through—I should be arbitrarily leaving out fifty others to which, whenever I take them up, I find myself in admiring hostage.

Merely to write out a list of authors and titles seems to brighten the prospect of the future, such is our respect for past successes and our invincible hopefulness. Brighten it for the reader, I mean. For such American writers to come as may be capable of filling out that prospect will be found, in their turn, keeping their distance from these family names and divining their own sources of counsel; and they will probably appear to us, in their stubborn effort at self-possession, intransigent and uncompanioned to the (probably) bitter end.

AFTERWORD (1970)

Certain of the above generalizations now seem to me excessively schematic, particularly those identifying the continuing circumstances of the making of American literature with the major historical forces active at the founding of the national society. And certain terms in the closing forecast of what might come next in American writing strike me as having been, even ten years ago, considerably out of date. It should have been clearer (and probably was, outside academic departments of literature) that the matter of a revolt against Eliot's critical magistrateship was pretty much a dead issue. Of course this revolt may have been unfortunate in its way: a new irruption of the old American antinomianism, with a new generation conspiring once more to ignore the best of its available teachers.

For other aberrations in tone and emphasis I will plead that the essay was drafted in the late 1950's when a great many national and international conditions that now seem always to have been with us had not yet declared themselves with entire distinctness.

But I make no apology for the names put down, in the first footnote, as wagers against a bleak future. I only regret not having had the wit, in 1960, to see that Mr. Norman Mailer should have had a place in this too cautious list. At the time I simply had not begun to take in the new series of "existential" essays and "advertisements for myself" already pointing the way to the achievement of *The Armies of the Night* (1968), the nearest thing to an old-fashioned Great American Book we have had in thirty-odd years. But I notice that the generalized description of how any new American writing "of permanent value" is likely to behave fits *The Armies of the Night* reasonably well.

The most serious flaw in the essay is its limitation to "imaginative" literature—novels and other fictions, poems and plays. Two serious omissions follow from this: the political writing of 1765–1790 and the argumentative prose of the era of Henry Adams, William James, and Thorstein Veblen, among others. A proper survey of American literary tradition would have to make room for these two gatherings of major talent. I have in fact written briefly about the literary achievement of the second in *The Ferment of Realism* (1965). But the effect would be, I think, to sustain the general argument about American literary history. For one thing, we may note how both of these extraordinary generations have lacked heirs of corresponding power and authority. In a sense we are still living off their dwindling capital—and paying for our failure to renew it.

"Building Discourse":
The Genesis of Emerson's *Nature*

"I like my book about nature," Emerson wrote in a much-remarked journal entry, "& wish I knew where & how I ought to live." The sentence is altogether characteristic. We can find in it, learning to look, both the subtle authority of expression in Emerson's best prose—the laconic fitness of thought and phrase which can release, yet at the same time almost perfectly conceal some momentous stroke of understanding—and also the tenuity and elusiveness that hang about much of his most familiar work. The entry is dated September 6, 1833. What he calls "my book about nature" existed at that moment only in his head. Short as it finally was, it would not get into print for three more years. The problem of "where & how I ought to live," words casually hitting off the central predicament of his life and vocation, he was never really to solve; characteristically, the act of identifying the problem in a satisfactory way, defining and isolating it by a transparent brevity of formulation, would somehow absorb the practical energy he would thereafter be willing to devote to it. The inward thought, the original expectation, were sufficient to the end proposed. What further busyness of execution could increase their value to him?

Written as an Introduction to the Chandler Facsimile Edition of *Nature*, 1968.

Perhaps every great talent, as it comes forward into its working life, generates some singular and appropriate obstacle to its ideal fulfillment. In any event, may we not see in this affair, at the inception of Emerson's literary life, the quintessential model for the whole of his extraordinarily influential yet somehow disappointing career as an American master? We are reminded how all of Emerson's work may be read as a kind of prolegomenon to some climactic accomplishment which was never quite to be realized, but the full virtue of which in any case could be traced back to the wholeness and sufficiency of his original conception of it. How then could the work of actually carrying it through seem anything except redundant and pointless? How could it escape that burden of personal embarrassment which, it was Emerson's inclination to feel, our commonest acts and choices in the world are perpetually bringing down on us?

The more obvious reason why this journal entry has attracted notice is that it provides a positive clue to the germination of Emerson's first book. It also suggests the amiable terms—"I *like* my book . . ."—on which this author preferred to live with his own work, and was perhaps determined to live, during its making; few other writers not swamped in complacency have been so fortunate. So it is the first half of the sentence that is regularly quoted. The second half, however, so casually and yet, upon examination, so gratuitously added, is what continues to hold attention: "& wish I knew where & how I ought to live." Either it is a *non sequitur,* worth noting in a writer whose more severe critics have sometimes intimated that the *non sequitur* was his chief rhetorical instrument, or it is a singularly revealing stroke of natural wit.

The problem of judgment here is typical. Once we begin to get the sense of how Emerson operates as a writer, our experience of reading him is likely to be full of double takes, and our admiration, sluggish and reluctant at first, so little taste remains with us for the mode of pastoral exhortation he seems to employ, springs forward by a geometric progression. It is typical, too, of the problem of Emerson that we may have to risk appearing fancy and sophistical to show off what we guess to be the full import of such deceptively casual remarks.

For does not this sentence in its easy, understated way strike to the heart of the specifically modern problem of the writer's occupation? Does it not anticipate that wrenching discovery about the vocation of art that underlies the whole revolution of "modernism" and stands at the center of our literary history since the displacement of classical-humanist norms: the discovery that the writer's, the artist's, life is not a life like any other of good report, needing only to be conducted by the common rules of reason, propriety, good professional discipline, but that it must itself become a new thing, a transfiguring re-creation; that first of all and above all, for the writer himself, *il faut changer la vie?*

The work and the life are one. But they are not one in the earlier Romantic sense that the work expresses the life in more or less of its natural totality. Rather, given the conception of a work of a certain order of virtue, the writer is taxed to re-create his whole temporal existence and to begin by considering as seriously as he considers the creative end he has in view precisely *where* and *how* he ought to live in order to undertake that end. *Ought* to live: the auxiliary of obligation is to be noted, surely not being required if the question in Emerson's mind was merely one of satisfactory domestic arrangements.

That Emerson knew himself, at thirty, to be burdened with the problem of vocation, as if his real service of life in the world was just beginning, is itself a fact of prime interest.* This burden is one that his first performances as an author inevitably had to labor under. If there is an uncharacteristic awkwardness of address in the book *Nature*—most commentators agree that there is—one may argue that it has its source here, in a need for self-justification as writer that is not directly relevant to the book's stated theme. Emerson, child of the nineteenth century, contemporary of Musset and Kierkegaard, was the first of his immediate line to be so afflicted. His father, uncle, grandfathers, and great-grandfathers had been ministers; in all the generations of his ancestry back

---

* The general shape this problem took for him and its consequences for his writing are well described in a valuable article by Henry Nash Smith, "Emerson's Problem of Vocation," *New England Quarterly*, XII (1939), pp. 32–67.

to the founding of Massachusetts, there were men who had shaped their lives to the ministerial calling, though like his father they might regularly suffer pangs of doubt whether there was any health in their own pursuit of it; and Emerson himself, properly schooled, had gone to Harvard and, after an interval of schoolteaching and miscellaneous reading, had enrolled in its divinity school in order to become a minister, in fulfillment of the college's chartered function, which was to perpetuate true Christian learning to posterity. In 1826 Emerson was approbated to preach by the Unitarian Association of Middlesex County. By the time he was ordained and established as junior pastor and heir apparent in the pulpit of the influential Second Church in Boston, in 1829, he was already marked out for distinction among the Unitarian churches, which in the early decades of the nineteenth century had assumed the intellectual leadership of the New England province and were guiding its modest revival of learning.

From the first, however, Emerson felt uneasy and constrained as a preacher and in pastoral duties. Yet some singular, barely statable pulpit charm and the gift, already studied and improved, of a direct, simple, natural-seeming eloquence won favor with congregations wherever he appeared. Poor health had been his excuse for declining the pastoral offers that came to him as soon as he began preaching.* Other causes were operating, as yet inconclusively. He had interrupted his theological studies to take a long winter journey of recovery, in 1826–1827, to South Carolina and Florida; this was shortly after his older brother, William, returned from two years at Göttingen and a disturbing interview with the aged Goethe to announce in a crisis of conscience that he was abandoning the ministry. Emerson's southern journey seems to have served the purpose of reconciling him temporarily to his expected career. It also involved him in a remarkable friendship with Achille Murat, the exiled son of Napoleon's

---

* Professor Jonathan Bishop, tracing out the events of these critical years, has persuasively argued that Emerson's various illnesses "oppressed him most as he prepared and began to practice the duties of the ministry, and left him for good only when he brought himself to abandon it." Such findings increase our sense of how profoundly Emerson's crisis of vocation was acted out. See *Emerson on the Soul* (1964), pp. 166–176.

redoubtable marshal and a "noble" and wholly virtuous example of something that up to then, Emerson admitted, he had supposed to be "only a creature of imagination—a consistent Atheist, and a disbeliever in the existence, &, of course, in the immortality of the soul." "My faith in these points," he added, "is strong & I trust, as I live, indestructible. Meantime I love & honour this intrepid doubter." It seems probable that what as much as anything else induced Emerson to accept the security of the Second Church's offer was his engagement to Ellen Tucker in the winter of 1828–1829; he was married in September, 1829, six months after his ordination. It also seems clear that Ellen's death from tuberculosis early in 1831 (with the prospect of an eventual settlement from her estate) released him to act out entirely according to his inward disposition the continuing crisis of commitment that led him in 1832 to resign his pastorate and abandon the calling to which he had been reared and educated.

Everyone agrees that it was not merely "a change in his opinions concerning the ordinance of the Lord's Supper," as the issue was reported to the Church, that brought this event to pass. Becoming established in the Second Church had only deepened his fundamental restlessness. On January 10, 1832, he wrote: "It is the best part of the man, I sometimes think, that revolts most against his being the minister. His good revolts from official goodness." On the 21st he urged himself: "Write on personal independence." Early in June he was more definite: "I have sometimes thought that in order to be a good minister it was necessary to leave the ministry. The profession is antiquated." The Unitarianism he served seemed to him "cold & cheerless," a cerebral faith that existed only by way of its opposition to the old Calvinism and was warmed by very little beyond the barren ardors of controversy.

More positively his continued reading in secular literature preoccupied him—Montaigne, Rousseau, Goethe, Schiller, Plato, Renaissance drama, modern history and fiction, the British quarterlies (where he first detected Carlyle's strong new voice), and in particular his immersion, after 1829, in Coleridge's *The Friend* and *Aids to Reflection,* in the poems of Wordsworth, and in French and English redactions of the new philosophy, and epistemology, of German idealism. He did not want merely to contract into some dreary new cycle of sectarian disputation; if he was interested in converting anybody, it was not on points of doctrine. He did not "think less of the office of a Christian minister," so at least he wrote his congregation, but he now had another kind of office in mind for himself.

In all Emerson's reading and free meditation, an extraordinary new understanding of the inward constitution of the creature, man, began to form. "There is a capacity of virtue in us, and there is a capacity of vice," he had written in April, 1831, "to make your blood creep." On October 1, 1832, full of the latest *Edinburgh Review* contribution of "my Germanick new-light writer whoever he be," he wrote: "Has the doctrine ever been fairly preached of man's moral nature?" and on the next day: "It is awful to look into the mind of man and see how free we are. . . . Outside, among your fellows, among strangers, you must preserve appearances,—a hundred things you cannot do; but inside,—the terrible freedom!" "Good it is," he added, "to grow familiar with your own thoughts & not shun to speak them." On the 14th: "The great difficulty is that men do not think enough of themselves, do not consider what it is they are sacrificing, when they follow in a herd, or when they cater for their establishment. They know not how divine is a Man." And further:

> Our best friends may be our worst enemies. A man should learn to detect & foster that gleam of light which flashes across his mind from within far more than the lustre of [the] whole firmament without. Yet he dismisses without notice his peculiar thought *because* it is peculiar. The time will come when he will postpone all acquired knowledge to this spontaneous wisdom & will watch for this illumination more than those who watch for the morning. . . . *A man must teach himself.* . . .

"Projects . . . sprout & bloom in my head," he wrote William Emerson in November, "of action, literature, philosophy." The difficult step of resigning his pulpit having been taken, at renewed cost to his still fluctuating health, Emerson considered another southern voyage, to the West Indies. This plan quickly gave way to the idea of a European tour, and he sailed for Naples in late December, 1832. In Italy the American pilgrim's familiar shocks of discovery came thick and fast:

that legendary Europe was not only hallowed monuments and noble scenes but beggars, pickpockets, filthy laundry blocking your view; that storied Naples was just another name for the same old world "of man & truth & folly," a name moreover which by its glorious associations made it all the harder "to keep one's judgment upright, & be pleased only after your own way"; that too much gawking at guidebook splendors, even cathedrals, oppressed you with the thought of your own "littleness" as a mere spectator and not a doer, so that to travel grandly is eventually to become self-vexed and self-chagrined; and that—a rising emphasis in his European journal entries— there truly is an American measure and an American difference which the free man of the new world may appeal to for inward assistance. "In Boston," he dryly wrote his Aunt Mary Moody Emerson, from Rome, "they have an eye for improvement, a thing which does not exist in Asia or Africa."

But it was not historical sites and architectural wonders, and certainly not the bothersome company he kept running into of clergymen and earnest seekers debating doctrinal issues, that he chiefly sought out in Europe but poets and men of letters: Landor, Coleridge, Carlyle, Wordsworth. The idea that his true vocation was that of "poet" had taken root in his mind. Seeing these men, he wrote on September 1, 1833, while waiting at Liverpool for his ship, "has comforted and confirmed me in my convictions." He had managed not to be disillusioned by his discovery of the ordinariness of their conversation—their petty worldliness, their passing displays of common vanity, their perfect unawareness of this and that important consideration and particularly of "that species of moral truth which I call the first philosophy." All this only increased their usefulness to him; the gap in his own case between circumstance and aspiration seemed less enormous.

He felt again the luck of being a man of the New World. America came back to mind as (in a line from the blank-verse "Improvisations" he wrote down when a few days at sea) that land "where man asks questions for which man was made." The "ignorance," as it seemed to him on reflection, of even these literary demigods of Europe concerning true religion; their confusing it with worldly institutions and observances; the degree to which their complicity with the given world of accredited thoughts made them reluctant to say plainly at every moment that "the purpose of life seems to be to acquaint a man with himself"; their inability to act consistently as men and writers on the revelation "that God is in every man"— these things sent him home in double exaltation. He had seen natural human greatness, superior always in essence to its customary manifestations, and he had freely imagined something even loftier and finer.

Yet Emerson, at thirty, was also aware that he had been challenged to meet his English worthies on their own ground. He took to heart Carlyle's warning that mere dissidence, mere rebellion, would not be enough, and that this might indeed be the only substance, so far, of the celebrated "American principle." It was because his new vocation was built upon a new life-faith, because it was, finally, religious, that Emerson's deeply conservative and deferential mind could embrace it so confidently. But what precisely was this faith and how was it to be articulated? The ripened and settled modes of understanding displayed in the forms of European literature, as in all the phenomena of European civilization, could not simply be disregarded. Hearing of some new message, "the men of Europe will say, Expound; let us hear what it is that is to convince the faithful and at the same time the philosopher," and they would, Emerson felt, be right. To find a way of satisfying this double audience—of incontrovertibly expounding as well as exhorting and advocating; speaking to the intellect as well as to feeling; yet expounding in such a way as not to lose the living pulse and nerve of the spirit's activity—was the literary task now before him. It was success in this task which would justify his new vocation, and which, in the achieving, would set him apart from the rhapsodic antinomianism of dissidence and self-assertion that was beginning to blaze up afresh in the New England province.

In the years following Emerson's return from Europe, the pattern of his outward career as an author was secured and with it a material solution to the problem of "where and how to live." During the winter of 1833–1834 he lectured, chiefly in Boston, on the uses of the study of nature and on his Italian travels, and he continued through the next two winters with lecture series on the lives of great men—he selected artists (Michelangelo, Milton) and spiritual heroes (Luther, George Fox, Burke) —and on the history of English literature. Thereafter the spoken lecture was both his chief source of earned income and the prose form he mainly used for his published writings. He moved from Boston to his grandfather Ripley's house in Concord in the fall of 1834; a year later he married again and, with his wife's income added to the Tucker legacy, settled into a house of his own in Concord.

Emerson's lectures, journals, and letters for 1833–1836 are crammed with formulations of his developing thought, that "main thought" which, as John Jay Chapman said, his writing "is never far from." For November, 1833, we find this journal entry: "Nature is a language & every new fact that we learn is a new word. . . ." In March of the next year: "The subject that needs most to be presented, developed, is the principle of Self reliance, what it is, what it is not, what it requires, how it teaches us to regard our friends." In September: "Perhaps you cannot carry too far the doctrine of self-respect." Bold undertakings are sketched that now and then anticipate literary innovations of a later time. Thus on November 19, 1833: "Wrote to Charles [Emerson] yesterday of the amount of meaning in life: *dum tacet clamat*. . . . If a susceptible man should lay bare his heart"—this, fifteen years before the entry in Poe's *Marginalia* that electrified Baudelaire and produced the purgative journal, "Mon coeur mis à nu." (Emerson himself would undertake this exorbitant task perhaps only in the great confessional essay, "Experience," and even there would choose to examine the data of his own life altogether impersonally.) In all that he writes during these years a double truth is regularly postulated. (1) The human individual stands at the center of the experienced universe and can find within himself (or not at all) the resources for whatever he is called to in life. (2) The surrounding universe—"nature"—supports him totally and continuously and speaks to him at every moment. The relation is dynamic: the universe of being may be trusted to communicate actively out of whatever force it is animated by to whatever of animate force resides in man, and thus *will* call him forth into his correspondent being.

We see, looking back into earlier journals and sermons, that something like this double truth has been with Emerson from the first, though his early expression of it was more conventional. Originally his stress was on how the "kindling excitement" man feels within himself, the power to transcend the common "weakness of humanity," comes from man's discovery that he may "lean on omnipotence" (May, 1828), or it was on how a "voice" speaks within man and satisfies his yearning for "a faith satisfactory to his own proper nature," telling him that "God is within him, that *there* is the celestial host." In this earlier form, of course, both thought and expression were still coming directly out of long-standing Puritan tradition, whose most creative participants—reconstituters of the central faith like Jonathan Edwards, adherents to new sectarian rites like the Quakers, Baptists, and Swedenborgians— had regularly moved toward some version of the thought announced in Emerson's first sermon, in 1826, that God "is not so much the observer of your actions, as he is the potent principle by which they are bound together." The New England theology had long since turned inward, psychologizing its essential witness, where it had not dried up altogether. And as much as any observable distinction of statement, it was the familiarity of Emerson's thought, its rootedness in regional and sectarian tradition, that touched the audience he was addressing, giving him in turn the confidence to speak his mind ever more bluntly and freely. He knew this himself (tallying his "advantages," he once set them down as simply "the total New England"), and his best critics have always recognized it. So Charles Ives, in whom the original energy of Emerson's thought survived perhaps the longest without dilution, being renewed in his inventions in music, shrewdly observed that the Emersonian "philosophy or . . . religion (or whatever you will call it)" was not simply an intellectual construction but a source of spiritual energy that acquired, for its adherents in covenant-minded communities like Concord, "some of the functions of the Puritan church."

The literary overform Emerson was using was the sermon; his lectures and, later, essays have the appearance of lay sermons. The old Puritan sermon was intended like any other to inspire the activity of faith and provided a regular place for spirit-lifting perorations. But in Calvinist New England, bred to the expectation of a reasoned faith and a learned ministry able to expound it, care was taken to ground this effort of inspiration and encouragement in rational demonstration, to support it with the other comforts of philosophic or doctrinal authority and sufficient argumentative proof. By the early nineteenth century, however, the old proofs from Scripture and the general framework of scholastic argumentation (a science no longer in itself considered to be divinely appointed, as it had been by the first Puritans) were not enough to persuade reasoning minds.

Between the founding of Massachusetts and the 1830's, a long revolution had taken place, intellectual as well as political and social. On the one hand new, empirically authorized, "scientific" descriptions of nature and of human understanding had gained acceptance and had become increasingly elaborate (and increasingly truistic) in the philosophically busy century after Newton and Locke. On the other hand, more recently, a sophisticated secular understanding of the historical origins of Christian worship had emerged, with the beginnings of the so-called "higher" criticism of religion. Now to the freest minds of the new age these new doctrines were not simply a troublesome challenge to the old beliefs. They were fascinating and absorbing in themselves. And Emerson was one of those post-Enlightenment minds who saw that, far from overthrowing faith, these doctrines might provide a powerful new endorsement of it—*if* rightly understood, rightly interpreted. Thus his broad interest in natural science, on which he lectured in 1833–1834 and to which he returned at the start of his series on "The Philosophy of History" in the winter of 1836–1837. In holding to the general structure of the sermon, so firmly established in New England as an instrument of reasoned inquiry as well as of declamatory faith, he was holding to a method of discourse which was reassuringly familiar to his audience, yet within which he could present his new understanding in, broadly speaking, philosophical as well as inspirational form.

The lectures he offered between 1833 and 1836 are literate and emphatic, and by every outward sign they were successful.

Each season Emerson was more widely in demand in eastern Massachusetts—he was also supply-preaching on invitation—and his platform reputation spread rapidly, culminating in the moderately precocious honor of invitations to deliver the Phi Beta Kappa address at Harvard in 1837 and the address to the graduating class at the Divinity School in 1838. But Jonathan Bishop is surely right in suggesting that these early lectures "fell somewhat short of fulfilling the fine promise he made to himself on his return from Europe to say nothing that did not wholly match his own purposes." In part this was probably because the subjects he lectured on were determined more than would later be the case by other people's interest and expectation (tell us about Italy, tell us about English literature). In any case these lectures, in print, seem rather too monotonously assertive. The arguments they advance lack natural flow; they do not yet do what Chapman said the mature Emerson always does at his best, which is to keep close, like the truest poetry, to the psychology of real life and real experience.

The fact is that the very conditions which gave the rapid opening out of Emerson's career in letters so natural and, as it seems, inevitable a configuration—first, that his thought by the fullness of his personal commitment to it had become second nature with him and was everywhere revealed; second, that the form of the sermon or inspirational treatise lay so conveniently to hand—were also, in subtle ways, obstacles to achieving a decisive eloquence. His tendency, never entirely overcome, was to say everything at once, to put his whole message into one masterful assertion, one comprehensive and immediately persuasive formula. Everyone recognizes this in Emerson. He is perhaps the nearest thing we have in Anglo-American literature to an introspective maxim-writer; he applies the New England predilection for the folk proverb (the form that Franklin, who represents another strain in Emerson's province inheritance, mastered first) to the subject matter of the great French moralists; and one notices that his European admirers, like Proust, who took several epigraphs from Emerson for *Les Plaisirs et les jours,* have accepted him as a master in this vein and have not thought to put him down, as Henry James did, as an author who "never completely found his form."* But Emerson himself acknowledged the need for a more sustained argumentative method that would be capable of overall "proportion" as well as brilliant local "ornament." In a journal entry of October, 1837, he admitted the characteristic fault weakening "that species of architecture which I study & practice, namely, Rhetoric or the Building of Discourse." "Profoundest thoughts, sublime images, dazzling figures are squandered and lost in an immethodical harangue."

This was a year after *Nature*, and presumably the entry reflects a sense of failure, or incomplete success, with that manifesto-like performance. It also suggests that what had chiefly delayed his book was uncertainty about how to organize what had become for him, by 1836, a very nearly self-evident argument. So, too, we may assume that Emerson's interest in science and the literature of natural history was in large part an interest in the special architecture of scientific formulation. Even more than the critical method of German philosophy, the method of modern science, with its forthright ways of collecting, classifying, and assimilating its data, challenged his practical ambition.

Certainly he recognized the relevance of the classificatory method of science to his own concerns as a philosophically truthful moralist.† The "two or three facts respecting science" that he set down in June, 1836, while hard at work on the actual text of *Nature* concerned method and the authority the method of science apparently derived from the constitution

---

* Josephine Miles' suggestion that among English authors the nearest to being a direct model for Emerson is "the aphoristic Jonson of *Timber*" is well taken. In the era that apotheosized Shakespeare—and Emerson yielded to none in this regard—his coincidental delight in Ben Jonson's literary craft is worth remarking.

Henry James's comment, we ought to remember, was made before the Edward Emerson-Waldo Forbes edition of Emerson's journals (1909–1914).

† Another way of putting this is that Emerson intuitively understood the idealism implicit in scientific inquiry: the scientist's axiomatic faith in the unity and intelligibility of nature.

In Chapter IV of *Nature* ("Language") we note that the Henry Adams-like proposition, "The axioms of physics translate the laws of ethics," comes immediately after a quotation from Swedenborg about the relation of the visible and invisible worlds.

of both the cosmos and the human mind. These "facts" were: "1. The tendency to order & classification in the mind. 2. The correspondent Order actually subsisting in Nature. 3. Hence the humanity of science or the naturalness of knowing. . . ." This "Humanity of Science," so conceived, was the subject he resumed as the first topic in his 1836–1837 lectures on "The Philosophy of History." Emerson seems to have decided that the propounder of a moral gospel must be as methodical as any scholar or scientist, must work out his own system of classification and make it stick. "We are always at the mercy of a better Classifier than ourselves," he wrote in September, 1836, claiming that "the pleasure arising from Classification" was what made "Calvinism, Popery, Phrenology [!] run & prosper." Such pleasure, natural to the human mind, was what confirmed from within any thoroughly artful description of experience: "The subjective is made objective." Thus, until an appropriate scheme of classification materialized, his own book about nature would hang fire. Without such a scheme, not even his abounding certainty, in 1836, that some immense spiritual reformation in which he would play a leading part was about to overtake his life and province could bring it forth.*

The very rush and incoherence of the journal entry in which a practicable structure for his book finally begins to take shape support this account of the history of its making:

> 27 March. Man is an analogist. [The same sentence
> occurs in the entry for March 21.] He cannot help
> seeing every thing under its relations to all
> other things & to himself. The most conspicuous
> example of this habit of his mind is his naming
> the Deity Father. [All the preceding sentences
> turn up, rearranged and recast, in "Language,"
> chapter IV of *Nature*.] The delight that man finds
> in classification is the first index of his Destiny.

---

* Henry Bamford Parkes, who wrongly identified Emerson's thought with that extreme tradition of antinomian dissent of which Emerson was in fact a singularly precise critic (in part through his undeniable sympathy with it), nevertheless was right with regard to the particular moment of 1836 in pointing out that "Emerson expected the reformation in the near future." ("Emerson," *The Pragmatic Test*, 1941.) Stephen Whicher gives a good account of the millennial fervors of this moment in *Freedom and Fate: An Inner Life of Ralph Waldo Emerson* (1953).

> He is to put Nature under his feet by a
> ~~true order of~~ knowledge of Laws.　　Phrenology
> Ethics again is ~~the living~~ to live Ideas
> Science to apprehend Nature in Ideas　　The
> moment an idea is introduced among facts the God
> takes possession. Until then, facts conquer us.
> The Beast rules Man.
> 　Thus through Nature is there a striving ~~for~~ upward.
> Commodity points to a greater good. Beauty is nought
> until the spiritual element. Language refers to that
> which is to be said.

Here at last are the classifications that open the way. "Nature," "Commodity," "Beauty" (with a subsection on its "spiritual element"), and "Language" become the successive chapters which fill out the first half of *Nature* as we have it; supplemented by "Discipline," a more general classification that, it is specified, "includes" the preceding ones, these classifications in fact compose the book's whole rising argument.

Professor Ralph L. Rusk, in the standard modern biography of Emerson, says simply that "chapters of *Nature* . . . were growing toward completion in his journals" all through the 1833–1836 period, but the journal evidence (which would be awkward to set out discursively) does not support this description of the book's emergence.* Emerson was already making use of his later method of assembling, rather than composing, his essays. But only two sections of *Nature* make really extended and detailed use of journal entries: "Chapter I" (untitled in the printed text but called "Nature" in the table of contents), which includes journal passages written in March and December of 1834, March and April of

---

* *The Life of Ralph Waldo Emerson* (1949), p. 203. Further on (p. 240) the less positive and rather more accurate statement is made that *Nature* "had grown slowly out of his journals, letters, sermons, and lectures."

In a letter of June 28, 1836, Emerson wrote that his "little book is nearly done" but also that his plan was "to follow it . . . with another essay, 'Spirit'; and the two shall make a decent volume." It would appear that the complete structure was not worked out until the last minute. On August 8 Emerson wrote his brother William that there was still "one crack in it not easy to be soldered or welded"—most probably this "crack" came after "Discipline" and was filled by the important opening paragraphs of "Idealism," where the argument turns off sharply in a new direction. He added that he hoped to finish within the week. On August 27, according to his journal, he received the first proof sheet.

1835, and January, February, and June of 1836; and the two passages attributed to the "Orphic poet" in the last chapter, "Prospects," which derive from a single sequence of entries for June 22–23, 1836. Even with these passages the most memorable phrases are not to be found in the original entry. In the climactic fourth paragraph of Chapter I, the great sustained dithyramb on man's experience in physical nature, the journal draft gives neither the breathtaking phrase about the vanishing of "all *mean* egotism" (which seems to me one of the irreducible formulations of a distinction central to the whole of Romantic and modern literature) nor the startling "transparent eye-ball" figure. And for the peroration at the end the journal draft lacks what is probably the best remembered sentence in the book, being the summary message readers were to take back into their active lives: "Build therefore your own world."

Nature, then, as a piece of writing, was synthetic in construction and far from seamless. From the traditional sermon it borrows the scheme of a predicative series of topics and subtopics leading to an inspiring peroration, and so permits itself a certain mixture of styles or voices; from contemporary learning the device of an original structure of classifications. Emerson himself showed no great satisfaction with the result. Once the book was out, he hardly spoke of it. He wrote to Carlyle in September of 1836: "This is only a naming of topics on which I would gladly speak and gladlier hear"—a description that fixes on the compositional element, the sequence of chapters and chapter headings discussed above, which Emerson himself cared for least. He never used this scheme again for meditative discourse. The topical divisions are not arbitrary; the arrangement they fall into is rational and progressive; but Emerson is not very interested in them and certainly does not feel bound to them. They are the scaffolding on which the fabric of vivid instances and affirmations is hung out—and hung out, except for a few key passages, quite casually. As in the essays, the local clusters and runs of eloquence and fervor, along with various maxims, are what we mostly remember from *Nature,* not the march of its argument.

Yet we can be misled if we conclude too hastily that

Emerson was only making a show of logical system in *Nature,* in deference to common expectation. The fact is that he worked forward according to two seemingly contradictory standards of truth. The old Calvinist suspicion of unmediated spiritual enthusiasm still carried weight with him. It might be true, as he affirmed in the "Introduction" (with a modern artist's natural pragmatism), that man "acts [the meaning he seeks] as life, before he apprehends it as truth," since man is wise not in the skillful exercise of his reasoning faculty but in the degree to which the whole incessant process of ordinary life has made supple and precise "the Hand of the mind" (the fine phrase used in "Discipline"). It might also be true, by the paradox Emerson would announce at Harvard a year later, that "books are for the scholar's idle times," and that Man Thinking has more important work to do than practice argumentation. Yet it remained axiomatic with him that every natural divination of truth *would* reveal itself, under scrutiny, to be rational and logically intelligible; and, as noted earlier, he continued to believe that it was a main part of the writer's responsibility to demonstrate this and thus to convince "the philosopher" as well as "the faithful."

But as it had become the very substance of Emerson's thought that truths of intellect were always truths of natural experience, so it seemed to him that the most important function of the writer was not to pronounce the truths but to activate the experience.* The result can be described in either of two ways. It is essentially philosophic discourse of which, however, a main rhetorical purpose is to conceal its own reliance on philosophic argument, fostering the illusion that what is said is wholly self-evident and naturalistic. Or it is essentially prophecy and exhortation (revelation of what is; encouragement toward what therefore must be done) that gains its decisive authority not only by surreptitiously appropriating concepts of systematic philosophy (in the manner of much of Wordsworth's psychological poetry) but by sub-

---

* This conception of effective discourse renews in secular terms the logic of the old evangelical sermon, and not just as vulgarly practiced. It had been Jonathan Edwards' concern as well as the Wesleyans' to make his hearers *live* the doctrinal truth he was preaching, through the sensible fullness and harmony of his rehearsal of it.

mitting these concepts to further critical refinement. Following this view, we see how Chapman's assertion that Emerson "bears no relation whatever to the history of philosophy" will have to be radically qualified, though we see what Chapman was responding to. John Dewey understood Emerson's tactics better (and the continuity between Emerson's thought and that of the major pragmatists is central to American intellectual history) : "he takes the distinctions and classifications which to most philosophers are true in and of and because of their systems, and makes them true of life, of the common experience of the everyday man." Emerson's prophetic criticism of life and human capacity is the more compelling because it is adjusted to philosophic premises as well as to experience and feeling, and it is the more complete because it includes a radical-empiricist critique of these premises.

Here Emerson's wit and irony play their part. They are conceptual as well as verbal. The more one recognizes how Emerson was at once forcing explosive philosophic issues upon the argument of *Nature* and yet keeping them at bay, the more one sees that even Chapman's tribute to the book's "extraordinary beauty of language" is less than adequate to its special distinction. A transcendental or idealist theory of phenomenal reality is obviously at hand as Emerson proceeds, and is the asset he seeks to convert to effective use.* But he understands that natural experience, rhetorically his final court of appeal, both endorses and subverts this theory, and that the skeptical argument against it has as much force to the sensitive intelligence as the evidences, mostly psychological and moral, in its favor. The argument he must disarm is thus an argument in his own mind and experience—his own and, he is sure, everyone's, as sentient and reflective beings. In the book, *Nature,* it becomes that argument with himself from which, as Yeats said, the true poet will make something beyond mere rhetoric. Emerson further sees that it is a wholly natural argument, that it is constitutional to the mind of man—by day, so to speak, experience is indeed material and sensual but by night it can turn fantastic and visionary—and so he

---

* Its sources—Platonic, Swedenborgian, Berkeleyan, German—have been widely discussed and need not concern us here.

is not disabled by it but sets about making it a positive resource.

That is to say, he writes dialectically, in the root sense. His sentences, as they advance, actively converse with one another. As Josephine Miles has said (*Style and Proportion,* p. 70), the usual connectives are omitted, but the connection is there. It is this continuous dialectical factor that overcomes the alleged discontinuity of Emerson's rhetoric, as it also helps to overcome the dispersion that naturally accompanies (as, say, in Alcott's writing) the effort to express purely a vision of experience as a universal hieroglyph: when everything is equally and endlessly significant, how does one ever decide which particular significance to bring forward next? Dialectical, even tautological, however, rather than syllogistic (Professor Miles's word): Emerson's writing proceeds from a way of talking with himself rather than from a reasoned scheme for completing arguments. Every really penetrating account we have of Emerson—invariably some essential division or doubleness of temperament is stressed—suggests that this way of talking was singularly personal. It is regularly seen, moreover, as the source of his peculiar combination of effectiveness (of voice) and insubstantiality (of demonstration). Chapman called him "the only writer we have had who has wholly subdued his vehicle to his temperament"—an ambiguous tribute, surely—while Ives remarks that "so close a relation exists between his content and expression, his substance and manner, that if he were more definite in the latter he would lose power in the former." For good or bad this is the way Emerson exists as a writer, and it is fundamentally, we see, the way of an artist. So William James understood the matter:

> . . . the man Emerson's mission culminated in his style, and if we must define him in one word, we have to call him Artist. He was an artist whose medium was verbal and who wrought in spiritual materials.*

—a judgment (applying, after all, to many poets and even narrative writers) which Charles Feidelson has perceptively amplified:

---

* "Address at the Emerson Centenary," *Memories and Studies,* 1911.

He was an artist in the medium of theory—in short, a dialec-
tician—and his doctrines are better regarded as themes of his
discourse than as elements of a system.*

Perhaps the best example in *Nature* of Emerson's dialectical art is also the most important passage philosophically;
it is the opening of Chapter VI, "Idealism." (See below,
Appendix I.) Up to this point Emerson has been filling out the
headings given in the breakthrough journal entry of March 27,
1836. Starting from a rhapsodic assertion in Chapter I of the
impact of what we commonly call "nature" upon our perceptions and feelings, he has enumerated in a rising succession
nature's practical "uses." As "commodity" it supplies us
materially; as "beauty" it satisfies the spirit's higher wants
and needs; as the demonstrable source of "language," and a
language itself, it both creates meaning and provides the
means of expressing, communicating, remembering meanings,
and is thus the specific instrument of our "knowledge" and
"power." In all of these ways it is a constant "discipline,"
educating us toward fulfillment of our innate capacity for
being. All aspects of Emerson's studied gift of eloquence—his
phrase-making, his witty mixture of pulpit hyperbole and
satirical colloquialism ("whilst we use this grand cipher to
expedite the affairs of our pot and kettle"), his active delight
in putting words to the inexhaustible variety and yet fitness of
things—contribute to making these successive assertions telling.

They contribute to something else, however: to keeping
in abeyance those "philosophical considerations" which he
himself intruded, not very relevantly, it may have seemed at
the time, in the last paragraph of his short introduction. Here
"nature" was defined in a different way, not as *what is*, which
variously speaks to us, but as *what we are not* ("all that is
separate from us . . . which Philosophy distinguishes as the
NOT ME"). It is object, we are subject—the definition is
Kantian and Coleridgean—and as it includes not only the
nonhuman physical universe but also the products of past
human action ("art, all other men and my own body"), we
see that Emerson's definition is epistemological: "nature" is
the name we give to what we find or might find, at each new

---

* *Symbolism and American Literature*, 1953.

moment, in our consciousness's continuous apprehension of things.

But how do we know where all this "really" comes from, or whether it is "really" there; whether our knowledge of it is true knowledge; whether its meaning to us has any objective validity? This is the particular philosophical question that Emerson, breaking with the comfortable academic philosophy of common sense realism which Harvard instruction and the Unitarian faith were based on, knew had to be faced. Since Berkeley and Hume the skeptical argument—that the names we give to what is objective to us have no foundation except in our act of naming, and that the speech of nature to our minds cannot be proved to be anything but subjective illusion —could not be ignored, particularly if a doctrine of "man's moral nature" and his duty to "teach himself" was at stake.

So in Chapter VI Emerson turned back upon his own demonstration to raise this awkward question, or rather, in the phrasing he uses (a doubt "perpetually suggests itself"), to indicate right away that the importunities of skepticism are intrinsic to experience. Such doubt always exists (thus the adverb) and it rises spontaneously (thus the reflexive). It is also a "noble" doubt: the higher part of our minds receives it. We see at once that Emerson is going to color and dramatize this risky step in his argument (self-imposed, but unavoidable) as richly as any other. Every phrase will count: every rift, to borrow Keats's famous charge to Shelley, not irrelevant here, is to be loaded with ore. The process has already begun in the more-than-transitional first paragraph of "Idealism," a striking example of rhetoric that is both idealizing and dangerously exact. "Thus is the unspeakable but intelligible and practicable meaning of the world conveyed to man the immortal pupil. . . ." "Unspeakable"; this despite all in the way of articulated meaning that an introduction and five preceding chapters have eloquently advanced. With the general argument explicitly joined on the plane of "language," the case for believing that nature can have effective "meaning" for us can hardly have taken a bleaker turn. But at the same time, "intelligible" and "practicable": this meaning cannot be spoken in so many words, cannot be captured in measured discourse, yet it can be grasped by the mind ("the Hand of the mind") and it can be acted on. This will be so insofar as man continues to be what he essentially is, "the immortal pupil," a being whose unique capacity for *education* is the one thing that can lead him out of the death cell of meaninglessness, of which the chief experienced symbols are the irreversible succession of time and the intrinsic separateness ("philosophically considered") of consciousness.

Emerson's tactics quickly become clear. He has raised, or turned to face, a shattering philosophic objection to everything he has been saying—the audible heightening of his language is the immediate sign of this argumentative crisis—but he is not necessarily going to answer it in the philosophic language usually employed. This "noble doubt," he means to suggest, represents a natural turn of mind and way of speaking, and it leads to certain further ways of speaking. That the tone of these has often been resigned or despairing is not his affair. It is by his own developed manner of speaking, on both sides of the issue at once and with the full resources of his rhetoric, that he will deal with it. He will deal with it melodramatically, histrionically; there will be a resounding verbal enactment of dealing with it, designed to produce an impression that it has been dealt with. That trickery and subterfuge are naturally in the air is suggested at once; I suspect that Emerson wanted the full range of connotation in the verb, "conspire," which ends the opening paragraph.

So he proceeds, subordinating one argumentative step after another to a manner of speaking that ironically exaggerates and even contradicts, but also getting the fullest supporting charge from the common words accompanying. "It is a sufficient account [not "true" or "complete"—we don't know that—just "sufficient"] of that Appearance we call the World [what could be more frankly skeptical?] that God will teach a human mind . . ." ["*Will* teach": if the sentence cadence is to come out right, can one avoid giving the auxiliary a positive emphasis?]. So far this sentence claims a lot, and all too simply—and Emerson now undercuts the substance of it by admitting flat out that all the instructed mind really gets in this divine schoolroom is "a certain number of sensations," to which, finding some to be "congruent" with others, it casually applies certain very simple names.

But in the circumstances what more can the mind do? Let us admit it: our impotence to tell whether these sensations and names are objectively valid is an "utter impotence." Yet such sensations do come to us, and have such intensity that the names we have arbitrarily given them are themselves strangely exciting to recall. And that being so, "what difference does it make"—what difference *to us*—whether these sensations "correspond with outlying objects" that exist apart from our apprehension? If Orion is not really there in the heavens (the choice of that conspicuous nonentity, a constellation, with its poetical name, serves Emerson's purpose here in an obvious way), then it is there in "the soul," which must itself be nothing less than a "firmament" if it can contain so magnificent an "image." That image, moreover, has such gorgeousness that we find it the most natural thing in the world to say that some creative power we are moved to call a "god" must have put it there. However we explain or fail to explain the matter, "the relations of parts" (the way *we* see it) "and the end of the whole" (the way *we* use it) remain the same for us. Whatever the situation may be in itself, it's all one to us.

Emerson is in fact being pointedly philosophical here, as precise about the cognitive mind's relation to the phenomenal world as anybody had learned to be by 1836. The philosophic supports he does *not* fall back on are noteworthy. He does not appeal to concepts of innate ideas or of metaphysical or ontological necessity, and his passing reference to "God" as the presumed source of our instruction is doubly undercut: by the unexalted phrase about "a certain number of sensations," as noted above, and by the almost derisive parody-echo of his second, lower-case appeal to divinity, "some god paints the image." The constitutive idea here is rather Kant's unity of apperception, the principle that what comes into our minds (whatever its source, and also whatever its effect on us: the impressions that create skepticism as well as those that create faith) must come in the same way, since it is received by the same organ, the same mysteriously separate and single instrument.

More than that cannot be said, except willfully. In the crisis of his argument Emerson maintains Kant's own reserve about knowledge of ultimate reality, being for the moment more discreet than many neo-Kantians. But he also knows the vivid splendor of our sensible perceptions and the consoling magnificence of our names and observations, and he thus counterpoints his second "what is the difference?" with a full-voiced evocation of the wonders we do perceive, land and sea, innumerable celestial bodies, "deep yawning under deep, and galaxy balancing galaxy." These may indeed be only "appearances," but if appearances so extraordinary do exist, how can man's natural "faith" in them—if that is what he is moved to—be anything less than "constant"? And even if they exist only in that appearance-registering mechanism, the mind, or even if (in the image of the stars that opens Chapter I) some of them should appear there only once in a thousand years, then the occasion surely requires no less a word than "apocalypse"—"the apocalypse of the mind"—and here, too, I think Emerson wanted both the proper meaning of revelation or uncovering and the vulgar meaning of some abrupt, utmost convulsion of natural existence.

Again we note that it is not to Emerson's purpose to specify his philosophic authority, and there is, for scholarship, a question how much of Kant he knew beyond French and English redactions and the gossip of the learned quarterlies. There is a question, too, whether naming Kant or any other "new" philosopher wouldn't have stirred up inconvenient prejudices in his audience, besides jeopardizing the whole scheme of arguing from "nature." Emerson does, however, somewhat uncharacteristically, make explicit the philosophic debate he is concerned here to re-create as natural to experience. He speaks directly of "the Ideal theory" and the common charge, attributed promptly to "the frivolous," that it affects "the stability of nature." And precisely at this point the intricate verbal dialectic we have been tracing stalls for a moment. The ironic back-and-forth of subject and predicate, substantive and modifier, gives way to naked assertion. "God" reappears, and what He will and will not do is set down as beyond argument, though the sentence as a whole is more charming than intimidating: "God never jests with us" and can be relied on to keep the "procession" of nature in step. (The special tone here is one that Emily Dickinson also mastered.) The next sentence opens down to the foundations of Emerson's purposes as a writer. It brings forward the main purpose of the whole book, which is to call man forth out of the sickroom of inaction into the kingdom of his created being. The substance of it is not metaphysical but psychological. The verb dominates: "Any distrust of the permanence of laws, would paralyze the faculties of man."* This "permanence" of nature may be only a hypothesis, but it is that one hypothesis that is constitutional to man, that his "wheels and springs are all set to."

Having put the real issue—active being or paralysis, life or nonlife—on the line, Emerson returns now to his usual mode of aphorism and figure-making, though not before admitting once again that "the question of the absolute existence of nature still remains open" and that nothing further can be said except that the particular impressions that do come to us do not in themselves "shake our faith." The rest of the book describes the natural behavior of that action of being which is creaturely faith. When toward the end of Chapter VI the question of "the reality of the external world" is resumed, Emerson argues simply from decorum: "But I own there is something ungrateful in expanding too curiously the particulars of the general proposition that . . ." At the last, admitting that "the ideal theory" is "that view which is most desirable to the mind," he flaunts this subjectivity as one of the theory's chief advantages, for the "desire" in question is, again, not gratuitous but constitutional; it is the mind's, and the heart's, proper response ("philosophy and virtue" together) to the compelling miracle of appearances.

The "self-concentration" of Emerson's style (to borrow again from Keats's description of the "modern" artist's character) seems to exist in close relation to an essential distrust of affirmative argument. Emerson shared, as did Thoreau, the Romantic (and theosophic) suspicion that silence might be more truthful to the nature of things than speech, though both writers were kept from carrying this thought to Carlylean or Symbolist extremes by their inherited loyalty, like Kierke-

---

* So in the Divinity School "Address": "O my friends, there are resources in us on which we have not drawn." And in "The Transcendentalist": "We are miserable with inaction."

gaard's, to the practice of edifying discourse.* The idea of
the purity of meaning in silence was a constant spur to writing
better—or to not writing at all. A sentence from one of
Landor's "imaginary conversations" stuck in Emerson's mind:
"no man ever argued so fairly as he might have done." His
invincibly high-minded Concord friends hardly encouraged
his trying. A journal entry for August 2, 1835, reports that his
gifted brother Charles had thrown doubt on the whole business
of keeping a journal, and he could only reply, "I must scribble
on," though the sentences end "in babble." Recording a long
conversation with Thoreau in November, 1838, Emerson reports himself "acceding" to Thoreau's assertion that the act
of writing usually betrays the thought and prevents the writer
from doing justice to the full human experience from which
his thought proceeded; here, Emerson added, was "the tragedy"
of all art, "that the artist was at the expense of the man. . . ."

The Concord atmosphere in the early days of the transcendentalist movement was oppressive with this kind of
deterrent perfectionism. The very effort to overcome it confirmed it. "Speech is the sign of partiality, difference, ignorance," Emerson had written a month earlier, "and the more
perfect the understanding between men, the less need of
words." So, too, with man's understanding of nature. What
does the "wise man" eventually see but that every fact contains all truths? The practical result is that the more we try
to speak some particular truth, the more our words fail us:

> . . . as we advance, every proposition, every action, every feel-
> ing, runs out into the infinite. If we go to affirm anything, we
> are checked in our speech by the need of recognizing all other
> things, until speech presently becomes rambling, general, indefi-
> nite, and merely tautology. The only speech will at last be ac-
> tion." . . . (October 12, 1838.)

---

* The writing of Kierkegaard, among their European contemporaries,
seems especially pertinent to that of the Concord transcendentalists. Perhaps not sweetness of temperament so much as the materially freer
equilibrium of Concord life in the 1830's—surely, for those able to take
advantage of the fact, the freest established society the world has ever
known; hence its writers' preoccupation with the subjective uses of
freedom—withheld Emerson and Thoreau from Kierkegaard's more savagely
ironic and subversive exercises in this traditional mode.

In *Nature* Emerson solves this insoluble difficulty in various ways. Precisely as his theme is abstract and ecstatic, he holds as much as possible to the concrete circumstances of ordinary life. His tact and charm are nowhere steadier than in these references to the familiar world of commodities, institutions, workaday feeling and common talk; the tone resulting is alive with the humor of an unexpectedly insistent worldliness. Here, too, the style endorses the thought. Charles Ives puts the matter well: "Emerson seems to use the great definite interests of humanity to express the greater, indefinite, spiritual values," and he stresses as Emerson's prime technical resource an "intuitive sense of values" that enabled him to "use social, political, and even economic phenomena as means of expression—as the accidental notes in his scale. . . ." The gradual change of taste in styles of prose argument effected by Romanticism and its inheritors has ratified Emerson's tactics. F. O. Matthiessen pointed out in *American Renaissance* how various touches in *Nature* (like the "pot and kettle" sentence quoted above) which were considered affected and coarse by some of his first readers, and altogether inappropriate to his dignified subject, have become the things that please us most immediately in reading him now.

But Ives was right in calling these effects accidentals. The major note is personal, elevated, and dramatic. The final message is a spoken command—"Build therefore your own world"—in a passage that turns on a forthright I-you strophe. The warmth of tone regularly invites consent, as the passing humor invites complicity. What we are made to do is not follow an argument but hear a voice, and a voice whose essential way of behaving is to project itself with full subtlety and force upon every argumentative occasion—militantly upon our inertia, sympathetically and humbly upon our doubts and fears, ironically upon conflicting pretensions, courageously ("courageous even to tenderness," Ives says) upon all that would paralyze us—so that the promise of adult health given in the last chapter of the book, the promise of "a continual self-recovery" through the "remedial force" of active spirit, is continually fulfilled on the page before us. For Emerson it was this manner of writing, self-projective, self-dramatizing, that had the best chance of being truthful. That it might also be called artful, sly, disingenuous, seems not to have worried him. By the measure of creaturely experience, artifice and insincerity had their uses, too, particularly for lofty persuasion. "There is no greater dissembler," Emerson once wrote, thinking specifically of the character of the poet, "than the sincerest man."

The great case of this projective and dramatic element of style in *Nature* comes in the long fourth paragraph of the first chapter. (See below, Appendix II.) The paragraph's general meaning is clear enough: by means of our vital "correspondence" with the whole of natural creation, we may come into our own truest being. The governing approach, however, is to dramatize this meaning as a fact of experience, to render the idea (of a transforming sequence of exhilaration and renewal) in sentences which have a positive content of psychological, kinesthetic persuasiveness. The paragraph thus comes to a climax in an image—the self as a "transparent eyeball" through which powerful currents "circulate"—that produces, I have always thought, the flutter of a singularly intense physical sensation. Phrase cadence apart, "eye" would have done as well, but "eye-ball" touches to the quick. The other metaphors which Emerson combined with the metaphor of *seeing* that he thus both starts from ("few adult persons can see nature") and so remarkably returns to are more benign, yet share, several of them, this element of gross physicality: in particular the metaphor of the snake shedding its skin and that of feeding and being fed (so "daily food" indicates by just what kind of natural process "a wild delight" can subvert man's "real sorrows," and "cordial" defines substantially the species of "exhilaration" that is promised).

But to take this passage as primarily a transcription of real physical or sensuous experience, and to judge its success by its power to make us believe that the moment rendered actually occurred at a particular moment to a particular man, is really to misconceive both its structure and the kind of truth it contains. (This is the way Jonathan Bishop appears to take it in an attentive and extremely interesting analysis that presents it as the record of an experience "of physical contact with the world" and connects its psychological details to various familiar states of "our body" and "our senses" in the condition

of "physical alertness": see *Emerson on the Soul,* pp. 10–15.)
The passage rather seems to me conceptual in organization and,
to a degree, parodistic in its language. Emerson is not necessarily writing about what demonstrably *did* happen or *will*
happen in physical fact but what *might* happen according to a
particular idea of the innermost nature of man—my own sense
is that the passage is like most of Emerson's writing in the
affirmative vein: it is fully effective only if you already know
what it is meant to convey and have heard something like it
before—and the whole of it continually modulates between
physical images and conceptual abstractions, the predicaments
of a concealed speculative thesis.

In fact the decisive leaps forward in the argument are all
conceptual, or ideological. One occurs in the bare main clause,
"all mean egotism vanishes," ending the vivid sentence about
"standing on the bare ground,—my head bathed by the blithe
air": a clause not to be found in the journal entry where the
sentence was first written out. In the journal this sentence ends,
"I become happy in my universal relations." That is no
triumph of style but it makes its point, and it would bear out
the experiential theme of delight, gladness, exhilaration.
("Joy" is Bishop's word for this theme, but it is worth noting
that Emerson does not in fact use the more static and Words-
worthian specification.)

Why did Emerson make this particular change? For all
his descriptive ebullience, his concern, I will say again, is less
to demonstrate the physical reality of an actual experience than
to project the idea, the concept, of a certain constitutional
transformation and purification possible to the self, the human
ego. It is to project the idea of a *virtuous* conversion. Thus
the telling qualification, "all *mean* egotism." For behind the
distinction thus introduced stands, historically, the long barren
struggle in the New England theology to distinguish between
true and false conversion, between the self that is indeed a
new being and the self that has merely come under some
passing excitation of the senses, the ordinary mechanism of
natural consciousness. Emerson is not interested in the old
form of this doctrinal struggle, but he instinctively feels the
seriousness of the issue it still poses, especially to a writer
concerned to close forever the old Puritan gap between

nature and grace, the creature and God; it is his burden as a New England writer to have to deal with it. "Egotism," a word he surely could have avoided but uses with Kantian exactness, takes this particular provincial bull by the horns. The word thus represents a raid with new philosophical weapons on an old argumentative stronghold which our time has pretty well forgotten but which Emerson's theologically minded New England audience was still mortally obsessed by.

The part played by older devotional concepts in the advance of the finished passage appears in another of these bare, unmetaphoric sentences that provide forwarding shocks, a sentence of special interest because it is the only one in the passage that thirteen years later Emerson would change, in fact turn completely around, in the second edition of *Nature.* This is the sentence, "Almost I fear to think how glad I am," that terminates the sequence, "a wild delight . . . glad . . . tribute of delight . . . good health . . . good fortune . . . a perfect exhilaration." Jonathan Bishop's analysis rightly stresses the flaunting of a paradox in this sentence, but his explanation, limited to considerations of physical feeling, is less than satisfactory. If the passage in general is to be taken seriously, something more must be involved in this intimate association of gladness and fear than "a certain anxiety as to whether the world will continue pleasing" (Bishop, p. 13). That kind of suburban anxiety would be trivial, and sentimental. What instead, describing the rush of exhilaration, the sentence literally points to is not the source of the experience in the sphere of natural feeling but the extraordinary quality it possesses in itself. It is of a fearful intensity, so "perfect" and so "wild" is the transport it brings; the self is overwhelmed by it and cannot recognize itself. What has been attained is not a certain sum of pleasurable impressions but a new condition of being.

Emerson does not linger over this climax. In the next breath the passage turns back to ordinary nature, to "the woods" and our familiar experience there—and there is a detectable awkwardness (registered in "too") in the transition. But the conceptual point has been made. What has come lightly to the surface here, again out of a long subtle tradition of analytic-confessional writing (and a score of Biblical texts),

is the recollected idea of the immeasurable fear and trembling
that are the creaturely burden of utmost revelation, and that
constitute the best argument to the believer that this revelation
is from, or of, "God."* Emerson's later revision of this key
sentence further concentrated its special emphasis. "I am glad
to the brink of fear," the 1849 text reads: it is not just that the
thought of such perfect gladness is "almost" fearful, but that
the gladness itself somehow opens into a chasm of fear.

Such sentences, in any case, are not really descriptive or
expository. They do not come, to cite again Bishop's careful
analysis, from a "watchful" attention to real physical experience, such as may be tested by a correspondingly realistic
watchfulness on the reader's part. Rather they are *projective*
and *performative*. They are their own subject; they constitute
an action that is itself expansive, creative of the thing adverted
to; they are a prose version of Romanticism's notion of a style
or voice in poetry that does not merely describe familiar
realities but originates new ones. The meaning they convey,
the truth of the new alignment of old conceptions which they
carry out, exists within this very act of statement. To put it
another way, the experience they project is grounded in a
structure of ideas about experience, so that primarily what they
celebrate is the suddenly revealed power and fitness of these
ideas—and the fresh power of mind that, audibly parodying
them in its own "other words," can thus renew them to active
consciousness. The result is a mode of prose argument for
which Emerson's younger contemporary Kierkegaard found
the appropriate name; it is "dialectical lyric," which is the
designation Kierkegaard gave to his own great study of "fear
and trembling." As with so many puzzling and seemingly ill-
disciplined writers of merit, so with Emerson, understanding
comes more easily when we have identified the formal mode he
was actually working in; and here we may recall Emerson's
own regular insistence that even when writing speculatively
he was fundamentally a poet.

The virtue of the whole long paragraph we are consider-

---

* Cf. Swedenborg on Divine Love and Wisdom, the two "transformations"
of spiritual life. Love desires and soars toward God; wisdom stands near
Him and trembles.

ing has to do not only with its occasional verbal pungency, its knifelike return upon its own advancing rhetoric, but also the consistency and thoroughness with which its component ideas act toward the proposed end. The projected experience of an inward conversion would not be complete or "true," for Emerson's purposes in *Nature,* if it was not shown to be convulsive of the whole being of man. Hence the extravagance of the "eye-ball" sequence, which follows immediately the statement about the vanishing of "all mean egotism." Why should we suppose this extravagance was not deliberate? Why is it not a fitting rhetorical climax? The primacy of *seeing* to the whole idea of sudden and exorbitant creaturely change—note the terrible exception admitted in the parenthesis, "leaving me my eyes"—is surely reinforced by the shocking physicality of the blunt anatomical name. The eyeball *is* peculiarly sensitive (psychoanalysis has observed its special association with castration-anxiety), and the image of the self as a transparent eyeball pierced by currents of being is meant, I think, to be abruptly painful. Elsewhere in *Nature* Emerson is soothing and benign, but at this exalted climax, as in most of the great developed passages in his work, he will not merely give comfort. The natural capacity of man is his subject, and the whole psychologically ambiguous burden of what may be in store for human beings must somehow be indicated, even if it wrenches discourse out of its ordinary tolerability.*

---

* Jonathan Bishop's criticism of the "eye-ball" passage makes much of the notorious caricature Emerson's friend Christopher Cranch "unerringly" chose to make of it. But Cranch, one must say, lacked literary judgment. His writing simply does not possess the critical penetration and authority of transcendentalist thinking at its best. Cranch's amusing cartoon, in any case, has little to do with the eyeball image as we reach it in context. It is rather an intramural response to the thought that the quick physical shock thus delivered has come from such an odd, kind, preacherly fellow as neighbor Emerson. Perhaps it is a charm against that shock.

It must be admitted that this whole eruptive sequence posed Emerson a further rhetorical problem. How would he return to the lower pitch of statement adopted for listing the uses of nature? It was a problem he did not really solve. The first two sentences immediately following the climactic assertion of being "part or particle of God" also have, in their brusque dismissal of friends and brothers, something naturally shocking about them, though the thought of course is Biblically sanctioned. But the various abstract assertions that finish out this long paragraph could just as well have come elsewhere in the argument, and in a different order, too, for they hardly touch one another.

Nature, published in September, 1836, made its mark not only in Concord and Boston. One copy went off to Carlyle in London, where, coming to the attention of men like Sterling and Monckton Milnes, it began to build the reputation that won Emerson a welcome in various Broad Church and non-conformist literary circles when he returned to England in 1848. In all, Emerson sent out about eighty presentation copies. By mid-October of 1836 he could tell his brother William that five hundred had been sold. Getting a book into print, in combination with his success at lecturing, "has bronzed me," he added, "& I am become very dogmatic." But he knew that this state of mind, in which he could identify the tenor of his own thinking with "the indisputable core of Modern History," was possible only because there were no audiences or reviewers at hand who could seriously test it: "To such lengths of madness trot we when we have not the fear of criticism before our eyes: and the literary man in this country has no critic."

Thereafter Emerson says very little about *Nature.* Its publication gave plausibility to his sense of himself as a man serving the vocation of letters, but he does not seem to think of the book as having much importance in itself. He is more excited, more lifted up in his own self-conceived being, by the birth of his first child on October 30: "Now am I Pygmalion." His memorable addresses at Harvard in the two succeeding years made more of an impact on public consciousness than *Nature*—in part because they had the support of his fine voice and public presence as well as of the institutional ceremonies they were composed for; in part because they were more openly controversial or, as was claimed, heretical. Certainly they had a greater effect on his reputation and subsequent career.

One may not agree with Stephen Whicher's view that *Nature* is an uncharacteristic production, "the style . . . stiff and *naif,* the organization over-elaborate, the thought gowned in unbecoming borrowed terminology." Yet Emerson's own apparent indifference to the book after publication, and his concentration thereafter on the more congenial form of the hour-long lecture-essay, are to be noted. And it is true that the ambitious scheme of the book as a whole, beginning with its title, may provoke a more particular sense of incompleteness and omission than do shorter performances on more limited topics. At several points in *Nature* the joining appears awkward and contrived (one such point, at the end of the "eye-ball" paragraph, has just been mentioned). There are other noticeable lapses. In the "Introduction" Emerson challengingly erects a critical test for new structures of thought:

> Whenever a true theory appears, it will be its own evidence. Its test is, that it will explain all phenomena. Now many are thought not only unexplained but inexplicable; as language, sleep, dreams, beasts, sex.

But we have to admit the virtual silence of *Nature* on all but the first of these "phenomena" (and on "madness," too, which was added to the list in 1849), a silence that is the more conspicuous if we put the book beside *Walden* and especially *Leaves of Grass.*

More important, although the opening definition of "nature" includes "all other men," the main expressive context is that of unitary beings alone in a physical universe: creatures of unconditioned subjectivity "embosomed for a season in nature." The social world, the great realm of "economy" that dominates the opening of *Walden,* appear only as incidental metaphors. Historical events reduce to heroic pictures showing virtue in the embrace of natural beauty; the trades and industrial labor of men signify only the spirit's abstract mastery of natural forces; "the rapid movement of the railroad car" is simply a means of introducing the eye to a new pace and rhythm of perception; ecclesiastical institutions, philosophic structures, have no more body than the original flash of spiritual insight they derive from; great centuries-old cathedrals are presented as emerging like shells, insects, and fish, out of a universal "sea of forms"; and when Caesar is mentioned, it is in the same breath and with the same rhetorical coloring as Adam. Invariably, to recall Charles Ives's comment, Emerson brings forward these allusions to the social and historical world with tact and precision, but insofar as his scheme always calls him back to considerations of the sovereign ego in unmediated relation to nature, they remain ways of speaking rather than substantial elements in the argument.

His proper subject, of course, is not "nature" in any customary sense but man, and "where & how," given the consti-

tution we find in him, man "ought to live." Full transfer to
this subject was made in Emerson's next published work, "The
American Scholar." It was made, characteristically, by way of
establishing a tautology, but one which served to ground his
new thought, his précis of the scholar's true vocation, in the
most venerable of philosophic precedents:

> He shall see that nature is the opposite of the soul, answering to
> it part for part. One is seal and one is print. Its beauty is the
> beauty of his own mind. Its laws are the laws of his own mind.
> Nature then becomes to him the measure of his attainments. So
> much of nature as he is ignorant of, so much of his own mind
> does he not yet possess. And, in fine, the ancient precept, "Know
> thyself," and the modern precept, "Study nature," become at
> last one maxim.

APPENDIX I

Thus is the unspeakable but intelligible and practicable
meaning of the world conveyed to man, the immortal pupil, in
every object of sense. To this one end of Discipline, all parts of
nature conspire.

A noble doubt perpetually suggests itself, whether this end
be not the Final Cause of the Universe; and whether nature outwardly exists. It is a sufficient account of that Appearance we
call the World, that God will teach a human mind, and so
makes it the receiver of a certain number of congruent sensations, which we call sun and moon, man and woman, house and
trade. In my utter impotence to test the authenticity of the report of my senses, to know whether the impressions they make
on me correspond with outlying objects, what difference does it
make, whether Orion is up there in heaven, or some god paints
the image in the firmament of the soul? The relations of parts
and the end of the whole remaining the same, what is the difference, whether land and sea interact, and worlds revolve and
intermingle without number or end,—deep yawning under deep,
and galaxy balancing galaxy, throughout absolute space, or,
whether, without relations of time and space, the same appearances are inscribed in the constant faith of man. Whether nature enjoy a substantial existence without, or is only in the
apocalypse of the mind, it is alike useful and alike venerable
to me. Be it what it may, it is ideal to me, so long as I cannot
try the accuracy of my senses.

The frivolous make themselves merry with the Ideal theory,
as if its consequences were burlesque; as if it affected the stability of nature. It surely does not. God never jests with us, and
will not compromise the end of nature, by permitting any in-

consequence in its procession. Any distrust of the permanence of laws, would paralyze the faculties of man. Their permanence is sacredly respected, and his faith therein is perfect. The wheels and springs of man are all set to the hypothesis of the permanence of nature. We are not built like a ship to be tossed, but like a house to stand. It is a natural consequence of this structure, that, so long as the active powers predominate over the reflective, we resist with indignation any hint that nature is more short-lived or mutable than spirit. The broker, the wheelwright, the carpenter, the toll-man, are much displeased at the intimation.

But whilst we acquiesce entirely in the permanence of natural laws, the question of the absolute existence of nature still remains open. . . . (Chap. VI, "Idealism.")

APPENDIX II

To speak truly, few adult persons can see nature. Most persons do not see the sun. At least they have a very superficial seeing. The sun illuminates only the eye of the man, but shines into the eye and the heart of the child. The lover of nature is he whose inward and outward senses are still truly adjusted to each other; who has retained the spirit of infancy even into the era of manhood. His intercourse with heaven and earth, becomes part of his daily food. In the presence of nature, a wild delight runs through the man, in spite of real sorrows. Nature says,—he is my creature, and maugre all his impertinent griefs, he shall be glad with me. Not the sun or the summer alone, but every hour and season yields its tribute of delight; for every hour and change corresponds to and authorizes a different state of the mind, from breathless noon to grimmest midnight. Nature is a setting that fits equally well a comic or a mourning piece. In good health, the air is a cordial of incredible virtue. Crossing a bare common, in snow puddles, at twilight, under a clouded sky, without having in my thoughts any occurrence of special good fortune, I have enjoyed a perfect exhilaration. Almost I fear to think how glad I am. In the woods too, a man casts off his years, as the snake his slough, and at what period soever of life, is always a child. In the woods, is perpetual youth. Within these plantations of God, a decorum and sanctity reign, a perennial festival is dressed, and the guest sees not how he should tire of them in a thousand years. In the woods, we return to reason and faith. There I feel that nothing can befal me in life,—no disgrace, no calamity, (leaving me my eyes,) which nature cannot repair. Standing on the bare ground, —my head bathed by the blithe air, and uplifted into infinite space,—all mean egotism vanishes. I become a transparent eyeball. I am nothing. I see all. The currents of the Universal

Being circulate through me; I am part or particle of God. The name of the nearest friend sounds then foreign and accidental. To be brothers, to be acquaintances,—master or servant, is then a trifle and a disturbance. I am the lover of uncontained and immortal beauty. In the wilderness, I find something more dear and connate than in streets or villages. In the tranquil landscape, and especially in the distant line of the horizon, man beholds somewhat as beautiful as his own nature. (Chap. I, "Nature.")

Melville's Later Fiction

The Rites of Story-Telling

Brimming over with the creative confidence and ambition he was pouring into the writing of *Moby-Dick*, Herman Melville, in the summer of 1850, published an enthusiastic appreciation of the stories and sketches of his fellow countryman, Nathaniel Hawthorne. This essay, the memorable "Hawthorne and His Mosses," is on the whole more revealing of Melville himself at this high point in his hurried public career than of the precise character of Hawthorne's fiction. But it is not superficial; nowhere does it allow us to think that its author has not read deeply into his subject's work, or that the encounter between reader and story-teller has not been exceptionally direct and full. Melville simply chose to describe in a familiar way his own free part, as well as Hawthorne's, in this literary encounter. He tells about Hawthorne by way of telling about his own participating excitement, and about certain high-flown thoughts—mainly of what it means that Hawthorne is an American and a man of the present day and hour—which this response has led him on to. What he has to say, under the licensing disguise of "a Virginian Spending July in Vermont," is not the kind of thing usually met with in critical writing:

Written as an Introduction to *Great Short Works of Herman Melville*, 1970.

. . . already I feel that this Hawthorne has dropped germinous seeds into my soul. He expands and deepens down, the more I contemplate him; and further and further, shoots his strong New England roots into the hot soil in my Southern soul.

In the era of Romanticism and, in the United States, of New England transcendentalism, it was everybody's custom to appraise works of literature in, broadly speaking, biographical terms. The value of the work was one with the spiritual or existential virtue of the man who had written it, and its function was to give voice to that particular quantum or reserve of virtue, to make it accessible as a source of common good. But Melville as usual overflowed the ideological convention he appropriated. The encounter of reader and author that he describes is not presented as simply a generally edifying or constructive social transaction. It is, in the metaphor used, that one particular transaction wherein life itself is generated and the existence of the race is continued in passion into the future. Hawthorne, we remember, may have intimated something of the same understanding of the consecrations of the story-teller's calling in a preface written the next year for a new edition of his *Twice-Told Tales* when he described his stories and sketches as "attempts . . . to open an intercourse with the world." To Melville it was not only the more solemn and profound of Hawthorne's tales or those touched with his peculiar "blackness" that reached out in this way. Pieces like "Buds and Bird Voices" or "The Old Apple Dealer," having their own subtle element of outgoing compassion and melancholy, rose, Melville declared, from "such a depth of tenderness, such a boundless sympathy with all forms of being, such an omnipresent love," that they too had power to open a direct passage from "the intricate, profound heart where they originated."

About story-telling as a social rite, procreative or otherwise, there is more to be said than Melville ventured to say in the Hawthorne article or anywhere else (though a few passing remarks in *The Confidence-Man* on the nature of fiction have gradually been recognized as extraordinarily discerning and comprehensive). What that *more* may be, however, is implicit in his own best practice. His work remains important as much for the ingratiating freedom and inventiveness of its formation, in particular its resourceful attention to the job of beguiling concrete audiences, as for the exemplary humanity of its themes. Indeed the quick responsiveness of compositional arrangement to, at once, the progressive extension of the story and the advance of the reader's expectation is what particularly fixes assent. Quite regularly these stories shift focus at some key point and momentarily put their emphasis on the story-teller's own resolute effort to work his way through the narrative occasion and to do it justice, to get it right—or else his willingness to fall silent where the event transcends casual understanding (as in Chapter 22 of *Billy Budd*) rather than falsify its profoundest truth.* As much as any ultimate weightiness of theme, it is, with Melville, this active sense of engagement and risk in the business of getting through his story that gives it plausibility as it goes forward, and in the process assists in opening it out until it becomes capable of bearing that particular weightiness.

A story well told, so that it has the power to fix itself in the imagination of those who hear it, always tells us two things. It says, "here is what happened," and it has its say clearly enough in this respect whether or not (as Melville's stories mostly do) it also takes on the character of parable or even allegory or, at the least, leads to certain meditative formulations that can stand as autonomous truths.

But it will also say something further. It says, "this is what it is like to have knowledge of such happenings, to see in consciousness that they can happen, to undertake the task of opening such knowledge and vision to others." Anyone who passes an ordinary amount of time in the sociable exchange of gossip and anecdote knows how much depends, for interest and for belief, too, on *how* things get said. The more so when the matter is serious: stories that ought to be important and

---

* In those with a first-person speaker who is himself a main character—here "Bartleby" is the best example—this effort merges with the character's dramatic struggle, sometimes comically reluctant, to act out the part that has fallen to him in the story. The story may thus issue in a kind of surprising conversion, an unsought-for transformation of consciousness and commitment.

consequential can be so poorly told, or really not "told" at all, that they quite lose currency. The most momentous events reduce to pointless fantasy or self-refuting rumor in the manage of someone who has too little feeling or care for the sequences of reality as they actually are absorbed into consciousness but merely blurts out their bare substance and result. Melville seems to have understood from the first, as well he might, given the strangeness of his first materials, that to tell a tale is to gamble or wager for the reader's, the listener's, continuing acceptance, continuing, that is, beyond the initial "suspension of disbelief" which is any willing reader's undertaking in the covenant of literature. It is a wager precisely for *confidence:* an offering of testimony that, by forthrightly embracing the pragmatic burden of verification, becomes the better able to persuade others that the game itself is decidedly worth playing, on both sides and for its own sake.

It thus looks, systematically or not, beyond each immediate narrative occasion. Its motives are, in a formal sense, ceremonial and confederating. For the story-teller conspires to draw his hearer into becoming not simply a believer in the one particular tale he is telling but a devotee of tales in general, a true aficionado. In some measure he conceives of transforming his casual reader into a reader-by-vocation, the necessary partner for his own elected service. ("The demand that I make of my reader," Joyce remarked, "is that he should devote his whole life to reading my works.") But in this task the story-teller serves not only himself but the common fortune. That is, he engages his readers actively, deliberately, into that vast unending civil process which all men and women are bound to by their character as, willy-nilly, historical and imaginative beings: the process of exorcising the immeasurable entail of past events and making imaginative provision, so far as can be done, for the uncontrollable onset of present and future. In a word he fills time, covenanting with his audience to compel time's successions at least a little closer to that ideal "fullness" in which the life we inherit and the life we imagine are not hopelessly out of joint.*

The aim of the story-teller's wager is also, of course, to

---

* One may say, risking misunderstanding, that the conspiracy of fiction is thus, ideally, a religious conspiracy: that is, a ritual enterprise for the

give pleasure, and share more or less promptly in the pleasure-giver's agreeable rewards. As with any art the covenant of fiction promises enjoyment here and now as well as provision, of the kind described, against past and future. That after all would be the common truth in Melville's sexual metaphor for his encounter with Hawthorne's tales—and one can find a further parallel with sexual logistics in the sense communicated in certain of Melville's own narratives that to enter fully into the engagements of story-telling can be, temporarily at least, transporting and exhausting. Except perhaps in a few special forms—like the *solemn deposition* we are offered in the "inside narrative" of *Billy Budd*—the whole vast genre of prose fiction is a genre primarily for entertainment. It is hard to think of a major novelist or story-teller who is not also a first-rate entertainer, in the vulgar sense: a master, according to choice, of high comedy, of one or another robust species of expressive humor, or of some special variety of the preposterous, the grotesque, the absurd. And Melville, certainly, is no exception. A kind of vigorous supervisory humor is his natural idiom as a writer, and one attraction of his shorter work is the fresh further display it offers of this prime element in his literary character.

A version of the "contemplative humor" that Melville celebrated in Hawthorne's work is one component in Mel-ville's prose comedy. But its major instrument is something broader and freer, something that on any given page is an end in itself. It is an antic humor, carried by physical gesture as well as meditative fancifulness. What chiefly propels it is, first, a sense of the special interest of those moments in life when, though the self-approving consciousness gives us one set of directions, the creaturely totality of our being mysteriously issues us an altogether different set that abruptly takes command and bends us this way and that, quite against our apparent will; and, second, the corollary sense that these are the moments when our history and destiny as moral beings are

binding together of minds and souls in space (otherwise divided and *un*civil) and in time (otherwise fractured and *un*historical).

For the reader, the case with the best stories corresponds to what André Gide once remarked of the Christian Gospel: "it is a question not of explaining it but of accepting it."

really determined. Some of the liveliest sequences in Melville's fiction occur when characters normally at ease with themselves and their resolved attitudes to life (like the fine old lawyer of "Bartleby") are overborne by some strange new phenomenon of behavior and carried quite out of themselves by sudden excitement. A passage in *Moby-Dick* nicely summarizes the dialectic of feeling that plays through such sequences:

> There are certain queer times and occasions in this strange mixed affair we call life when a man takes this whole universe for a vast practical joke, though the wit thereof he but dimly discerns, and more than suspects that the joke is at nobody's expense but his own. However, nothing dispirits, and nothing seems worthwhile disputing. He bolts down all events, all creeds, and beliefs, and persuasions, all hard things visible and invisible, never mind how knobby; as an ostrich of potent digestion gobbles down bullets and gun flints. And as for small difficulties and worryings, prospects of sudden disaster, peril of life and limb; all these, and death itself, seem to him only sly, good-natured hits, and jolly punches in the side bestowed by the unseen and unaccountable old joker. That odd sort of wayward mood I am speaking of, comes over a man only in some time of extreme tribulation; it comes in the very midst of his earnestness, so that what just before might have seemed to him a thing most momentous, now seems but a part of the general joke . . . [breeding in him] this free and easy sort of genial, desperado philosophy. . . . (Chap. XLIX, "The Hyena.")

The passage gives us in epitome both the broad character of the fictional world projected in most of Melville's shorter fiction, and one of the main ways suggested, though not the only one, of looking at this world and surviving what is seen. As a piece of writing it effectively illustrates its own point. The thing that is to be said is said with a lively humor which convinces by piling up a quick abundance of freshly expressive detail. But it is also said in a manner that presses beyond the conventional limits of comic ingratiation. We feel at once that the "hard things" spoken of are somehow no joke, for all the slapstick of the ostrich image; that *waywardness* and *desperation*, though not necessarily incompatible with a "philosophy" which is genially "free and easy," are something more in this case than figures of speech.

The fact is that Melville's humor is inseparable from that strong imaginative intelligence supporting his gravest undertakings in fiction. The impressions of life and destiny it delivers are not materially different from what emerges in those works of his, like "Benito Cereno" and *Billy Budd*, where comic extravagance is subordinated almost completely to wit of another kind, the wit of moral and psychological understanding *and* of joined narrative sequence which tragic action even more exactingly requires of the writer who attempts it. It is on this ground, among the intense images of spiritual passion and change given to us in Melville's (formally) most original tales, that we most feel his greatness as a writer, and that his work seems finally to surpass in concentrated power and truth even so masterful a humorist as Dickens, from whom in the 1840's and 1850's Melville, like Dostoevsky, learned many excellent lessons.

The themes and actions of Melville's shorter tales and the truths they predicate are very likely as profound as interpretive criticism has persistently assumed them to be. He, too, in his broad American way, was a Victorian "sage" who may be read for the wisdom in him. For the most part these themes and actions are also clear and explicit in presentation. Melville liked to get things properly explained as well as build up symbolic hints and portents, and when he speaks figuratively, the figures drawn are agreeably circumstantial and definite.

Particularly in the tales of 1853–1856 there appears to be, first of all, a steady burden of autobiographical statement. Nearly all remind us somewhere that they are the work of a writer whose career in literature seemed by 1853 to have fallen on evil days and who himself, toward the end of his work on *Moby-Dick*, had prophesied that his life had come "to the inmost leaf of the bulb, and that shortly the flower must fall to the mould" (letter to Hawthorne, June, 1851). One after another presents an action of withdrawal, resignation, defeat; of stoic endurance and passive suffering; of isolated and constricted spirits living on, though sometimes with a strange cheerfulness, after wrenching disasters; of measures taken, usually too eccentric to be generally serviceable, against hardly avoidable catastrophe.

The whole frame of action has become less splendid and spacious. Only now and then are glimpses still given of the

kind of "far-off, soft, azure world" ("The Piazza") that figures so grandly in the early Polynesian books and in *Moby-
Dick*. Instead these stories offer, as settings, a series of houses
and habitations—the walled law-office and the Tombs in
"Bartleby"; the shadowy, decaying slave ship in "Benito
Cereno"; the queer misshapen houses of "I and My Chimney"
and "Jimmy Rose"; the grimly secluded paper factory which
is the "Tartarus of Maids"—that are closed-in and oppressive
in the extreme. So the earth itself is presented, in "The Encantadas," as a "great general monastery" and "Potters Field."
The lives of the main characters correspond. Instead of heroic
"knights and squires" and figures of "immaculate manliness"
of the kind liberally provided in *Moby-Dick*, we find persons
of "desperate fortune" ("The Encantadas") who are "afraid
of everyone" ("Jimmy Rose"), men who appear "flayed alive,"
wracked by trouble as if by "the ague" ("Benito Cereno").
Characters may imagine themselves happy and secure, yet be
in reality "like the man who, pipe in mouth, was killed one
cloudless afternoon long ago in Virginia, by summer light-
ning; at his own warm open window he was killed, and remained leaning out there upon the dreamy afternoon, till
some one touched him, when he fell" ("Bartleby"). "Nature's
pride"—the irreducible force of life that is the last inward
resort of human dignity—is identified only as a perverse counterforce to "nature's torture" ("The Encantadas: Sketch the
Eighth"); it persists as a source of treacherous hope, "a hope
which is but mad," depriving its victim even of the consolation
of "a sane despair."

As in his earlier books Melville's statement of these themes
is typically reflective as well as figurative and dramatic. In
the stories he wrote after 1853 there is still enough of the ob-
stinate seeker after truth and a "definite belief" (as Hawthorne reported him at their meeting in England in 1856) to
furnish texts for all manner of philosophical debate. Melville
continues to frame his narratives as, among other things, tests
of the validity of various great received propositions of religious and moral knowledge. The central New Testament
commandment to "charity," for example, is as directly ques-
tioned in "Bartleby," the first work published in the 1853–
1856 period, as it notoriously is in *The Confidence-Man*, the

last in this run. But what now becomes equally prominent is the resigned or dryly humorous suggestion that the one sure thing in life is the overturning of received propositions. "Somehow, too," the narrator in "The Apple-Tree Table" remarks, "certain reasonable opinions of mine seemed not so reasonable as before." When the stuff of new awareness materializes, it is not necessarily clarifying. "Truth comes in with darkness," is the concluding strophe, as it may be called, of "The Piazza"; and it comes there with the haunting expression of a particular face, the concrete recollection of one or another puzzling old story.

An increasing reserve and restraint are to be felt in these tales with regard to philosophical assessments, and are felt moreover as a positive resource. Certain high dramatic moments are deliberately left undescribed; they become in fact the more impressive through the narrator's pointed refusal to take them up in his regular fashion. A profounder tact, a more intense respect for persons and what will ultimately be required of them, seem chiefly responsible for this change of manner, rather than any doctrinaire skepticism or ironic derogation of traditional understanding. "The half shall here remain untold," Melville writes at the darkest point in his narrative of the Chola widow, Hunilla. "Those two unnamed events which befell Hunilla on this isle, let them abide between her and her God. In nature, as in law, it may be libelous to speak some truths." The very greatest fictions, perhaps, cannot withdraw into silence in this way. But it is possible to feel a singular humanity, and civility, in writing that chooses to do so, out of a measured confidence in its own sufficient strength of intimation; an objective discretion and tenderness which, like that of mutually tolerant lovers, are life-supporting rather than otherwise.

From 1856 to 1885 Melville gave up prose fiction, as he gave up, in time, the thought of any further public career in literature.* But in certain renewed experiments of his final

---

* The principal work, however, of this long interval, which was devoted mostly to writing poetry, is a kind of philosophical novel-in-verse, *Clarel* (2 vols., 1876), offering a remarkable new gallery of fictional characterizations and life histories.

years, made possible by his retirement at the end of 1885 from the drudgery of a routine job in the New York Customs House, the tact and forbearance of judgment he had come round to in the middle 1850's are resumed almost as if there had been no interruption. In his last major effort—the long narrative of the handsome sailor, Billy Budd, and what befell him and one or two other "phenomenal men" in the year of the British fleet's Great Mutiny—these qualities become sources of exceptional power. The philosophical restlessness of earlier times seems quite gone, though not the probing curiosity. Melville's old interest as a story-teller in framing experience into meditative axioms and queries is still a prime motive, so that one way of grasping the general form of *Billy Budd,* as the poet Eugenio Montale recognized, is to see that it moves forward, in Montale's terms, not only as a *tale of adventure* crystallizing into a *mystery play* but also as a *critical essay* and *Platonic dialogue.* But the narrative voice is no longer that of a man who can imagine himself either gaining or losing by the outcome of his inquiry. Rather, the various propositions about life which the events of the story yield up are valuable as they help to specify more precisely the quality of manhood celebrated in its main characters: the rare natural beauty and nobility of spirit in Billy Budd, the doomed "peacemaker," and the austere rectitude of the fatherly Captain who under the rigidities of the martial law must be Billy's executioner.

With these last remarkable figures, plus the malignant yet finally pitiable Claggart, for a time their antagonist, the table of personalities and life histories constituted by Melville's later fiction is complete. Ever since *Billy Budd* was first published, in 1924, readers have felt strongly its unity with Melville's earlier work. In occupying the ground of tragedy it resumes the ambiance approached in "Bartleby," "The Encantadas," "Benito Cereno," and in the climaxes of *Moby-Dick.* Yet the last word in this moving story is not tragic in accent, though it comes to us as a death song. It is, instead, Billy's gentle, absolving plea to be allowed as much of beauty and ease in death as he was blessed with in life—and no reader who follows Melville through the full circuit of his life and work can be other than grateful that there could be this music at the close:

I remember Taff the Welshman when he sank,
And his cheek it was like the budding pink.
But me they'll lash me in hammock, drop me deep,
Fathoms down, fathoms down, how I'll dream fast asleep.
I feel it stealing now. Sentry, are you there?
Just ease this darbies at the wrist, and roll me over fair,
I am sleepy and the oozy weeds about me twist.

The Confidence-Man

Herman Melville's strange and puzzling prose "masquerade,"
The Confidence-Man—in Elizabeth Foster's words his "vale-
dictory as a professional novelist"—is one of those books that
makes of the reader's own bafflement a part of its essential subject matter. It openly teases us with its apparent inconse-
quence, and then, in flashes of insight that have the abrupt
simplicity of an authoritative and final wisdom, it teases our
impatient expectation of an order and sequence that we would
hardly think to demand of our own behavior, our own habit
of consciousness. It teases our frivolity, our deep-rooted bad
faith as critically principled readers, in seeking the reassurance of stable and, so to speak, manageable argument without
giving up the privilege of being richly diverted and entertained. Or, as Melville himself dryly puts the matter in one of
those penetrating remarks on the nature of fiction and our absorption in it that we find scattered through *The Confidence-
Man*, it catches us, too, looking "not only for more entertainment, but, at bottom, even for more reality, than real life
itself can show."

The book before us is simply "a work of amusement," so
Melville tells us in the same passage: strange then that we
should lay any sort of aggressive critical demand upon it, that
we should require of it a higher consistency, a more perfect
rationality. Almost in the same breath, however, and with a
breathtaking access of seriousness that typifies the book's un-
even rhythm of demonstration, the uncertainty of the whole
enterprise, for writer and reader alike, is suddenly joined to

Reprinted from *Landmarks of American Writing*, ed. Hennig Cohen,
Basic Books, 1969.

the profoundest mysteries of our life and our consciousness as spiritual and imaginative beings. How shall novel-writing itself escape this very restlessness, this infinite duplicity of human consideration, in equal parts self-deceiving and self-transcending? A negative answer is inescapable, but Melville, in this book, is beyond exclaiming over it. He makes his point quietly: "It is with fiction," he remarks, "as with religion; it should present another world, yet one to which we feel the tie."

A writer who has come to see his occupation in these extraordinary terms is either on the verge of an extraordinary final mastery or is himself near the breaking point. And it has in fact been hard to separate the special impression *The Confidence-Man* makes on us from our knowledge that its publication early in 1857 marked the end of Melville's life as a writer of books and the beginning of the withdrawal and resignation of his later years. *The Confidence-Man* is the last extended work of prose narrative that Melville published in his lifetime; the last, therefore, in that astonishing succession of writings that fill out the brief, brilliant decade of his public career as an American author. When it appeared, he was still a young man, not yet thirty-eight. Yet how much he had already written. Between the Polynesian traveler's tale of *Typee* in 1846 and the frantic allegorical romance of *Pierre* in 1852, he had published seven full-length books, one of them his masterpiece, *Moby-Dick,* and between *Pierre* and *The Confidence-Man* he had been hardly less prolific, filling *Putnam's* and *Harper's* magazines with a vividly imagined series of tales and sketches. It might be noted that by 1857 Walt Whitman, born the same year as Melville, was only just past the beginning of his career as an American poet. If Melville had reached a point of professional exhaustion, there was good reason.

Various outward circumstances also played their part in bringing his career to a crisis. A fire at Harper's in 1853 that destroyed the undistributed stock of his earlier work was more than a symbolic check; it had made difficult any significant recovery from the loss of popularity and cash profit he had suffered with *Moby-Dick* and *Pierre*. And publication of *The Confidence-Man,* the reviews of which were not wholly discouraging, was immediately overtaken by the financial panic of 1857, Dix and Edwards, his new publishers, failing within the month. These causes, however, seem incidental. The real trouble was inward. Melville's family knew it, and sent him on a European tour in the fall of 1856 to regain his health and balance. Hawthorne knew it when they talked in Liverpool that November, and saw also that there would be no easy recovery for him. But the book itself, as it has been impossible for readers not to feel, may be the strongest testimony of all.

For of all Melville's books *The Confidence-Man* is in every way the most problematical, a remarkable claim in the case of an author whose most ambitious earlier work had been greeted by some reviewers as presenting evidence of serious derangement. In the first place nobody can be sure that the book is finished. It doesn't distinctly end; it appears only to break off, all too much like its author's career for the analogy to escape notice. On the other hand nobody is sure that this makes much difference. *The Confidence-Man* seems the kind of book that has one great thing to say and that says it, through an ingenious yet oddly repetitive series of incidents, over and over again.

We may not be able to agree on what precisely this message is, but we feel formally the single-mindedness with which it is delivered. We become conscious that what we are observing is the repetition of one consistent species of action, the forced renewal of one uniform perspective. The actual narrative does show a certain progression forward. One scene does more or less prepare another. The mystifying man of confidence drops hints and pointers that ready his victims for his next manifestation in a new disguise and that establish these successive disguises as familiar and expected before he re-emerges wearing them. But to say even this may be assuming too much. For it is not at all clear whether there is indeed just one such confidence man, wearing different disguises, or a whole boatload of confidence men distinguished only by an increasing subtlety of performance. The succession of figures who come before us does not match exactly the list offered in Chapter iii by the black cripple who begins the main sequence of episodes, the list of those who will declare their faith in him. And some of the personages he names resemble characters who appear later as antagonists of the confidence man and, eventually, his further victims.

Indeed there is a sense in which everybody on board the Mississippi steamboat where the action of the book takes place appears as both confidence man and victim—purveyor-dupes all of some visionary distortion of the enterprise of life, some interior hallucination, in which each has persuaded himself to invest heart, soul, and mind (not to mention cash in hand) beyond any margin of security. The progression of the book is as arbitrary and mechanical as a dream, and there is a dream-like stammering and obsessiveness in the conversation of its characters. The steamboat itself, ironically named the *Fidèle*, is a ship of fools (it sails on the first of April)—"a piebald parliament," Melville writes, continually receiving "additional passengers in exchange for those that disembark; so that, though always full of strangers, she continually, in some degree, adds to, or replaces them with strangers still more strange"; all moving, whether they know it or not, toward a common end, or, as Melville obliquely puts it, "involuntarily submitting to that natural law which ordains dissolution equally to the mass, as in time to each member."

This haunting, slow-motion confusion of human movement and impulse, as of blind men bumping against blind men (not even "battering" each other, as in Yeats's more heroic vision), is the substance of every scene; it takes the place of a plot. An impression grows, becomes dominant, of mankind milling slowly about in a state of hypnosis, self-enchanted, under the compulsion of a seedy, shabby regimen of petty fraudulence and distrust. The confidence man himself is strangely content to play his games and tricks for very small stakes. His operations as the agent for phantom coal companies and charitable funds, selling nostrums called the "Samaritan Pain Dissuader" or the "Omni-Balsamic Reinvigorator," are the more mystifying in having no other tangible motive than "two or three dirty dollars." Yet those few characters who may appear for a time morally superior to the rest—like Pitch, the bluff, cynical, self-reliant Missouri bachelor, or the mystical philosopher Mark Winsome, embodiment of a smug version of the Transcendentalist ethic of self-serving optimism—seem, before we are through with them, fools or knaves of an even deeper dye, since it is presumably a greater potential for virtue that has been corrupted in them.

And we are offered no escape from this heavy-footed masquerade of human fraud and folly. The two figures in the book who stand wholly outside its floating theater of action— we are told about them in stories within the main story—are far more terrifying than any who appear on board: the coldly ferocious Goneril, jealous and vindictive, more cuttlefish than woman, whose very touch both stabs and freezes; the Indian-hater, Colonel John Moredock, sober, upright, citizenly devotee of a murderous private religion of unending vengeance. The moral world of *The Confidence-Man* is of a paralyzing obscurity. To become involved in it is to be drawn into a slowly darkening whirlpool where all conventional wisdom is sucked down and obliterated; and all the paired opposites by means of which we customarily conspire to keep balance— reason and insanity, folly and wisdom, drunkenness and sobriety, enthusiasm and lethargy, sincerity and charlatanism, honesty and deceit, love of man and hatred of man—become synonyms and meaningless jargon. It is a world from which the blessings of grace and of moral certitude appear to have been withdrawn, for we are conscious more of the absence of certain virtues, or elements assumed to be necessary to virtue, than of the power of malign alternatives. It seems fitting that the book's terminal image should be that of an extinguished lamp.

Now, that there are contradictions and loose ends in the fabric of the narrative is something to be kept in mind. Melville *was*, apparently, ill and in low spirits while writing it. We can imagine how, even as he carried forward his caustic general scheme, he might have begun to turn away in self-disgust from the effort to complete it, from the sheer vanity of composition. One's very absorption in writing, all that effort to improvise new images and figures for a pattern of human conduct that never finally varied, might itself seem a confidence game of the most absurd kind. Yet everywhere the vision that is projected appears uniform and complete. We seem to have been introduced into an autonomous civilization that in some queer way is in harmony with itself, however dismal a harmony it may be. But it is a civilization to which we cannot easily find the vital key, and I am speaking now not of the dense outward particulars of the book's action, which compose a clear enough moral satire on the degradations of a wholly commercial and entrepreneurial society, but of the character of this vision itself, this way of representing humanity that confronts us at every turn.

For the deepest meaning of the book is the atmosphere of mind it registers and proceeds from. Deeper than the satirical "comedy of action" with which we are outwardly occupied—and here, again, I borrow terms from Melville's own commentary—lies the "comedy of thought" that, for one thing, never tells us, as such comedies customarily do, what ground of fictive abstraction the events and characters are meant to occupy. *The Confidence-Man* is full of colorful, seemingly emblematic figures of essential human behavior, yet it is a book which can also casually raise doubts "whether the human form be, in all cases, conclusive evidence of humanity," and whether the basic attributes by which we identify humanity—feeling, reason, natural sentiment—may not be quite unsuitable to the conduct, the plain endurance, of life as we know it.

The total instability of human character and behavior is a basic premise, governing fictional form as well as moral knowledge. The talk of the confidence man himself is full of oblique warnings on this score. "Don't be too sure what I am," he tells one supposedly self-possessed cynic. "You can conclude nothing absolute from the human form." And to another he defines the mind itself as, first of all, "ductile." "We are but clay, sir, potter's clay, as the good book says, clay, feeble, and too-yielding clay." Hence "the mystery of human subjectivity in general," from which all lesser mysteries and dubieties follow; and hence the common possibility of such freakish manifestations as the friend and aider of men, the true philanthropist, who is always surly and cynical in the extreme, or of his even more freakish opposite, the "genial misanthrope"—"a new kind of monster," as the confidence man coolly defines him, made possible by the sinister general advance of "refinement and softness" in modern life. Inconsistency and mutability are the laws of life—they are, for example, the single truth revealed by the otherwise mystifying little story of Charlemont, in Chapter xxxiv—and therefore must also be the rule for human discourse and communication. The great masters of narrative and dramatic literature excel, Melville notes, in nothing so much as this rendering of irreducible inconsistency. Shakespeare is the model for all in being at one and the same time "enlightening and mystifying"; to those intent on full clarification he has a strange power to "open . . . eyes and corrupt . . . morals in one operation," though the wiser reader will say no more than, with conscious redundancy, "This Shakespeare is a queer man."

All such turns and spirals of argument indicate, we can say, a further intensification of that general picture of human behavior which characterizes all of Melville's writing, more or less, at first turned mostly to comic but increasingly, though never exclusively, to tragic ends. Man is a creature subject to galloping contagions, a creature whose very vitality takes the form of a surrender to the epidemic distemper of the moment. In *The Confidence-Man* it is the contagion of suspicion and distrust, erupting periodically in fits of violent misanthropy or the self-hatred of true melancholy; a distemper that is made the more significant because it is also shown to be not at all unwarranted or irrational.

But there is, to repeat, a curious lack of dramatic emphasis and concentration in developing this general picture. If there is critical agreement on anything about *The Confidence-Man* it is on this point: that the style rather than the story is the surest measure of what the book has to say, and the chief indicator—more than the broken, enigmatic narrative sequence—of its general import. It is a strange, halting, self-referential style, full of hesitation and qualification, yet now and then flashing out with aphorisms, slogans, obscurely symbolic images and descriptive figures, that do fleetingly light up the moral perplexity of the whole. The movement of the writing thus typifies the procession of events and the vacillation and instability of the characters involved in them. The line between irony and double-talk, between grim insight and palpable absurdity, is sometimes drawn very fine. "He who comes to know man, will not remain in ignorance of man": by the time we reach this sentence late in the book we may, as baffled as the character who speaks it, be hard put to decide whether it is evasive nonsense or oracular wisdom.

The confidence man himself is the principal exemplar of this style, and questions about the meaning of the book are questions finally about his identity and mission. Who is the confidence man and what does he propose? The book is prodigal of clues, hints, obscure proto-definitions, though many of these reflect not so much the confidence man's own character as the character, the distorted and suspicion-ridden incomprehension, of the crowd that judges him. He is, to others, a quack, a fool, a knave—yet perhaps also, one onlooker remarks, noting that certain money dispensed by the fellow was, after all, "good money," an "original genius"; in any case "a queer and dubious man," and therefore the likelier candidate for being some kind of Everyman; a stranger in motley, in his jaunty final disguise as the fantastically costumed "cosmopolitan"; a "man-charmer," so one of his befuddled victims, the crusty barber of the steamboat's business deck, afterward remembers him. Insofar as he persistently offers a doctrine for men to live by that flies in the face of worldly experience, presenting himself as "the Happy Man" in a world where disaffection is so reasonable an attitude, he is an "extraordinary metaphysical scamp," preaching benevolence, charity, and trust in a way that somehow tempts men into an even deeper disbelief in them. "I am Philanthropos, and love mankind," he tells the barber, but the barber's reply carries equal weight: "Sir, you must excuse me. I have a family." Nothing disturbs understanding more than the confidence man's own way of identifying his purposes. "I am for doing good to the world," he says, "once for all and having done with it"; here, an audible violence of idiom and the grammatical ambiguity of the pronoun combine in a way giving support to a later charge that this confidence man is the most treacherous of all dealers in truth: one who "puns with ideas as another man may with words."

Or is he something worse than a philosophical punster and scamp? In her excellent edition of *The Confidence-Man* Elizabeth Foster has set out a carefully assembled case for seeing this character as the devil and for understanding the

book as a demonstration of how Antichrist has wholly super-
seded Christ as the ruler of this world and how "the devil
makes use of Christian idealism for his own ends." This black
"allegory," as Professor Foster is willing to call it, is the means
by which Melville develops his satirical attack on the whole
range of optimistic philosophies, religious, humanitarian, commercial, flourishing in his century. Such a reading of the book
is entirely plausible, and so for that matter is the considerably
more dogmatic view advanced by Newton Arvin that *The
Confidence-Man* is "one of the most *infidel* books ever written
by an American; one of the most completely nihilistic, morally
and metaphysically."

The evidence is abundant, and a reader who comes to
think otherwise may be driven to the dubious expedient of
saying only, "It just doesn't read that way to me." Certainly
if the mysterious man of confidence *is* the devil, he is a very
ingenious and aesthetically pleasing addition to the whole
gallery of modern fictional devils. Yet it can also be argued
that, far from tempting the world and its citizens into any fall
from grace or leading it into unrighteousness, the confidence
man merely adapts himself to it for the duration of the voyage.
He does not himself give direction to the world's custom. He
only falls in with it and plays its games, and more than once he
is struck and abused for his pains. When occasionally he takes
some small measure of material revenge, it is invariably in a
way that satisfies us, for he does so by tricking his opponent
into some appropriate self-contradiction and the loss at most
of only a few coins or bills; the pettiness of the retaliation is
nicely proportioned to the essential meanness of the offense.

At the same time he talks far more than he tricks, and far
in excess of any cash return. He talks, talks, talks. He functions
in the book as essentially a promoter of discourse, a "talking
man" as one character calls him, and thus a teacher in his
way—for, he immediately replies, "it is the peculiar vocation
of a teacher to talk." "What's wisdom itself," he goes on, "but
table-talk?"* What he offers, however, is not doctrine, in the

_____

* The sentence following makes clear the allusion here to the great case
of the Last Supper: "The best wisdom in this world, and the last spoken
by its teacher; did it not literally and truly come in the form of table-
talk?"

ordinary manner of teachers. Rather, it is the image of a way of life, but one that, far from beguiling men into evil ways, is so austere and forbidding when you see the point of it that those few who begin to understand it retreat from it even more violently than those who merely greet it with their ordinary suspiciousness. The name for it may be "confidence," but it is a confidence in circumstances and prospects that is only to be maintained by an unending process of testing, a constantly open-eyed examining of all signs and indications, a process of engaged watchfulness that has no resolution and from which there is, in life, no release.

Moreover, as a proposed way of life it comes guarded with warnings that, worst of all, are directed against itself as well as all other things; for it is the confidence man himself who, in the last chapter, speaking words from the Apocryphal Son of Sirach, seems to connect the teacher of confidence with the spirit's subtlest enemies. Perhaps the purest definition of this way of life comes (Chapter xvi) as a paraphrase of the teaching of St. Paul in I Thessalonians 5:21: "Prove all things; hold fast to that which is good." Typically the Biblical verse alluded to is one that follows closely after another notable warning about the false teachings of the children of darkness. Those who see the full consequences of this teaching must be truly appalled; and though it is not the kind of teaching we usually associate with the devil, the impulse of those who hear it is to curse it. "But to doubt, to suspect, to prove," a sick man grasping for cures dolefully protests, *"to have all this wearing work to be doing continually*—how opposed to confidence. It is evil."

Perhaps so, but I myself would write this man down as the first modern critic and garbler of the book's projected meaning. For what can also be said on this score is that characters unambiguously identified as doers of evil, devils in human shape, do indeed enter the book—I have already mentioned them: the wife Goneril and the hunter Moredock—but they are not brought aboard the *Fidèle* and do not participate in its running action.* The immediate world of *The Confidence-*

---

* We note that these two figures are given, as described, the distinctive characteristics of Melville's other "devils," in both earlier and later work: that is, the absolute single-mindedness or monomania, and the pure,

Man is the midworld of common, circumstantial human weakness. For all the book's opening out toward spiritual horror and darkness, it occupies the ground of comedy; in style, in narrative design (or the lack of it), in its ultimately monotonous substance of demonstration, it holds itself back from the kind of meaning claimed for it by the interpretations cited above.

Here again our understanding is governed in part by the curious structure of the book. We feel throughout that the confidence man is not only a character of a different order from the others in the story as, to be sure, the devil would be, too, but that he remains apart in his own self-conscious being from the midworld of the *Fidèle* and his passing complicity with it. He remains apart just as, formally, the first and last chapters, and thus our first and last glimpses of him, stand apart from the central mass of the narrative. These chapters enclose the book like the supernatural framing chapters of one of the great panoramic Chinese chronicle-novels, chapters which evoke directly the larger context of meaning of the often chaotic events of the main narrative. In these framing chapters in Melville's book, the confidence man plays a different part from that of his usual masquerade, though one obviously germane to it.

We see him first, in the opening chapter, as the mute lamblike "stranger" going about the deck of the *Fidèle*, displaying on a slate the great legends about charity from St. Paul's letter to the Corinthians: that charity thinketh no evil, suffereth long and is kind, endureth all things, believeth all things, and never faileth. Like one of Silone's mysterious heroes he is described as having "come from a very long distance," with still some further way to go. His aspect is taken to be "somehow inappropriate to the time and place," and he is treated by the other passengers with a hostility that progresses from annoyance and jeering to shoves and punches until, having gone through his series of inscriptions about charity, he withdraws into "motionless" privacy. We do not see him again in this manifestation; and in the forty-odd chapters that follow, on the rare occasions when charity is

---

helpless, vindictive malice that Melville would eventually specify, in a late poem, as the one unpardonable human affliction.

urged as a rule for mankind, it is savagely mocked. "To where it belongs with your charity! to heaven with it!" one paragon of suspicion cries out; "here on earth, true charity dotes, and false charity plots." And in the next breath he mocks the great avatar of charity himself: "Who betrays a fool with a kiss, the charitable fool has the charity to believe is in love with him. . . ."

But the speaker here—a gimlet-eyed, sour-faced, wooden-legged cynic, a "shallow unfortunate" whose speech is a surly croak—is not a character likely to be entrusted with the last word. With regard to subsequent episodes he is right enough; through most of *The Confidence-Man* Christian charity is honored only in the breach. Yet it seems to me that the singular brilliance and vividness of that pageant-like opening chapter are never positively dispelled. The bearer of the inscriptions may, in his more usual performance as confidence man, be dubious and equivocal, but the inscriptions themselves are not touched by this change of style. The command to charity so remarkably erected stands over the whole book and carries through it with positive force. Mere improvised fictions, however ingenious in their tracing out of an epidemic demoralization, cannot overthrow the claim it makes on the germ of humanity within us.

Surely Melville did not intend them to; nothing we know about the courage of his intelligence, his power as a writer to hold contradictory ideas and feelings in expressive balance, requires us to suppose so. No mere pattern of words can put down the force of true charity, for it is of that order of things, like "true religion" (Chapter xi), that is "in some sort independent of words." Man is clay, feeble, ductile, too yielding, but holy charity is not. It is itself a mysterious stranger and pilgrim in its passage through men's consciousness; it is a force superior to its daily betrayals and bides its time. In this it is like Providence; if our conviction of it "were in any way made dependent upon such variabilities as everyday events," this conviction would fluctuate, Melville writes, like "the stock exchange during a long and uncertain war." But it is not so dependent.

Feeling the force of this term, a force undiminished by all the frauds practiced in its name, we are required to ask whether the bearer of it, the confidence man himself, is indeed the double-dealing devil or Great Beast that our apocalypse-minded criticism has pretty regularly assumed him to be. It is possible that he, too, bides his time, in a world which does not encourage him to do anything else. In the last chapter he leaves the public quarters of the boat, for the first time since Chapter i, and goes into the semi-obscurity of the gentlemen's cabin, where he finds an old man sitting alone "in peace" reading a Bible. The old man is such a one as we have not seen before in the book, one who makes no effort to impose himself on the world and who looks out on it not with fixed suspicion or hostility but with a kind of muddled and ingenuous trust that seems very near to foolishness. A man of seventy, he is described as looking "fresh-hearted" as a boy of fifteen, doubtless, the passage insists, because he has somehow remained "ignorant" of what the world really is. But seeing him, the confidence man abruptly changes his usual manner; he "tones himself down." Talk follows, and it is as riddling as elsewhere. The old man is confused and made sad by new reports of uncertainty and deception, and credulously buys a traveler's lock and a money belt from a preternaturally sly and worldly-wise boy-peddler. But through this scene the confidence man acts with a restraint, and a kindliness, different in tone from what has gone before. He eyes the old man "with sympathy," and answers his declaration of an ultimate trust in the power of God with a remarkably straightforward commendation of the worth and true comfort of such trust, for him who can maintain it. And at the last, as the cabin lamp burns low and is extinguished, he "kindly" leads the old man away, out of the obscurity of the place to the haven of his stateroom.

Is there a possibility that this kindness and sympathy are, for once, real kindness and real sympathy, plainly given and plainly received? Have we not come finally upon a meeting free of the tension and combativeness, though not of the equivocality, of all that has preceded? The turn the narrative has taken is not heroic or dramatically momentous; it will not be the basis for a new affirmation that will sweep over the domain of the book and resolve all its multiplying duplicity. Nevertheless it is a turn. An act of kindness *has* been done; charity, strangely untouched by everything that has happened since the deaf-mute first raised his slate, has been reasserted. The long pageant, in which a quite rational self-interest and misanthropic suspicion have played at graceless, sour odds with the simple instinct of fellow feeling that makes men seek the comfort of one another's company, has come to an end; and we are left with these two—the cosmopolitan stranger and the old, befuddled figure of trust—in a relation of kindness and mutual consideration: a hopeful, benignant ending after all. It, too, is a "masquerade," but there may be more comfort and cheer in it, or at least less terror, than we quite dare to think.

POSTSCRIPT

Pascal, a great framer of dilemmas and paradoxes, would say that we cannot expect the three orders, *l'ordre des corps, l'ordre des esprits, l'ordre de la charité* to come together; for the absolute realization of charity, that is, Jesus Christ, is, from the world's point of view, invisible. The sign of his glory is his humility, the sign of his richness his poverty, the sign of his rule over men its invisibility; and the sign of Divine power, his resurrection, is *secret*, not an event within the order of the world.

—J. M. Cameron, *New York Review of Books*, November 6, 1969.

The Art of Jewett's *Pointed Firs*

Somewhat of a curiosity in American letters, the considerable reputation of Sarah Orne Jewett's *The Country of the Pointed Firs* survives and holds its own in a less and less congenial era —as the best work of a scrupulous minor artist forgivably overpraised by her friends; a "little masterpiece" (Edward Garnett's verdict) but within the limits of the "local color" school. Willa Cather's generous estimate represents the kind of claim that has been made for the book. What she said has the ring of extravagance:

> If I were asked to name three American books which have the possibility of a long life, I would say at once, 'The Scarlet Letter,' 'Huckleberry Finn,' and 'The Country of the Pointed Firs.' I can think of no others that confront time and change so serenely.

She wrote this in 1925 to introduce her own selection of Sarah Jewett's work, in devotion to the memory of a writer who had befriended her at the start of her own career. In other circumstances would she have claimed so much? In the expanded version of her introduction published eleven years later, in *Not Under Forty*, these sentences are omitted.

Reprinted from THE NEW ENGLAND QUARTERLY, March, 1959.

But before discounting them we ought to consider what precisely they assert. Willa Cather was claiming for *Pointed Firs* a special quality, not of magnitude or power or importance but of durability, of freedom from vicissitudes of taste, therefore presumably of artistic truthfulness and wholeness. To make her point she invoked for comparison two books which, like Jewett's, are distinctly "regional" but which possess, each in its own way, a formal coherence, a consistent intensity, that transcend their particular substance and setting. The achievement is one for which Willa Cather would have had a personal and professional respect, her own novels being aimed at some such category of transcended regionalism. Grouping *Pointed Firs* with the masterpieces of Hawthorne and Mark Twain was her instinctive tribute to the American masters in her own line of work. It was by concentration on the local, the long familiar, the particular, that each had achieved the formal authority which is the precondition of significance as well as of permanence.

On the other hand, each had had to find his bearings as an artist and performer (no quick process) and to approach his material from a broader ground of experience, before the crowning achievement was possible. "One must know the world *so well* before one can know the parish," Sarah Jewett once wrote to Willa Cather, in context less sententiously, Cather tells us, than it may sound. As such knowledge is measured, Sarah Jewett, though she had lived as much in Boston as in Maine and had traveled abroad, scarcely knew the world well. If she was finally able in *Pointed Firs* to lift what she did know to the formal order of accomplished art, she earned the triumph by her single-minded devotion, through thirty years of work, to her narrow materials, the spare life and setting of the Maine coast, as much as by acquaintance with major society. And as in her life she was both native and outlander, so through all her work runs a pattern of contrast between the in-world of the coastal villages, economically atrophied, and the bustling prosperous out-world from which the summer visitors come and into which the young, the active, the ambitious, invariably escape. To compare the initial full statement of this contrast in *Deephaven* (1877) with the more penetrating, and disturbing, intimations of *Pointed Firs,*

twenty years after, is to gain a measure of her development as
an artist.

In *Deephaven* the summer visitors, two Boston girls, are
the central figures, and the record of village life is the record
of their self-consciously sensitive observation. They sympathize with the village in its evident decline into poverty and
stagnation, and relish its lingering charm and beauty. But
they are looking in from outside. A positive class distinction
between visitors and natives is all but asserted, and the visitors'
patronizing approval, though well meant and not quite offen-
sive, is less attractive than Jewett seems to have realized. Similarly, though her intention was clearly to pose, through the
simple integrity of village manners, a pastoral criticism of
the outer world, the fact that this criticism is delivered by
outsiders, who will not stay, dissipates its force and leaves it
vague and indecisive: "we told each other, as we went home
in the moonlight down the quiet street, how much we had
enjoyed the evening, for somehow [*sic*] the house and the people had nothing to do with the present, or the hurry of modern life."

In *Pointed Firs* the dispositions are altered. The emphasis
is no longer divided, half on proving the observer's sensitivity.
It is all on what she observes and apprehends—on the great
presences of the natural landscape and on the figures in it
who accept her into their community and tell her, enact before
her, its almost buried life. Her sensitivity remains important
in one respect only, that it opens the life of the village to
her: her landlady, the herb gatherer Mrs. Todd, trusts her to
keep shop; silent ruined men speak to her; she is allowed to
be sympathetic with the "old ways"; and at the great tribal
reunion which climaxes the book she may participate as an
adopted member. But she never fully belongs, and there is no
question of her staying. When she leaves in September, she
must accept the rebuke implicit in Mrs. Todd's disinclination
to stop for good-byes. The whole book has given an indelible
impression of a community that is dying, however luminously;
but the narrator, as if to underscore what she is made to feel is
a betrayal of privilege and trust, now applies the metaphor of
death not to the village but to herself:

. . . the little house had suddenly grown lonely, and my room looked empty as it had the day I came. I and all my belongings had died out of it, and I knew how it would seem when Mrs. Todd came back and found her lodger gone. So we die before our own eyes; so we see some chapters of our lives come to their natural end.

The import of this, however, is equivocal: her departure is a kind of dying but one which, precisely in departing, she can outlive. And the final passage of *Pointed Firs,* though simpler and less obviously eloquent than the ending of *Deephaven,* intensifies the ambiguity of feeling well beyond the pathos and nostalgic allegiances of the earlier book. Sailing out of the harbor and bay in early September, the narrator notices how rain has made turf and woods green again, "like the beginning of summer ashore"; and having thus established the still vital beauty of the place, she looks back to see that "the islands and the headland had run together and Dunnet Landing and all its coasts were lost to sight." The disappearance of the town into the landscape confirms the theme of decay; yet the beauty and vitality of the setting assert a superior fortune; and we cannot say whether there is gain or loss in the departure, whether we are escaping death or being cut off from some rare, transforming condition of life.

What is unmistakable here, in comparison with *Deephaven,* is the greater emotional energy and also the greater spareness, the concentration, the restrictive simplicity of statement. Less seems attempted, more actually is secured. The advance is strictly formal: the basic materials which compose the *Pointed Firs* volume (1896) are all in *Deephaven* or in the stories Jewett collected in *Tales of New England* (1894). No new judgment is offered, no different point of view arrived at. The difference comes, on the one hand, in a mode of narration suited as never before to the special character of her apprehensions and, on the other, in a simple sustaining structure within which she could both elaborate and concentrate the thing she had to say.

It may be surprising, considering Jewett's reputation for craftsmanship, to observe how little she had been able, up to *Pointed Firs,* to master an art of narrative. She set, of course, high standards for herself: not the current fashion of local-color sketching but the momentous example of *Madame Bovary* supported her choice to write about "simple country people" and dwell upon "trivialities and commonplaces in life" (letter of 12 October, 1890). She matured as a writer in the shadow of Howells and Henry James, and measured herself, as they did, against the nineteenth-century European masters. The new lesson of realism, truthfulness of observation and rendering, was what she started from. The weakness in her early work is of another order—and I am not thinking simply of the patchiness of *Deephaven*, pieced together from magazine sketches. Her stories are deficient precisely as stories; she simply does not manage narrative well. Her most scrupulous observation and delineation cannot conceal, and tend rather to underline, the clumsiness and contrivance of the action. Sequences of unconvincing fantasy ("A White Heron"), co-incidences and fatalities unsupported by a Hardy's profound intuition ("A Lost Lover"), clichés of melodrama ("Marsh Rosemary") are what carry her stories along, from each carefully rendered situation to the next.

It might be argued that she studied too exclusively the sentence of Flaubert which she kept pinned to her work desk: "Écrire la vie ordinaire comme on écrit l'histoire." She might better have taken note of Mark Twain's "How to Tell a Story." The suggestion is not facetious; the mode of narrative Jewett did finally come around to in *Pointed Firs* is much closer to that celebrated by Mark Twain (and stock-in-trade with a host of regional yarn-spinners, journalists, and public entertainers, apprenticed like Twain to a thoroughly artful popular tradition) than to the technique of Flaubert or Henry James. The first-person narrator in *Pointed Firs* tells no stories herself; rather, she sets down stories which are told to her. And much of their "meaning," in fact, is in the struggle of the teller, himself participant, to do justice to the thing he has to tell; and their truth is confirmed in the wavering rhythm of his effort to express himself as his story seems to require. It is in these stories-within-the-story that the major themes of the book are contained; the narrator's part is simply to describe the teller and the situation, to provide the occasion, to give notice of the passing of time—and, at the beginning and end of the book, to lead the reader sympathetically into the legended world of Dunnet Landing and safely, if equivocally, out again when the time comes. Jewett, it might be said, solved her inability to master a Jamesian art of the short story by abandoning it.

Or she realized at last that what she had to tell was one story and one story only, one that all her earlier ones, we see now, lead up to or provide analogies for. Another way of describing her success in the Pointed Firs is to say, in these terms, that she had finally discovered within her materials—anecdotes, incidents, scenes, special cases—the essential legend that was there for her to tell, and found for it an appropriate form. The lineaments of this legend are set down all through her earlier work and letters, and it may be useful at this point to describe them, before going on to describe the structure she set them into in Pointed Firs.

The great event determining all others—rarely treated directly but persistently there as a shaping pressure—is the economic disintegration of the coastal towns, the withering away of the enterprise that gave them life. These towns, unlike the up-country farms and villages more characteristic of the work of Mrs. Stowe and Mrs. Freeman, did once belong to the great world of affairs and owned an oceanic vitality and breadth of prospect.* "Since the Embargo" hangs over Jewett's work like "before the War" over chronicles of the South. There remains no practicable future, and no promise in the present: "all the clocks in Deephaven, and all the people with them, had stopped years ago," and a sandbar fills the harbor mouth. The personal and family energy that went with commerce and community affairs is spent now in nostalgia and regret, in the breeding of "characters," or—as with Yeats's Sligo peasants and fishermen—in the cultivation of visions and voices; when the world of enterprise is sealed off, what remains for restless

---

* A number of Jewett's sketches are set in country villages and farms, but the sea and its harbors and opportunities are almost always there in the background, if only as an outlet, an enlargement of prospect, vanished into the past perhaps but still haunting the present.

minds but the development of unmarketable psychic powers?*
All the signs, however picturesque, betray the long retreat
into backwater stagnation. The wharves rot, the warehouses
fall apart; and though the cottages and their kitchens, cup-
boards, and flowered borders are kept spruce and trim, they
are lived in and tended by the old, the retired, the widowed,
the unmarrying, the sick, the mad, the "uncompanioned."

The people of the region are its strictest measure, and
still another sign of the perfection of Jewett's utterance in
Pointed Firs is her concentration on persons, her resistance to
distracting scenic details. Landscape and local custom, the
anonymous picturesque, are strongly present but now in the
background; the burden of meaning is carried by specific personal histories. The types of character she worked with would
not have been unfamiliar to her readers. It is a commonplace
concerning the later New England local-color writing that
young people rarely figure in it—few children, almost no young
men, even more rarely a young couple. In *Deephaven* an unusual passage of open satire describes an evening lecture on
"Elements of True Manhood," an inspirational discourse "directed entirely toward young men, and there was not a young
man there." Young men of energy and hope are sure to be
from the outside, like the young hunter of "A White Heron,"
and are likely to represent a certain coarseness, a positive danger to the delicate balances of backwater life. For the homegrown the one remaining hope of manhood is to break away
into the great world, again with the imputation, usually, of
coarseness and self-ruination, as with the "lost lover" of Miss
Horatia Dane. Those who stay are the weak and pathetic, the
half-men, shiftless and full of "meechin' talk" like Jerry Lane
of "Marsh Rosemary," whose "many years" older wife knows
herself to be "the better man of the two."

"Ef *I* was a man . . ." she snaps at him contemptuously

---

*See the chapter "Cunner Fishing" in *Deephaven*. In Yeats's *Reveries
of Childhood and Youth,* with its references to the time of Galway's
prosperity in commerce with Spain, there is a corresponding evocation of
bygone economic vigor and the pathos of its passing, and of the warp and
eccentricity that set in by default. The histories of the small ports along
the Maine and Maritimes coast and that of a town like Sligo have more
than a little in common.

—and despairingly. There is no more striking symptom of the blight that has settled on the region than the recasting of customary social roles, particularly the roles of the sexes. The superiority of Jewett's work in the local-color genre—and here, too, *Pointed Firs* marks for her a distinct advance—appears in the combined bluntness and subtlety, the overwhelming indirection, with which she presents a norm of distorted, repressed, unfulfilled or transformed sexuality as an index to her essential story. When there is a marriage, it is like that of Ann Floyd and Jerry Lane: the weak boy marrying for protection and security the vigorous spinster who has the competence and strength of a man. That the marriage is childless and ends in desertion does not come as a surprise. More often there is no marriage at all, simply the desertion, as in "A Lost Lover": here the elderly heroine, whose lover was long ago supposed lost at sea but really ran away, has come to be regarded as a widow and, on the basis of this lie, a person of consequence in the village and in her own eyes; she has achieved position and respect, at the cost of playing a woman's full part.

The men do have the choice to go, though it may destroy them, and only the already defeated or crippled, the childish or womanlike, stay on. But for the women the only choice, the sacrifice required for survival, is to give up a woman's proper life and cover the default of the men, to be the guardians and preservers of a community with no other source of vitality and support. In a society without a future the woman's instinct to carry on the life of the tribe can only be fulfilled by devotion to what remains, and her energies must go to preservation of the past, to intercourse with nature, to disguising and delaying the inevitable dissolution. This is the ambiance even of a story like "A White Heron," in which the heroine is only a little girl. In the presence of the hunter, "the woman's heart, asleep in the child," stirs with a premonition of the power and release of love; but in defense of her mysterious sympathy with wild creatures and her secret knowledge of the heron's sanctuary, she refuses his appeal like a profaning courtship (in his offering her money there is again the imputation of grossness); and the suggestion is made that her whole life will turn on this renunciation.

The story of the region would not be honestly told if the

sexual warping were not brought into it, but it would not be fully told if that were made the main, the decisive, theme of it. Sexuality figures, rather, as one among several of the great natural contingencies determining the forms life must take in this life-abandoned society. Old age and death are another: it is with the aged that the force of decay registers most poignantly. External nature provides the others—thus, perhaps, in the final clarifying of her vision, Jewett's choice of title; and thus, in *The Country of the Pointed Firs*, the steady counter-pointing of personal and tribal histories by the invoked presence not only of the landscape but of season and weather, too, and the incessant audible movement of the sea in its storms and calms, its tidal rise and fall.* Only society is dying, only *human* life: water, rock, woods, birds, vegetation are alive and, in the time we are allowed to look at them, surpassingly beautiful. The season is nearly always early or full summer, and rarely later than the first touch of fall; it is as though winter, reinforcing all too harshly the testimony of the region's economic life, were too terrible to contemplate.

Framed by the vitality of the landscape and the inanition of human affairs, a fight for life goes on through all Jewett's work. The sexual warping is subsumed by this more general tension between the signs of natural power and the signs of impotence and death. In *Deephaven* the one show of "business-like" community life is for a funeral. Ironically the dead man is to the mourners a figure of awe and envy rather than of regret; he is "immeasurably their superior now. Living, he had been a failure . . . but now, if he could come back, he would know secrets, and be wise beyond anything they could imagine, and who could know the riches of which he might have come into possession?" The circumstances of life are such that one must either covet death or (like courteous, bewildered, mad Miss Chauncey in perhaps the best single chapter in *Deephaven*) "disbelieve" in it. The struggle to delay extinction appears, in Jewett's people, exhausting. Human life cannot survive in its customary forms and must be absorbed into the timeless cycles of nature. And even nature may

---

* It is remarkable how near the book comes to the literary naturalist vision of life as determined by the play of great impersonal and uncontrollable forces in nature and society.

be ambiguous. Even summer is not to be trusted. There is an "early summer-tiredness that belongs to New Englanders of the old stock," Sarah Jewett wrote to Sara Norton in 1898. Summer she described ("The Courting of Sister Wisby") as the season which to the New Englander "must always last," must become permanent; that it does not, her own birthday came the third of September to remind her. And in the opening paragraphs of "Sister Wisby," set in late August, she expressed the grievous ephemerality of the upper New England summer with a positively Hawthornean apprehension: under the "cool cloak of bracing air,"

> Every living thing grows suddenly cheerful and strong; it is only when you catch sight of a horror-stricken little maple in swampy soil,—a little maple that has second sight and fore-knowledge of coming disaster to her race,—only then does a distrust of autumn's friendliness dim your joyful satisfaction.

So *Deephaven* ends in falling leaves and bleak autumnal days, though perversely, at the moment of departure, the sun is out again and Indian summer beginning: "we wished that it had been a rainy day." Even in the finest weather the tide will ebb and the sea turn rough, though in the closing sentence of *Deephaven* it is imagined moving and speaking "lazily in its idle, high-tide sleep."

Aspects of the structure of *Pointed Firs,* the definitive order Jewett here devised for her materials, have already been mentioned. There is the main sequence of action and of time —as the book ends with the narrator's departure in early fall, it opens with her arrival in June and moves through the phases of a summer. And there is the counterpointing of human undertakings with the natural setting, a pattern of notation which appears on nearly every page. Spelling this out in full detail, however, would be impractical and not really very helpful, since we would still have to identify the art that keeps it from lapsing into pathetic fallacy; also, this is the part of Jewett's craft which she mastered first and which will not in itself account for the superiority of *Pointed Firs.* It is enough to say that her observation of setting—of the changes of sea and sky, the colors of the landscape and the old buildings, the variety of scenes and views—being accurate and economical, is always convincing, and moreover is never used to claim any feeling or implication not already established in the human sphere; it fills naturally the pauses which mark the passing of time in a place with so much time on its hands.

The principle ordering device is no more complicated or esoteric than those so far mentioned; it is simply the arrangement of chapters and episodes. The twenty-one chapters of *Pointed Firs* (in the only version printed in the author's lifetime; other Dunnet Landing stories were added by later editors) fall into six distinct groupings; thus, between the brief opening and closing sequences there are four main episodes which form the body of the book. Each has, within a scaled-down minimum of incident, its distinguishing quality of feeling and its particular scope of suggestion; and their arrangement, though perfectly casual, does not seem indeliberate.

The first three chapters form the opening section and are used chiefly to get the narrator established in Dunnet Landing and in her own role there. She arrives, she introduces Mrs. Todd, she settles on a vacant hilltop schoolhouse as her place of work. Nothing more has happened, though in a few phrases some of the main themes have been announced—in the "mixture of remoteness, and childish certainty of being the centre of civilization," which is her first impression of the atmosphere of the village, its whole actual history is suggested; in the few sentences on Mrs. Todd's practice of the mysteries of herb lore we are given a first casual symbol of the devices human energy is put to merely to survive in this place; and in the story Mrs. Todd tells the narrator, as intimacy grows between them, of the man she had loved as a girl but could not marry, we are put in touch with the primary myth so many of Jewett's stories of this region make use of, of the man who went out into the world and the woman who stayed behind.

The next three chapters (iv–vi) carry the first of the four main episodes, centering on Captain Littlepage and the story he has to tell. He is seen first at a funeral (which furnishes in a few lines a paradigm of all the counterpointing of people and place—the "futile and helpless" procession winding along the rocky shore under the "clear, high sky" of "a glorious day early in July"), a mysterious figure, aged and worn, "the one strange and unrelated person in all the company." He comes then to the schoolhouse, and as he talks, quoting Milton and Shakespeare and speaking of the old days and the old stock, we are shown a character of intelligence and refinement from which the original strength and air of command have not entirely disappeared. It is he who most bluntly points the contrast between past and present, between the lifeless provincial isolation of the village now and the days when its men, and their wives and children, too, "saw the world for themselves" and "were some acquainted with foreign lands an' their laws." And it is he who declares the plain bitter truth which all the gentleness and sympathy of the narration cannot mitigate, that it is "low water mark now here in Dunnet," and that "there's nothing to take the place of shipping in a place like ours." "There's no large-minded way of thinking now," his lament goes on, and though coming out of the narrowest of circumstances, rises in its own colloquial voice to some of the phrasing, even something of the manner of judgment, of Yeats's oracular "Second Coming": "the worst have got to be best and rule everything; we're all turned upside down and going back year by year." It is Yeats's vision of chaos particularized, given a local history and habitation.

Yet the story Littlepage tells has the effect of ratifying this disaster, this drawing in of the village on itself. It is a tale of "strange events," of an encounter with the outer world so bewildering and terrific as to break a man's strength and wither his ambition. It is a tale within a tale, of a vision in uncharted northern waters of a great town peopled by ghostly human figures that glided out of sight when approached but attacked a boat's crew of men as they tried to get away. "A place where there was neither living nor dead," Captain Littlepage says, "a kind of waiting place between this world an' the next." In some ways this is the boldest and most decisive passage in the book, for it secures that reference to the life of male action and encounter without which the narrator's sympathy for backwater Dunnet would seem myopic, sentimental. It is simply an old man's hallucination, yet also a fable of the ungovernable anonymous forces which have closed the village off from life and the world. This fearful midworld is what those who go out from a Dunnet Landing must enter; good reason then to choose to stay home, even though it must be to wither and stiffen in a setting which, in its mild and permissive way, is only another kind of midworld, halfway over to death.

Mrs. Todd has a rational explanation for Captain Littlepage's stories: too much reading has affected his mind. Yet the narrator makes a point of showing her disturbed by them, and at the beginning of the second of the four main episodes, we are brought up short by the same metaphor: the sunlight falling on Green Island, where Mrs. Todd's mother lives heartily on, "like a sudden revelation of *the world beyond this* which some believe to be so near" (my italics). The analogy to Littlepage's city of ghosts seems unmistakable. Ultimately, in *Pointed Firs,* there is no disguising what sort of equivocal refuge from the onset of life and death even the loveliest sanctuary provides.

But for the most part this second episode (chaps. vii-xi) sounds a less troubled note. Here indeed we feel at its strongest the power of nature along this coast to sustain an equable condition of life. The action is of the simplest: on one of the fine mornings of early summer, the narrator goes out to Green Island with Mrs. Todd for a day's visit. The loveliness of the island and the vivacity of its octogenarian mistress, Mrs. Blackett, set the tone for the idyll of these chapters. If Dunnet Landing is provincial and isolated, what must Green Island be, "so apparently neighborless and remote"? A world unto itself, the narrator says, "a complete and tiny continent," a place where "it was impossible not to wish to stay on forever," a retreat fostering "that final, that highest gift of heaven," that "perfect self-forgetfulness" which is the secret of Mrs. Blackett's power of survival. The pasturage is thin but sweet; there are wild flowers and shrubs, sheep and fishing weirs, and the trim, immaculate, hospitable house with its unused best parlor and sociable kitchen; and from the height of land, in the climactic passage closing chapter ix, a grand view opens out over the whole coast: "It gave a sudden sense of space, for nothing stopped the eye or hedged one in,—that sense of liberty in space and time which great prospects always give."

Life and space, an unconstricted prospect—these are the notes sounded in the Green Island chapters. The opposing conditions are not forgotten, and are to have their due soon enough; here, however, they are softened, and serve to make what is to be valued at Green Island the more attractive. Treated differently, Mrs. Blackett's son William, the child-like man of sixty whose mother must still speak for him in company, could have been used to overset all that is claimed through the old mother and her snug retreat. Instead Jewett is concerned to give in William the impression of a life which, far from having been wasted by its circumstances, has found its only possible security there. The one positively disquieting note is in the story Mrs. Todd is moved to tell, being caught off guard by the charm of the moment and place, of her courtship and marriage long ago—of her inability to love her honest husband as she was loved, of his death at sea and the long widowhood in which their marriage has come to be no more than a dream to her. So even in this sanctuary of life and space, death and time intrude, in deprivations and constrained adjustments.* But at the end of the episode the narrator comes back to the wide view from Mrs. Blackett's bedroom, a "place of peace" and "quiet outlook upon field and sea and sky," and to the pungent savor of the herb garden mixing with the sea wind, the signs of an ineradicable vitality.

The next section exactly reverses the major and minor themes of the Green Island sequence; in this counter-idyll death and time are the keynotes, and life and spaciousness belong only to the indifferent presences of nature. Significantly we come forward in these chapters (xii-xv) into dry August, past the freshness of early summer. Again a story is recalled from older times, the stage being set in the intermediate twelfth chapter as the narrator listens to Mrs. Todd and her visitor Mrs. Fosdick tolling the past, recording the lives and the changes, deaths without entrances. Their story is of "poor Joanna," and like the preceding episode has its corroborative setting: this is Shell-heap Island, a forbidding inaccessible place with "a different look from any of the other islands,"

---

* Just here we have the much-cited image of Mrs. Todd as an "Antigone alone on the Theban plain," possessed by "an absolute, archaic grief" in the contemplation of unfulfilled tribal pieties and duties, a figure often praised but more for verifying the classical seriousness of Jewett's art than for its obvious appropriateness to her main theme.

and the object, with its Indian relics, of much local superstition and legend: "a dreadful small place to make a world of."

Here in solitude lived Joanna Todd, "a sort of nun or hermit person"—and as Captain Littlepage's story may be taken as a parable of a man's options in this country, Joanna's is an archetype of the woman's. Hers is the region's primary fable, of the girl "full o' feeling" who lost her man to the outer world and whose life was closed off before it had begun; in desolation she put off alone for Shell-heap Island, never to return. The rising tempo of the old woman's recollection is deftly used to establish the gravity of the story. At first reluctant to tell it out, Mrs. Todd soon takes it up with the absorption and unself-consciousness of a ritual performance. She had been one of the first to see Joanna after her withdrawal out of the world; and one of the freighted climaxes of the book comes in Mrs. Todd's account of how, after a blundering minister had spoken his cold word, she caught up Joanna in her arms and begged her to come back into life with her. Joanna's refusal, her conviction that she had "committed the unpardonable sin" ("We don't seem to hear nothing about that now," Mrs. Fosdick remarks), is like the obsession of Captain Littlepage, pitiable perhaps but not lacking nobility. Without ignoring anything of the eccentricity and barrenness of these lives, Jewett succeeded in *Pointed Firs* in heightening them, not to tragedy exactly, but to a moving solemnity, confirming as by a pageant, a *tableau vivant,* their impersonal necessity and their vulnerability, despite all show of endurance, to time and death.

As before, a balance is kept in this episode between the contrasting themes. So Joanna's utter "loneliness of sorrow" comes to us through Mrs. Todd's robust compassion. So, too, in a coda to her story, in which the narrator pays her own visit to Shell-heap Island, time and death, though not denied authority over life, are briefly displaced as the sheer physical presence of the island brings Joanna's story alive in the narrator's imagination; and in a final passage that recalls the eloquent last paragraph of Chapter 58 of *Moby-Dick,* Joanna's life is presented as no more than the familiar norm of our human condition: "In the life of each of us . . . there is a place remote and islanded, and given to endless regret or secret happiness; we are each the uncompanioned hermit and recluse of an hour or a day; we understand our fellows of the cell to whatever age of history they may belong."

One more main episode remains, as the season now draws on to an end. Again the keynote changes; now the stress is back on the sedulous human bustle and not, for a time, on its constriction and fatality. This is the Bowden family reunion, plainly symbolic, on which virtually the whole population of the region converges as if to renew its stubborn hold on life. There is room now for relaxations of humor, for genre comedy, as the clans gather and their "characters" go on display—the doctor's rivalry with Mrs. Todd's herb practice, Cousin Sant Bowden's military drill-mastering, the huddling over family resemblances, and so on. But the cheerfulness and bustle speak for deeper forces, too, and the narrator is prompt to interpret them: they indicate "the hidden fire of enthusiasm" which is not yet gone out of the New England nature but, "once given an outlet . . . shines forth with almost volcanic light and heat," breaking through "the granite dust in which our souls are set." The "transfiguring powers" we are asked to credit to this occasion are verified in the narrator's account of the solemn slow procession into the waterside picnic grove, moving for all the world, she observes, like a company of pagans going out to worship some "god of harvests":

> It was strangely moving to see this and to make part of it. The sky, the sea, have watched poor humanity at its rites so long; we were no more a New England family celebrating its own existence and simple progress; we carried the tokens and inheritance of all such households from which this had descended, and were only the latest of our line. We possessed the instincts of a far, forgotten childhood; I found myself thinking that we ought to be carrying green branches and singing as we went.

A focal passage, clearly—and though the reunion subsides into crotchety gossip and frayed tempers, its weight of suggestion carries through. For once, before straggling back to their isolated individual struggles merely to endure, these people have acted together as a living community and asserted their life as a continuing race. Against "the waste of human ability in this world" which their lives betray, they have made at least a show of the "reserve force of society."

After this, the common fate having been conspired against by this ritual of postponement, the narrator may take her leave. But the end of the book is not quite yet. If I am insisting on the deliberateness of form in *Pointed Firs*, I do not mean that it is rigidly or arithmetically calculated. There is one more chapter (xx), before the last, that does not belong to any particular phase of the summer, as do the episodes already described, and that does not take in charge any one particular concentration of feeling. It begins as little more than a character sketch; indeed the first rendering of Elijah Tilley ("such an evasive, discouraged-looking person, heavy-headed and stooping," chirping in suitable dialect about "haddick" and baked potatoes) seems mildly condescending like nothing else in the narrative so far. But as it moves into Mr. Tilley's house and the openhearted flow of his talk, the dignity of an unobtrusive pathos is resumed, and we are given a summary image of the equivocal devisings life has come to in this place.

He is one of the last survivors of the old time, one whose mind now seems "fixed upon nature and the elements rather than upon any contrivances of man." Like Mrs. Todd and Mrs. Blackett, Littlepage and Joanna, he has found his own way of holding on against the ebbing of the old vitality. His life, however, is different in one respect from all the others, in being wholly devoted, quite unreconciled, to the lost forms of human society that once sustained it. His main energy and skill go to serving the memory of his dead wife and keeping up their house as she left it—knitting, mending, making shift, missing her without abatement, and talking of nothing else. His recital becomes an elegy not only for the dead woman and for their life together, but for all the lives and households in the country of the pointed firs, by this old man who has come to be both wife and husband in his house (as William Blackett is both son and daughter in his) and by this shift has forestalled to the limit of his capacity the ruinous work of time; a "ploddin' man," as Mrs. Todd must say of him, but also, through the entirety of his absorption, a transfigured one. A final image of Mrs. Todd, in the short last chapter, catches up the implication of Mr. Tilley's manner of life and indeed of all the personal histories which Jewett's book is constructed from—we see her as a figure "mateless and appealing," yet "strangely self-possessed."

All form is "significant," but some forms, to borrow a cadence, are more significant than others. A demonstration of structural wholeness does not prove, nor does it explain, the impressiveness of a piece of writing. Examining structure or design, we find ourselves judging substance and implication as well—and no doubt operating from prejudgments (usually unspoken though not necessarily not understood) as to interest and worth. There is nothing illegitimate in this. How else do we identify the specific gravity and bearing, the importance, of a work? We judge certain perceptions more commanding than others; we scarcely bother to *raise* questions of art or the lack of it unless our serious attention is commanded.

What is it then in Jewett's *Pointed Firs* that does so command attention, that secures the impression not only of integrity but of importance, and so of the durability Willa Cather claimed for it? The book, we observe, proceeds through a sequence of personal histories and personal encounters. Yet the specific events, one by one, are too slight to produce much more than anecdotal pathos; what gives them body and interest is their insistent revelation of a more general order of existence. Particular persons have been put sharply before us, yet our feeling for their lives, though warm enough, is curiously impersonal; our interest in them is less as personalities than as examples, as case histories.

In this respect *Pointed Firs* is no special case. In most of the best "local-color" writing, as even in more ambitious work like Anderson's *Winesburg*, the interest in character is negligible—that is, as "character" is properly understood in fiction: persons moved through a convincing range of human response to moral (behavioral) decision or commitment. Instead there is an interest in line-drawing, or in caricature—a sociological interest, essentially. If *Pointed Firs* is exceptional as a work of art, it is so only through perfection of its genre; in substance and implication it is sociological, and historical. The powerful compulsions of American civil life have always been too ambiguous and diverse, and too relentlessly novel, to be easily registered and identified; what the restricted focus of "regionalism" has provided in our literature is a way of bringing them to expression and putting them in some sort of objective judgment. So a great part of what holds us to a *Pointed Firs* or a *Winesburg* is the clarity and accuracy of their testimony as to the experience of these compulsions and urgencies which in our civilization have traditionally worked (so witnesses as different as Tocqueville and Poe, Mark Twain and Henry Adams, Jewett and Anderson, have told us) to sap private morale, obliterate individuality, and transform persons into grotesque natural phenomena.

To say then that *Pointed Firs* is a masterpiece of the local-color school (its only peer would seem to be "Old Times on the Mississippi") is not at all to talk it down. The work of this school, the bulk of it produced between 1870 and 1900, constitutes a potentially powerful criticism of the main directions of American life. Set sometimes in the past and recalled from the perspective of a transformed present, and sometimes in some backwater of the present seen from the turbulent mainstream, these books hold up for inspection (occasionally satirical, more often affectionate and elegiac) some local pattern of community life which has already vanished or is on the point of vanishing and which in its isolation and decay gives off a luminous but pathetic (if not terrible) beauty—the flush of dying. These are the "jolly corners" of American life (Henry James, not equipped to look in the usual places, found them at Washington Square as well), and in the best of the literature that celebrates them there is not only a compassionate response to their ill fortune but also a knowledgeable criticism of what has overtaken them. In the very best the criticism returns upon the region itself—the jolly corner proves to be the very center of dread—and we find expressed a fatalism beyond nostalgia or irony, a sense of American life as requiring, as being *founded* upon, the pitiless extinction of the past, the violent extirpation of amenity and beauty and of every temporary establishment of that truly civil order which is the earliest of American dreams.*

---

* It does not seem accidental that the fashion of local-color writing coincided with the heyday of agrarian populism and the beginnings of

The art of *Pointed Firs* reaches this order of revelation—a rare enough achievement. The very conditions in our civilization which provoke such books and such judgments act also to deprive them of body and cogency. Instead of an intelligible and practicable criticism, what we are likely to get from even our most conscientious talents is self-pity and hysteria. Performances and lives which in England, under similar provocation, have traditionally turned eccentric yet still can make themselves felt along the central axis, have tended rather in our centerless country to fly off the handle altogether. A hysterical assertion of special fears and delusions, and of special privileges and immunities from the main course of our democratic, technological, acquisitive society underlies more than just our local-color writing. Not only New England spinsters but national dignitaries—statesmen, evangelists, bankers, editors of great newspapers, men of letters and scholarship—are driven to extremes of nostalgic fantasy, and yearn for imaginary pasts with a violence matched only by their will to overlook the real one. The claiming of permanence and sovereign value for the most obviously adventitious and unsavory conditions is the national disease of what more than one of our writers has divined to be a nation of confidence men, self-deluded and destroying.

The consequences for the imagination are immense and inescapable. Is there one among our significant writers whose very life has not been a self-conscious, energy-consuming struggle to get and stay on some sort of center without going dead? Is there one of our classic books which is not in good part a critique, or a confession, of this hysteria, an exposure of these false parturitions of the spirit and of the civilization that compulsively generates them? Ours is a literature that springs, when it springs at all, from violent contradictions of idealized feeling, that makes a specialty of sudden fruitions and melancholy aftermaths, that knows—with ambiguous exceptions like

---

muckrake journalism. All responded to the same intuitions about American society. Where populists and muckrakers put out warnings of what industrial, metropolitan, corporate society was getting the country into, the local colorists projected images of what the country was being led away from, what was being destroyed in the process. Frequently there was a pooling of effort, as in Mrs. Freeman's *The Portion of Labor* or Lincoln Steffens' charming account of his California childhood.

Henry James—no middle ground between extraordinary originality and equally extraordinary tastelessness, self-imitation, banality. A pragmatical literature, we might call it, one rarely able to live (and this is a source of strength as well as a limitation) except in immediate contact with its undistilled and unprimed sources of feeling. So all but a few of its finest books, and *Pointed Firs* is a perfect instance, ground their strength and appeal, and find their form, not in some objective order of thought or judgment but in a tenuous *ad hoc* balancing of intense and contradictory emotion, a balance or tension which, as it can give surprising authority to a style like Jewett's that otherwise follows a conventional rhetoric, requires in the first place a rare artfulness to get control of and maintain; which may achieve for the space of a single work the creating and sustaining force of some deep-grounded formal idea, yet will barely submit to argument or rational analysis.

Jewett's ultimate art in *Pointed Firs* is to sustain this creative balance of crossed feelings; to make for her materials a claim of value and permanence but to show it as a hopeless claim. Readers of her letters and other work know that she was not free of certain "hysterias" of her time and society.* Her judgments of present and past antedated her proving them in her art. But prove them she did—by making them as impersonal as the sympathy we are brought to feel for her characters; by suffusing them with the durable colors of legend, the solemnity of history. *The Country of the Pointed Firs* is a small work but an unimprovable one, with a secure and unrivaled place in the main line of American literary expression.

* See Ferman Bishop, "Sarah Orne Jewett's Ideas of Race," *New England Quarterly,* xxx (June, 1957) .

Edmund Wilson and His Civil War

From soon after 1920, when he began contributing critical articles to various New York journals, Edmund Wilson has been a conspicuous and influential figure in American letters. When some years ago he took the risk of reprinting in two fat volumes close to two hundred periodical essays written between the early 1920's and late 1940's, and written each time with the steadfast journalistic purpose of producing something readable and plainly interesting, the result confirmed a rough sense that had been gathering in the the minds of readers for a quarter of a century: that for nearly every important development in contemporary writing Edmund Wilson was in some way a spokesman—an arbiter of taste, a supplier of perspective, at the least (to adapt his own phrase for Hemingway) a gauge of intellectual morale. Time and again, reading *Classics and Commercials* (1950) and especially *The Shores of Light* (1952), one would find that judgments formulated under pressure of the weekly deadline had proved to be both just and durable; that they somehow contained that sense of the matter which academic historians of literature, with all the advantages of hindsight, were still groping after.

Read as a lecture at Cornell University, June, 1962; several paragraphs are reprinted from EDMUND WILSON, University of Minnesota Pamphlets on American Writers, No. 67.

This in turn renewed the respect long granted the earlier series of books of critical commentary in which Wilson, with the instinct of a skillful publicist, had concentrated the attention of inquisitive common readers on some significant general development in the arts, or in contemporary history, and in the understanding of both. There had been *Axel's Castle* (1931), with its matter-of-fact demonstration of how the difficult modern practice of symbolism and formal experimentation clearly belonged to the mainstream of European literary development; *To the Finland Station* (1940), attempting a kind of natural history of revolutionary Marxism; *The Wound and the Bow* (1941), casually assuming a natural alliance between the criticism of literary works and the psychological inquiry into their authors' motivations; and *The Triple Thinkers* (1938), open-mindedly alert to the great variety of ways in which that queer monster the artist (along with that even queerer monster the artist *manqué*) could manage to be seriously interesting. In theme no one of these books was particularly like any of the others. But all bore the marks of the same firm and vigorous hand. Almost never did Edmund Wilson repeat himself, in the tiresome manner of the special pleader, the critic with one string to his bow. In fact, this diversity became established as one of the principal merits of Wilson's writing; this, and his evident willingness to do the spadework necessary for dealing intelligently with each new subject. His constant virtue was to write as if literature and the discussion of literature were not a bit less various and interesting than life itself, and not a bit less important; that is to say, not less worthy the full attention of that ideal civil intelligence to which no actual phenomenon appears without significance, deserving to be looked into with the appropriate concern.

In so operating Edmund Wilson never bothered much to disguise his prejudices and the play of personal taste and distaste in his reactions. More than once he was led to assert unfashionable judgments which he could not carry off in the argumentative detail. Actually he made a strength of this defect, if such it was; in the long run it seemed a further guarantee of that personal engagement with his subjects which gave weight to his opinions even among those who might find them finally unsatisfactory.

But what has been the guiding principle of Wilson's literary journalism? That there is one seems to me beyond doubt, though at the time of Stanley Edgar Hyman's dubiously motivated polemic in *The Armed Vision* (1948), it was apparently possible to count on a general impression to the contrary; perhaps it still is. In operation, moreover, the principle or, better, purpose that I find in his work seems on the whole more alert to the actual situation of literature in the present age—as an affair of *these* writers and *this* reader, struggling within such and such practical circumstances—than, say, the more methodically formulated principles of those American critics whose work may be grouped with, or was schooled in, the so-called New Criticism.

What Edmund Wilson's writing has always served—and here we may think of all he has done besides criticism: travel books and social reportage, a novel, a collection of stories, several plays, parodies and topical verse in abundance, editorial introductions, reminiscence, personal opinion, educational theory, studies of culture survivals like the Zuñi and Iroquois, and chronicles of quite unclassifiable matters such as the discovery of the Dead Sea scrolls or his own discoveries as a student of Hebrew—is nothing less than Literature itself, in the broadest, the proper, sense of the term. He *believes* in literature as a humane activity, an index to civilization. Or, if "belief" seems the wrong sort of word, he trusts it to the point of choosing to live by it. (Recall his celebration, in "The Historical Interpretation of Literature," of all those before him who truly revered "the priesthood of literature.") And in so doing he bestows upon it and positively renews for it something of that vital efficacy, within the fabric of civilization, the idea of which we usually think to associate only with the great imaginative masters but which must survive at a lower level of everyday effort if it is to survive at all. Edmund Wilson does not limit "literature," in the manner of university assignments and publishers' anthologies, to prize performances in standard genres. He spreads his net to anything written in such a way as to convey some measure of accurate knowledge and foster some sort of useful understanding; in such a way, too, as to maintain the serviceability of ordinary language to both ends. He is genuinely interested in what is being done and whether it is being done well.

This generosity of attention deserves the praise it has received. Clearly there have been, among his contemporaries, more deeply reflective critics, more original inquirers into theoretical issues. But has there been anyone who has done so much to keep the whole literary establishment going? Wilson's great service is to have been (to borrow the handy mistranslation of Malraux's title) a museum without walls—a museum of idiosyncratic design in some respects, but open to all, immensely stimulating to visit regularly, and generally reliable in what it mounts for display.

Now if we consider the matter, it may seem curious that a literary critic should be singled out for praise in these terms. There should be a dozen Edmund Wilsons—readers of books whom we can trust to do their job with reasonably open and informed minds, reporting accurately on what they have read and bringing to their work a range of interests no broader than what ought to be possessed by any accredited university graduate; who know a few languages and can learn more; who are interested in past history and contemporary society, in philosophy, religion, art, popular entertainment, human character and psychology, nature and scientific method, and so on; and who in particular (as distinguished from technicians and clerks) have a trained feeling for the catalytic power of imaginative inquiry organized into responsible forms of presentation, the feeling, that is, for literature. But there is only one such figure that we can so quickly think of, and that this one continues to be widely known as our "most important critic" is a matter of particular interest. It bears looking into further.

I have mentioned Wilson's evident willingness, as the curious American phrase goes, to do his homework.* Of course his learning is pragmatic. He finds out what he needs to know

---

* I think this is a real and major virtue, and do not endorse the objection that much of this *ad hoc* learning is at second hand. It has been suggested that Wilson relies heavily on the writings of less well-known and more conscientious scholars and does not always make clear the character of his borrowings. On this point it may simply be said that Edmund Wilson does not write with the thesis-candidate's built-in anxiety about originality and property rights; that he accepts the collaborative nature of

to develop his argument and then works up that knowledge. That the resulting display of erudition over a wide range of topics astonishes many academic scholars is a comment on academic scholars, who as a class at least, as Wilson has justly remarked, do not like to read very much. He should not be too severe on this point, however. A mind of taste and imagination can get nearly as chary of reading new work as creative writers are—a notoriously lazy or evasive breed when it comes to reading. The temptation is to skim, as Wilson admits is the case with himself, or, with masterpieces, to put off and put off again the renewed encounter; for when you know how absorbed it is possible to get and what fundamental changes in apprehension may follow from giving your whole attention to a great work, you may after a while start inventing excuses not to.

My point is simply this: the importance we rightly attribute to Edmund Wilson's work is one more sign of the continuing disorder not only of criticism but of the whole estate of literature in our time. Behind us in the earlier twentieth century lies a brilliant creative period, and, somewhat nearer, an exceptionally inventive period in criticism and literary theory; yet all the while our confidence in the efficacy of letters and of fresh creative effort in general has been silently withering. What has been lost is not just a conviction that literature will help to bring us a better life, that it will transform society or fulfill personal development or even, in Arnold's poignant claim for poetry, "interpret life for us, console us, sustain us." Worse than that: we find ourselves less and less able to believe that literature has sufficient power even to manage its own survival and maintain some minimal and admittedly useless existence *en soi*.

---

knowledge; that his service to literature-in-general includes keeping up with scholarly writing and testing it like other serious work, so that characteristically a book like *Patriotic Gore,* on the literature of the Civil War, offers among other things a kind of rough survey of the quality of academic scholarship in the field of his concern.

On the other hand, in a review of *Patriotic Gore* (*New England Quarterly*, December, 1962), Professor Charles H. Foster noted that in transforming *New Yorker* review-essays into the chapters of his book, Wilson had often "trimmed away" references to the scholarship on which his findings were partly based and in several instances had puzzlingly obscured the provenance of his interpretations.

At the death of Yeats in 1939, Auden could say casually that poetry makes nothing happen, being confident that it would at least survive "in the valley of its saying"; but demoralization has now gone radically deeper, if not yet all the way. Edmund Wilson has successfully resisted this demoralization, without sacrificing his specifically literary intelligence. It may well be that such resistance has taken a certain obtuseness and vanity on his part—the same amount needed, say, to support his pretensions as a writer of verse and drama —stemming from that self-assurance which Alfred Noyes would remember from Princeton in 1914–1915 (see *Two Worlds for Memory*), making Noyes doubt "whether it had ever occurred to him that he could possibly be wrong." The defects of Wilson's solid virtues are considerable and must be thought about.* But the essential fact remains: that he has served the collective enterprise of literature in his day with an extraordinary energy and faithfulness. By continuing to act as if it was alive and kicking, he has helped it as much as any writer of his time actually to remain so. His whole career has been a kind of optimistic gamble: he has bet on literature and its survival—literature as it was in those rich epochs of human creativity that produced the work his own strong appetite as a reader was nurtured on—and he has never seriously hedged this bet.

It may be added that he has always done his job with a contagious show of willingness and spirit. The way he characterized himself in his "All-Star Literary Vaudeville" of 1926 identifies his outlook still. He is one who has felt "a certain human sympathy" with all manifestations of literary activity, "even with those of which, artistically, he disapproves." It is a source of deep gratification to him when literature is "sold" to the public, and he is happy to be known as one who "on principle, in the face of alien attack . . . will stand by even the least intelligent, the least disinterested, of its salesmen: he has served in that army himself."

---

* They have always been there. If they had not, it is questionable whether Scott Fitzgerald would have accepted Wilson as, so he said, his "literary conscience." The real threat to his own integrity of mind and imagination that a more original, more profound intelligence would have posed, Fitzgerald would surely have found intolerable.

If there remains a persistent core of doubt about Wilson's value as a critic, it surely concerns his working method, and the depth and freedom of mind from which that method derives. He is essentially descriptive in his approach. He tells the story of lives and careers, he summarizes plots, he paraphrases arguments and tabulates symbols; he practices psychological portraiture, classification by genre, structural comparison, and other incidental skills. But he does not analyze, or sufficiently persist in analysis; he does not measure and weigh the constituent ideas; he does not inquire, except biographically, into the whole logic and mode of existence of the works he surveys. In short, for all his devotion to the idea of literature, he does not address directly the specifically literary, architectonic virtues his arguments assume. His interest regularly turns off to the special matter of the psychology of literary behavior. What was it like to have been this or that author at the moment of composing such and such a work? On this ground, taking literature as a species of personal expression, Wilson addresses himself to what appears before him, what is given, and describes it according to his lights. But he is without the tenacity of interest—the interest not only in what is but in what could be or might be or even should be—that makes the great critic, the writer on literature who will transform taste and alter the very foundations of critical judgment.

There is point to such reservations—certainly we must distinguish between Wilson's service to critical understanding in his time and the service of a Coleridge, a Henry James, an Eliot—but first the virtues of his manner may be considered. Who his models have been is not difficult to discover. He has been explicit about them, and insofar as they have also served as models for his justly admired prose style, with its clarity, efficiency, and steady forwarding energy, we cannot say offhand that they have been bad models. One of the most important was his teacher at Princeton, Christian Gauss; and in Wilson's memorial account of the style of Gauss's teaching we find a clear statement of his own critical procedure. The special quality in Gauss, Wilson writes, was "the unusual fluidity of mind that he preserved through his whole career." As against a dogmatist like Irving Babbitt, Gauss was the kind of teacher "who starts trains of thought that he does not himself guide to conclusions but leaves in the hands of his students to be carried on by themselves." Moreover, "his own ideas on any subject were always taking new turns: the light in which he saw it would be shifted, it would range itself in some new context." Gauss knew a great deal about a great many things, and had the knowledge of languages to back up his literary and historical learning. But he carried this learning unostentatiously. His easy manner, his level voice, Wilson says (apparently without irony), "made a kind of neutral medium in which everything in the world seemed soluble."

The result was an impression of "extreme flexibility and enormous range," of a mind whose powers could be brought to bear with equal force on any important subject, and in describing Gauss's method Wilson is clearly projecting a view, and an accurate one, of his own. Gauss, he writes, was "able to explain and appreciate almost any kind of work of literature from almost any period. He would show you what the author was aiming at and the methods he had adopted to achieve his ends." And he had "a knack of fixing in one's mind key passages and key facts." At the same time he was distinctly at his best in presenting an established figure whose relative stature and significance might be open to more questions than he cared to deal with but whose claim to attention was not in the least in doubt. Rousseau is the example Wilson cites, and in his account of how Gauss would highlight the main incidents in Rousseau's career—a writer whom students were likely to find boring—"by a series of incisive strokes that [nevertheless] involved no embroidery or dramatics," we see what the technique was. Gauss would bring a Rousseau forward to the turning point; the moment when, going to visit Diderot in prison, he decided to compete for the essay prize on the question whether progress in the arts and sciences had tended to corrupt or to purify society; that moment when he set out for the "Finland station" of his life's progress. Gauss also set a standard for style that Wilson respected and mastered: "he made us all want to write something in which every word, every cadence, every detail, should perform a definite function in producing an intense effect."

Another of Wilson's models of critical procedure (leaving aside models of style and intellectual temper, like Shaw,

Samuel Butler, Renan, H. L. Mencken) was Saintsbury, and again, professing admiration for Saintsbury's *Encyclopædia Britannica* articles, he gives us a clear passage of self-definition, praising those "wonderful feats of condensation that manage, in summarizing a lifetime, to include a maximum of detail and, in their briefly expressed comments, to hit all the nails on the head." Saintsbury was "perhaps the only English critic, with the possible exception of Leslie Stephen, whose work is comparable, for comprehensiveness and brilliance, to the great French critics [Taine in particular] of the nineteenth century." But Wilson also remarks that unlike these latter, Saintsbury "has no interest in ideas"—and we recall our core of doubt about Wilson's own performance. He himself clearly has had an *interest* in ideas. But it has been an oddly acquiescent and derivative interest. He observes ideas, like natural phenomena; he wonders what compels men to take them up, and he is impressed by the power that derives from them; but he does not seem to *think* with them, or about them, or make them, even provisionally, his own. He does not seem to have imagined what exactly it means to say that thought, in our own case as well as for those history presents, must be proved in experience.

Wilson has always seemed admirably free of ideological prejudice and precommitment, and especially alert to how other lives and minds may be warped by them, which is one reason why he has been so effective a natural historian of the literary life. But there is something perfunctory about this liberal curiosity of his, something curiously automatic and self-enclosed. What Santayana said once about American open-mindedness in general applies to it: that it can too easily turn into "a habit of doting on everything"—everything, that is, that happens to have caught its attention; that it derives from a personal assurance it never stops to test, which is that "the forces that determine fortune are not yet too complicated for one man to explore"; and that it trusts its own casual habituations as it trusts nothing else, because it has always been able to do so "safely and prosperously." Reading a lot of Edmund Wilson's criticism at one time, what we may come to notice is less and less the free play of this curiosity and the insights and discoveries it leads him to, and more and more the *a priori* assurance it rests on—and in this regard the model for his

critical method and the mind which most resembles his own
(or which his own most resembles) is that of his father, the
Red Bank, New Jersey, lawyer to whom, a few years ago, he
devoted the last section of his personal memoir, *A Piece of
My Mind* (1956).

For it is very much a *type* of mind that Wilson's writing
gives voice to, a distinctly American type perhaps, at least a
familiar and important one in both American literature and
American public life. An otherwise excellent study of his
career written some years ago by Norman Podhoretz labeled
him "the last patrician," which is of course inaccurate; whoever our American patricians may be, they have not had a great
deal to do with our serious literature. His mold is rather his
father's—the mold of the independent, freethinking professional man, in this case of the type of the town or small-city
lawyer (a newspaper editor or certain types of businessman
would do just as well; a doctor, teacher, minister less well) ;
the man of broad but not particularly fine taste, with a strong
and confident habit of mind and with pride in his judgment,
who is skillful at dossiers, presentations of essential evidence,
summings-up; something of a dissenter but according to no
easily predictable pattern; conservatively radical, out of an
unshakable assurance as to his own position; a leader of
opinion used to making himself listened to, but not likely to be
aware that among those who know him well, as opposed to the
general public, a kind of silent resistance is steadily building
up; a champion not so much of the lost cause as of the accidentally unpopular or unfashionable one, whom we visualize finally
as Edmund Wilson portrays his father: "explaining at length,
but with an expert lucidity, some basic point of law or government."

He is curious, this type, and he is unshockable, but while
it is impossible not to admire him, it is equally impossible to
admire him without considerable reservation. For we see that
his curiosity and liberality are of a special kind. These are the
postures of the professionally privileged and established old
resident—we picture him on a balcony or at an upstairs window
overlooking his town, the county seat perhaps or some larger
capital—beset sometimes by a degree of uneasiness at certain
changes in progress below but not compelled to add them all

up and arrive at a genuinely new sum. There he perches, coolly examining the credentials of old-timers and newcomers alike as they pass in review; examining them shrewdly and fairly, to be sure, but nevertheless with the limited purposes of a descriptive chronicler of settlement, and tending to accept at their own valuation those who speak his language and who, in his own best manner, manage to look after themselves. Here again Wilson's portrait of his father mirrors his own case and identifies something central to his whole effort as a critic:

> The reason for his success [as a lawyer] was undoubtedly that he never undertook a case which he did not think he could win, and that his judgment about this was infallible. In court, he attacked the jury with a mixture of learning, logic, dramatic imagination and eloquence which he knew would prove irresistible. He would cause them to live through the events of the crime or supposed crime, he would take them through the steps of the transaction, whatever this was, and he would lodge in their heads a picture that it was difficult for his opponent to expel.

Such a man is hard to argue with; one can only point to what has been left out of account, provided of course that one has sufficient knowledge of the case oneself and has not been hypnotized into overlooking the omissions.

This breed of the professional, moderately freethinking and highly self-regarding, middle-class intelligence, a breed long dominant in American cultural life though latterly having more and more trouble keeping its balance and adjusting to irreversible changes in status, is an exceptionally interesting one, particularly in literature, of which it has been almost sole producer and consumer. Of course it no more constricts its best representatives than any class background. For this reason it shows most purely in the second-best and third-best. Among contemporaries James Gould Cozzens has been a pluperfect representative of it, which is to suggest his characteristic virtues as a novelist and also his startling limitations. Wright Morris is another, much more congenial but, by comparison, somewhat weightless. Certain woman novelists who made their way into professional careers seem conspicuous examples of it: Edith Wharton, in an exotic sort of self-made way not at all incompatible with being a social lioness or with an ability to criticize the breed with a vengeance in her cold-hearted male characters (small wonder Edmund Wilson wanted "justice" for her) ; Willa Cather and Ellen Glasgow more obviously. John Dos Passos has had an odd and eventually debilitating lover's quarrel with its outlook. Faulkner's alter ego in his later books, the lawyer-monologuist Gavin Stevens; that part of Hemingway that never escaped being his doctor-father's son and the apprentice to several cynical-sentimental city editors; Wallace Stevens through a number of fantastic disguises—all seem birthright communicants of this breed of mind. It forms the collective fate they have had, as individuals, to overcome.

Now this mind has many admirable virtues. It is intelligent and accurate. It can be trained into great practical skill. It will give steady, efficient, profitable performance. It admires things worth admiring; it has a sense of "excellence" (a favorite word in its pedagogic-administrative department, as with Mr. John Gardner) ; it is alert to prevailing tendencies. It understands Darwinism and Freudianism—it used to understand Marxism—and modern anthropology and the theory of the genetic code and epistemological paradoxes and the notion of relativity. It is at ease with literary and philosophical classics, and is given to quoting Shakespeare, Milton, the Bible (particularly Job and Ecclesiastes) , the Golden Treasury, Dr. Johnson, Voltaire, and others among what Mr. Cozzens once referred to, unaffectedly enough, as "the best minds of sixty centuries." It only lacks the ability to see beyond itself. And it is not so much without the power to do this as without the inward incentive, the imaginative will. For it is finally an arrogant and airless mind. It is acquainted with a great many ideas and sends its children to schools where great ideas are cherished and enshrined in a dignified curriculum; it has in fact taken over the universities; but ideas become things to it, counters to score with. Its besetting sin is, in a word, *knowingness,* which is its substitute for imaginative freedom and the passion of irreversible creative conviction. And whatever else knowingness is good for, it cannot cure itself; it cannot intercede against those particular afflictions, "complacency and resentment," which Camus in a late essay identified as peculiar to the writer's, the intellectual's, course of life.

Far more than any prejudice or self-assurance in opinion, it is this element of knowingness that bothers us in Edmund Wilson's writing. There is a kind of incapacity to imagine that what he knows or has found out by inquiry is not the whole essential story, and that what others see, which he himself does not see, may nevertheless really be there. Like his father, Wilson accepts the system he works within, in this case the literary establishment and its custom. He does not fundamentally question it; he only aspires to master it (which he is willing to work hard to do) and then to have his mastery acknowledged. When something comes into view that he cannot, fairly promptly, conceive any practical reason for, and when it persists in its inadaptability to his formulas of understanding—chief among such matters being certain works of poetic and religious imagination, and certain obdurately alien styles of behavior: Russian, English, even those Indian cultures with which his intention is to be sympathetic—liberal curiosity may give way rather abruptly to irritation and withdrawal. Irritability indeed appears to be Edmund Wilson's characteristic vice; and my point is that this is not merely a fact of temperament but the characteristic intellectual expedient of a whole identifiable class.

Even within the ranks of this class there are notable exceptions. It is illuminating to compare recent books like *A Piece of My Mind* and *Patriotic Gore*, as they are retrospective and historical, with, for example, Mr. Rexford Tugwell's recent essay in autobiography, *The Light of Other Days* (1962).*

---

* The comparison is not arbitrary. Tugwell and Wilson have much in common. Both were born in the 1890's and educated in the years just before the First World War. Both, in their chosen fields of work, have been something more than technicians and specialists: Tugwell's long series of books on politics and social and economic theory surely deserves critical examination. Moreover, they happen to share the interesting background of upstate New York; American regions do need to be taken into account. There are also suggestive differences: the differences, first of all, between a summer home on the edge of the Adirondacks and village life in Chatauqua and Niagara counties, farther west and later settled; between a lawyer's son and the son of a factory manager and petty entrepreneur; between the Hill School and the Masten Park High School in Buffalo, not to mention Princeton and the Wharton School of Economics; between post-Episcopal freethinking and birthright Congregationalism, with its institutionalized belief in the covenanted community; between an observer's speculations about political responsibility and the thing itself; and so on.

Tugwell, we feel at once, is not in Wilson's class as a writer; he is awkward with narrative and has little flair for the clinching image, the figurative instance. His book is not finally *written,* as Edmund Wilson's work always is. But the pattern of events and changes it puts on record is, I think, imagined, thought out, understood, with a thoroughness that goes distinctly beyond what Wilson has ever driven himself to.

Tugwell casts his account in the form of an inquiry: how did the pattern of life and change I grew up within produce the particular persons it did produce? and what in general were its resources for creating persons, and democratic citizens? Collaterally what was there in this pattern that led us blindly to the tragic decision of Hiroshima, a decision taken by men of my generation and my kind? was there nothing in our lives that could have kept us from that error? It is a very serious and exceptionally interesting inquiry, comparable in value, for all differences in scale, to Edmund Wilson's into the literature of the Civil War. But the first thing we notice in Tugwell's inquiry is that he includes himself in it. He conceives himself to be as much the creature of the conditions he describes, as vulnerable to them and determined by them, as anyone else. In this his imagination extends one crucial step further than Wilson's, whose conception of the realm of history and its destructive modern progress may remind us of Eliot's comment on Ezra Pound's conception of hell, that it is too exclusively a realm for other people. Tugwell is at best merely adequate as a writer of sentences and chapters, but he has taken this essential imaginative step of considering the life he has known as a tragedy in which he himself has been a responsible participant, and not as a mistake due to the panickiness, the self-delusion or animal stupidity, of some other people who ought to have known better.

Yet whatever else Edmund Wilson has lacked—and a good deal *is* missing of the equipment necessary for the kind of historical criticism he aims at—he is exceptionally acute at one main part of the critic's job, the most important part, probably, for a literary journalist, and certainly an indispensable one for the kind of book he has chosen to write in *Patriotic Gore.* He is consistently quick and shrewd as a judge of individual men. More exactly: he is a shrewd judge of the *testimony* of individual men. In this respect, too, he is his father's son. He is a good judge, that is, of men according to their manner of expression in words; according to the fictive image of themselves their writings project. In *Patriotic Gore* what he writes about Grant and Sherman on the basis of their written memoirs is perceptive and just. But the kind of panoramic historical criticism he has attempted in his major books has to be something more than cross-examination and the sorting out of documents, and we notice that what Wilson says of these men by inference from their conduct in the field and from the general evidence of their behavior in life or of their children's behavior is very much less satisfactory. When it is not the cliché of common gossip, of hero worship or slander, it is mostly a kind of behaviorist fantasy. This or that happened to a man in his formative years and is the key to all his subsequent conduct. Wilson has a sharp ear for the points at which a man's casual language reveals or betrays him, and can usually be trusted in descriptions of where and in what ways a writer has put himself into his books. But this is not the same thing as understanding the historical life, or even the full creative act of mind, these books come out of and ambiguously refer to, in which respect his critical findings tend to lapse into a sophisticated kind of moral positivism or name-calling.

This responsiveness to documents is the sustaining virtue of *Patriotic Gore,* a volume that bids for a place in Edmund Wilson's work alongside *To the Finland Station.* It, too, might be subtitled "A Study in the Writing and Acting of History." In *Patriotic Gore* we are shown, one after another, the reactions of individual men and women, in journals, letters, novels, memoirs, speeches, and life histories, to the national crisis of the Civil War (and coincidentally to another great crisis, less central for Wilson only because it is not compacted into a single brief period of public violence: the collapse in America of the old, zealous, apocalyptic Calvinist religion) . The book is not a history of the war. It is not even a full history of the literature of the war, its announced subject; Whitman's *Specimen Days* and *Democratic Vistas* are only the more startling of its omissions. But I agree with most of the book's reviewers

that *Patriotic Gore* comes closer than any other commemorative
Civil War book of our own time to succeeding in that effort
which, from the first, Whitman said never could be accomplished, the effort to get the real war into the books.

Patriotic Gore is not, however, Edmund Wilson's masterpiece, as Alfred Kazin and Robert Penn Warren, among others,
have called it. On the contrary we are reminded once more,
in reading it, that Wilson is not and never has been a writer
likely to produce a "masterpiece" of any kind. In the mass it
seemed to me at first, and seems again on rereading, a curiously
dull book, nearly impossible to follow along consecutively for
any great length, though fine to look around in a chapter or
two at a time. Dull, I mean, in the special way that any bulky
deposition of evidence which has not been shaped by the
continuous organizing force of disciplined critical reflection
and argument is bound to be dull. It lacks an objectively coherent compositional scheme, the kind of scheme which in
Wilson's best earlier books was created for him by his subjects
and the terms of discourse already surrounding them: in *Axel's
Castle* the modernist literary revolution and its rich critical
literature, in *To the Finland Station* the actual drama of a
great ideological and historical revolution working itself out
on the central stage of modern history.

Brought together in book form, the constituent essays of
Patriotic Gore produce a divided impression. There is, once
more, the breadth, the versatility, the serious readiness of
interest, qualities the mere existence of which strikes a new
blow against the mandarin and the parochial in literary understanding. But what also comes through rather forcibly is the
case-making pragmatism or opportunism of the interpretive
approach. We read one or two chapters and feel, here is the
writer, the critic, who supremely wants the actual, the important, the vital, to be made secure in our understanding,
and the known circumstances of their existence to be in no way
evaded or misrepresented. But as we read on we begin to
suspect that too often what the exposition is really seeking
security for is the accident of the writer's opinion—and Wilson
remains a man of sharp, hedgehoggish opinions, aggressively
held. The lively, versatile sense-of-what-is-interesting begins to

appear as something less admirable, a kind of vanity about being heard and making his point, some point, any point.* What is missing is a sustained pressure toward full discovery, a free overriding force of reflective contemplation.

Instead, briefs are filed—brilliant ones, mostly, which for the moment carry the day. The author comes before his readers as a skilled trial lawyer before a jury, as the man who by his own word has got the significant evidence and into whose hands that evidence may be safely entrusted for evaluation and disposition. The scheme of judgment and interpretation in *Patriotic Gore* (it operates differently for different men and different occasions) is improvised to follow the emphasis the author has decided to develop, and it is invariably an emphasis *ad hominem*. So instead of reasoned analysis we get, if the term may now be used neutrally, a sophisticated kind of intellectual McCarthyism (I am thinking of the late Senator's ways of presenting documentary evidence), that is, an arbitrarily assembled and potentially endless series of facts and quotations strung together according to an essentially visceral or sentimental response to them. For biographical portraiture this can be a compelling method, particularly for minor and scarcely remembered figures, like the various authors of *The Valley of Shadows* or *A Confederate Girl's Diary* or *Bricks Without Straw*. But for placing individual lives, public or private, in full and accurate relation to a great collective event like the American Civil War, it is not enough. It only caricatures reality.

Two broad themes of general interest do emerge in *Patriotic Gore,* and both have to do with Wilson's laudable insistence, in the midst of what he refers to as "this absurd centennial," on the war's actual violence and destructiveness.

The first is his persistent attack on the quasi-religious fanaticism with which the war was conceived and fought, particularly in the North. The valuable result of this emphasis is the detail it leads him into. From Mary Chesnut's remarkable

---

* I leave out of account here the wastefully overwritten Introduction, the extreme stridency of which tends to cancel out much of what is reasonable and (roughly) true in its denunciation of American and Russian national behavior.

diary, for example, instance after instance of wanton destruction is drawn out, and we are made to feel, *this* is what war really does to those caught up in it. From a survey of the strange post-1861 writings of Hinton Helper, whose book *The Impending Crisis* was second only to *Uncle Tom's Cabin* in crystallizing Northern opinion, Wilson emphasizes weird details of crankery and paranoid obsession, and, we are warned, *this* as often as not is how the men of the hour, the leaders of "opinion," really think. The systematic ruthlessness in action of a Sherman on one side, a Stonewall Jackson or Mosby on the other, is stressed no more than it deserves. And the fiercely cautionary note first sounded in the Introduction—that the great reason for avoiding any war, even in what seems the noblest cause, is that "as soon as the war gets started, few people do any more thinking about anything except demolishing the enemy"—can hardly be overworked in the 1960's, to an American audience.

But this emphasis on the war's destructiveness is also mixed up with another of Wilson's old causes, his lifelong animus against religion, which seems to him incapable of leading anywhere except into hypocrisy and bloody-mindedness.* In *Patriotic Gore* this animus leads Wilson to misconceive the fervor and dedication of the Abolitionists, whose agitation in any case was surely not the one great cause of the war's special violence but a counterattack against the institutionalized human violence of the slave economy. And it is a

---

* His attitude toward religion involves a kind of inverted fundamentalism, as in fact he courteously gave Dr. Frank M. Cross of the McCormick Theological School the space to point out in *A Piece of My Mind*. Wilson addresses the matter of religion as literal-mindedly as a four square gospeler. Nothing beguiles him more than contemplating, as in the case of Calvin Stowe, the inevitable incommensurability of belief and conduct, particularly in the form of the convinced old-believer's obsessive concern for temptations of the flesh. This relish, which he shares with Cozzens and Penn Warren, for news of reverend men of the cloth pawing female parishioners and visiting brothels, and in general for "horrid disclosures" about respectable men with secret vices, bottles in their desks and the Lord knows what in their back closets, suggests unresolved private compulsions as well as the cramped spiritual history of a whole Anglo-American generation of painfully self-liberated men and women. Wilson also has, it should be said, a considerably more valuable crypto-Protestant relish for the everlasting scandal of the churches: I am thinking of the section on "Religion" in *A Piece of My Mind*.

main factor in his ambivalence about Lincoln. Wilson honors Lincoln above all other leaders of the time (as well he might), and yet insists on the bleakest view of his conduct in office. The stress is on the mystical, prophetic dignity with which the President as if by his own choice sent thousands upon thousands of young men to death. The most interesting expression of this view comes out, significantly, in the chapter on Alexander Stephens, the Confederate Vice-President. In effect Wilson simply assimilates into his own point of view Stephens' case against Lincoln as an agent of despotism, a naturally good man brought to "unjustifiable usurpations of power" and "high crimes against society and humanity" by the pressure of historical necessity—at which point, noticing that Lincoln is nevertheless made personally responsible for all this (an idea just true enough to be really absurd; we can all agree that under a Buchanan things would have happened differently), we recall that Lincoln was Edmund Wilson's father's hero, and that in *A Piece of My Mind* Wilson wrote at some length of how his father had identified himself with Lincoln, the hypochondriac lawyer who became the only guardian of true republican virtue.

Given the stress on the war's carnage, it may be surprising to discover that the sentimental hero of *Patriotic Gore* is Grant—"Butcher" Grant as he was long remembered in Northern towns whose volunteers had been swallowed up in the ponderous frontal assaults of the Wilderness and Cold Harbor. Grant of course makes the perfect pragmatic hero, as is suggested if we combine the description of him by Charles Francis Adams, Jr., as in military affairs a man "of the most exquisite judgment and tact" with Alexander Stephens' remark that as a leader he "does not seem to be aware of his powers." The main evidence for Wilson's view of Grant is the *Personal Memoirs*: an impressively executed work (as Matthew Arnold was one of the first, grudgingly, to allow) but as one-sided, really, as the war memoirs of an Eisenhower or a Montgomery, though in a much more tolerable prose style. Wilson does point out that one thing which cannot be learned from the *Personal Memoirs* is "all the cost of the war." Grant had a genius for the laconic that was surrealistically refined, and one's conclusion is that Edmund Wilson, that Cato of documents, is taken in by it, by the man's almost perfect *speechlessness.*

In the case of Sherman, on the other hand, where revealing private documents are more plentiful and unreserved, Wilson operates less as a trial lawyer than as a hanging judge. Sherman comes as near as anyone, apart from the Abolitionists, to being the book's villain—although the Atlanta-Savannah-Columbia campaign was surely a less costly contribution to ending the war than trench warfare and direct frontal attack; property can be reconstructed but not human life. The fine qualities in Sherman are mentioned only to be disregarded: his personal loyalty to Grant; his exemplary practical imagination in refusing the Presidency in words that ever since have been used to call the turn on dark-horse flirters and connivers after that or any other high office; his exceptional strategic inventiveness, as the Northern officer whose fieldwork in this first mass war European military students particularly admired. But Wilson's only reference to this is to plant innuendos about Sherman's responsibility for the Nazi blitzkrieg.

The second broad theme of *Patriotic Gore* is of more strictly literary interest, but the whole long first part of the chapter on the novelist DeForest is devoted to it, and as Wilson is primarily a critic of literature, it bears looking into. This chapter is entitled "The Chastening of American Prose Style," and the argument is that the shock and strain of the war and its bitter realities rescued American letters from verbosity and magniloquence; that, through the emergence of a "language of responsibility" among men who in the war had been "obliged to issue orders," standards were established of plainness, simplicity, clarity, directness, honesty, concision, and the like. For those who had seen active service no other style was stomachable. On the other hand, among those who did not serve, preeminently Henry Adams and Henry James, "the effect of the war may be traced in the development of the opposite qualities—ambiguity, prolixity, irony—that reflect a kind of lack of self-confidence, a diffidence and a mechanism of self-defense."

This is surely one of the oddest theories a well-regarded critic has ever set hand to. Is it meant to be taken seriously? Decades before the Civil War most American authors of stature were consciously trying to bring serious literary expression closer to the directness and nervous energy of common speech. That effort is a main part of what distinguishes them from the run of Brahmins and Knickerbockers, who, following neo-classical principles, thought of the popular idiom as being only for comic use. And it is an effort that forms one of the great central undertakings of literary Romanticism. (Historically the cult of serious or intense plainness goes even further back, to fundamentally religious origins; to the English Bible and the highly rationalized protocol, in matters of expression, of the dissenting sects of the seventeenth and eighteenth centuries, Quakers and Methodists in particular.) But what in their several ways Emerson, Poe, Thoreau, Melville when not deliberately rhapsodizing, Whitman in his verse-lines, even conservative Hawthorne, were trying to achieve was not just simplicity and plainness but *exactness,* a profounder accuracy, a more complete fidelity to the whole spectrum of creaturely experience and the motions of the mind in participating in it. In pursuit of these expressive ends, what may look like verbosity and magniloquence, along with a complex syntax, are sometimes required.

Wilson, however, whose own efficient prose has always had not only the concreteness and raciness but something of the intellectual slovenliness of summary journalism, does not appear to see the necessity for this distinction, or the rare virtue of the result. He seems to want not just simplicity of statement but simplemindedness. One is puzzled, in any case, to know how the great sentence-cadences closing the Second Inaugural —surely the supreme expression of the "language of responsibility"—fit his description of the approved new style. With Adams and James, moreover, Wilson has simply confused qualities of style with qualities of address and thought. Unquestionably these latter become more complex and subtle as the work of both men develops—and that of course is their distinction as writers, that they worked out styles to express this growing complication of thought, this mastery of the intellectual instruments of irony and ambiguity; it is what makes them more impressive as writers of English prose than DeForest, Ambrose Bierce, or even Oliver Wendell Holmes,

Jr., Wilson's elected heroes in this little morality play of stylistic purification.*

What, finally, may we say of *Patriotic Gore*? First, it is a very curious book with respect to what it appears to aim at being, an "inside narrative" of the collective experience of the Civil War. Second, because of its erratic amplitude, its massing of circumstantial detail, and its underlying passion of judgment, it is as good a book as any Wilson has written for identifying the kind of writer he has been and the value that attaches to his major work. He has presented himself as a historical critic, but he does not have what can properly be called a historical imagination. His address to past events and documents is in no way different from his treatment of what is current. It is essentially biographical, being shaped, like his criticism, by a preoccupation with the psychology of the individual case. And in just this respect it expresses with confidence and energy the outlook, in the broadest historical view, of middle-class individualism; the outlook of that class on whose patronage and participation so much of modern literature and the whole enterprise of modern journalism have so long depended. But when applied to a great national catastrophe like the Civil War, or to the impending crisis of our own apprehensive moment in history, what it precisely lacks is Lincoln's, or Whitman's and Melville's, religious and tragic sense of the war as purgatorial, an inescapable collective trial, a conceivably just though necessarily inscrutable working of something that for lack of any more satisfactory word may as well be called Providence.

Edmund Wilson not only resists this sense; he fears and resents it, which is to say that he fears and resents those conditions of life—they are not just wartime conditions—which

---

* The real charge against Henry James as a stylist is Edwin Muir's, that with his insidious mastery of colloquial idiom he "infected criticism with a vocabulary of hints and nods" and fathered a "question-begging" terminology from which the discussion of literary form has not yet recovered; against Henry Adams, that with the condensed annalist's style for treating men and events which he developed in the nine-volume *History* and perfected in his *Education*, he is the great ancestor of the wool-pulling antistyle of *Time* magazine.

make the religious and tragic sense of life reasonable to some men. Some fundamental deficiency in meeting experience drastically limits his understanding, just as it approaches the deepest waters. That queer pleasure he has always taken in listing all the superficial resemblances of men to animals and insects begins, in its indiscriminate repetitiveness, to appear less and less the expression of a ruthless iconoclasm and moral honesty and more and more a whistling in the dark to keep up the courage of his dogmatic rationalism.

We see (to repeat) that his judgment operates best on the *words* people leave behind them, but that as his examination draws him on into speculation about the reasons for these words, the human motives, actions, and necessities they refer to, this verbal positivism—the quality that gives his literary chronicling its admirable particularity and common sense—becomes more obstruction than asset. We notice, too, that his comparisons and definitions in books like *To the Finland Station* and *Patriotic Gore* are nearly always in terms of other books and that he is most effective in comparing minor instances to guaranteed classics: thus the Chesnuts are like the Bolkonskys in *War and Peace,* an episode in their life is like Chekhov, and so on. When such comparisons do not turn up, he seems at a loss to know what to think. And we may begin to feel that perhaps Wilson's praiseworthy belief in the efficacy and validity of *literature* (which I began by calling his great virtue as a practical critic) is damagingly related to a profound distrust of life and all its disconcerting profusion of appearances; a distrust of the mind's freedom to act among them; a binding insecurity that issues in the countermeasures of aggressive annoyance and chronic irritability. It may well be sound tactics for a peripatetic journalist to write from defensive annoyance and irritation; it can guarantee directness and authenticity of relation; but it is a handicap to the prosecution of serious historical and moral argument.

Yet to say such things may be to say something a good deal stronger than the case requires or deserves. The point may rather be, simply, that Edmund Wilson has been a journalist and remains a journalist. It would be churlish not to add that he has been an extraordinarily valuable one. All who have to do with literature have played parasite to his writings, his discoveries and revaluations, and are too much in his debt to allow much complaining. He has been one of his time's indispensable teachers and transmitters of important news. His work reminds us how much we depend on these jobs being done and done well, how impoverished we are when they do not get done.

But he has held to his career of literary chronicler at a cost. At his best he has remained one of the many pensioners (the universities now are full of them, with less excuse) of the brilliant creative era in literature and the arts of the earlier twentieth century. That great legacy, however, is running out —as efforts to pass it along to new generations as if it were intact must increasingly discover. The need is no longer for summaries and translations, the critical techniques Wilson remains a master of, but for reformation and renewal. Yet it may be said that even though he can no longer expect to have an active part in any such new development, he will still be felt as an assisting presence. His books seem to me as likely as any mere criticism of the past fifty years to keep alive for younger writers a practical image of what it is that lies open for them to do.

Witness and Testament: Two Contemporary Classics

Matter of interest for literary historians: have any recent American books made a stronger impression on the consciousness of people who read than *The Autobiography of Malcolm X,* published posthumously in 1965, and *The Armies of the Night,* Norman Mailer's chronicle of the Pentagon march published in 1968?

Characteristically, both books are part and parcel of the civil turbulence of the past decade in American life. To begin speculating at this point in time about their ultimate place in literary history may seem a bit precious. Yet to speak of them merely as books that have a cultural and topical importance, or even as documents whose testimony has already shaped our understanding of our time's history, is to do less than full critical justice to the literary achievement they represent. Calling them "classics" is not merely pitchman's slang. I am simply persuaded that these two books do in fact have a central place in the continuing major history of American writing; that they are works of formed imaginative argument as powerfully developed and sustained as any we have had during the past quarter century; works organized and deepened by imaginative

Read at the English Institute, September, 1970, and reprinted from NEW LITERARY HISTORY, Winter, 1971.

conceptions of the story to be told which have in the end not only a tough interior truthfulness but also, emerging as determining themes, a visionary force, a transforming authority. And what precisely do we mean by high literature if not work of this character?

Both books are aggressively personal in focus and, like much current poetry, confessional in their tactics of statement. At the same time they are books which quite obviously first won a hearing, and are now firmly lodged in the paperback market, by reason of their topicality. The two authors in their different ways have been public men with a vengeance; and what they write about in these books are matters as central to the public life of our time as any we can think of—the black revolt, the fight against the Vietnam War, and all that each signifies in the moral and civil history of American society. Thus we are likely to respond to them in rather special ways. We may intensely *want* to find them forceful and impressive; we feel that they could be weapons, each one, in a great cause. We read them therefore with a certain indulgence. We ask them only to be just good enough, to give what encouragement they can to struggles which we know will not be won merely by writing and reading books.

A great many books have recently been claiming our attention in this way; and it is of special interest that literary men and women, as distinct from plain journalists, have been drawn into writing them, as if to satisfy some new, or revived, test of occupational seriousness. So we find an old-school man of letters like Robert Penn Warren turning out a collection of interviews on segregation and race consciousness; a book it is possible to think as nicely fitted to Warren's raconteur's talent as any he has ever given us. From a younger novelist, Jeremy Larner, comes one of the livelier accounts of Eugene McCarthy's campaign in 1968; from Susan Sontag, an impressive report on the impact of a visit to North Vietnam. Those novels and poems, too, that show some special boldness of ambition are likely to have, or move toward, the form of public statement, like Saul Bellow's latest novel, *Mr. Sammler's Planet,* or Joyce Carol Oates's *Expensive People* ("a hatchet," says her narrator, "to slash through my own heavy flesh and through the flesh of any one else who happens to get in the way"), or Robert Kelly's "long poem about America in time," *The Common Shore,* of which the opening section is called with proper ominousness, "The State of Siege."

Black writers especially seem compelled to accommodate their effort as writers to public, civil ends. More or less inevitably their books are received as public documents first of all, and perhaps they come to be written out largely according to that expectation. (Black North American writers, that is, as against those from black Africa and the West Indies, who in the main seem freer to be read and to think of themselves as primarily novelists, dramatists, poets.) Thus it was with particular regard to black American writers and books that the critic Richard Gilman formulated, not long ago, an argument concerning the kind of writing I am discussing, and the response proper to it, that touches directly on my present concern.

Mr. Gilman was addressing himself to Eldridge Cleaver's *Soul on Ice,* another best seller for topical reasons, and the critical line he took was deliberately provocative. With such books, he said, the first thing we professional readers of literature have to do is suspend altogether our ordinary standards. In a word, these books are not for us. The conditions under which they are written are conditions of constraint and desperation literally unimaginable to nonblacks, and the special service they perform for their authors and for the community of black readers is such that our trained habits of judgment simply do not apply—*cannot* apply—and must be discarded, being not only inappropriate but in present circumstances socially and humanly destructive. *Soul on Ice* is not just another work of literature; it is nothing less than "an act of creation and definition of the self" on the part of a man totally estranged from us and our cultural privileges and assumptions. We have indeed, as Mr. Gilman nicely puts it, to "make room" for *Soul on Ice,* "but not on the shelves we have already built."*

Now this argument, from a critic whose general good sense I very much respect, can be criticized in various ways. Socio-

---

* Mr. Gilman's essay, and a further reply to some of his critics, are reprinted in his collection, *The Confusion of Realms* (1970).

logical and, in a fashion, philosophical ways, chiefly. If books like *Soul on Ice* derive from civil and psychological conditions so vastly different from those assumed by standard literary criticism, if they represent an act of mind so remote from ordinary literary performance, will anything such criticism chooses to say make a difference one way or the other? Will it in fact keep those books from doing their special job? or will their authors really be beaten into silence and their own proper readers turned away by comments that by definition are so immensely irrelevant? Also, wouldn't this argument apply equally to other special classes of books? Mr. Gilman himself, in correspondence following his essay, sensibly acknowledged the force of objections that the same sort of thing may be said of women's literature, books by women about the special experience of women in our society, or of the literature of homosexuality or of criminality. How much we would lose, for example, if Genet's writing was automatically exempted from critical interrogation.

Mr. Gilman might have been challenged even more centrally, I think, by reference to the literature of religious experience and religious indoctrination; the work, for instance, of an author like Thomas Merton, whose liberating influence Eldridge Cleaver very handsomely acknowledges in his book. Here in particular the writer's work is subordinated to doctrinal and sectarian purposes, and most frequently represents or symbolizes just such an act of self-creation and self-definition. But have we really no way of discriminating objectively between Thomas Merton and, say, Mary Baker Eddy, or in a nineteenth-century context between Mrs. Eddy's writing and Newman's or Kierkegaard's, with regard to the discursive authority each possesses and to both the mediate and ultimate consequences of an absorption in them? Most broadly, is it really impossible to enter imaginatively, rationally, the world of discourse of people whose outlook and life experience are substantially different from our own, and whose stake in the making of books differs correspondingly? Isn't Mr. Gilman's argument at some point profoundly patronizing? does it mean anything that the suspension of critical valuation it calls for would be especially suitable to children's writing or to the writing-for-therapy of the mentally sick?

The matter would be interesting to thrash out on these grounds; it could lead into wide-ranging sociological, perhaps political, debate. But the objection I particularly want to make is more strictly literary, though not for that reason less serious. Mr. Gilman's argument seems to me characteristic of a good deal of well-intentioned concern these days with the matter of "relevance," the relevance of traditional disciplines of thought to present social needs; a form of it crops up all around the mass of current writing and thinking about the teaching of English in schools and colleges. It involves, I suspect, a strangely limited understanding of what constitutes the species "literature" and of what is involved in the consideration of literary "form"—to leave aside its curious historical forgetfulness about the whole main set of the Romantic and post-Romantic ethos, that great rallying ground of the anticlassical, antihierarchical "confusion of realms" that Mr. Gilman has taken as his critical theme.

To quote him again, "we have all considered that the chief thing we should be working towards" in literary criticism is a certain state of "disinterestedness," of " 'higher' truth and independent valuation," and so forth; but who precisely is this "we"? in what cork-lined chamber of adjudication does this "we" hang out? Am I right in detecting here the presence, as a main term of argument, of an odd parochial confusion in understanding and applying the modernist dogma of the "autonomy" of literature; some queer residue of the classroom rigors of the famous "new criticism" and the legendary purity of its disregard for questions of intention, effect, social implication? Mr. Gilman's argument turns, I think, on a position I doubt he himself would tolerate for a moment—on a strict separation of "literature" and the considerations appropriate to it from *any* writing done in the service of extraliterary causes or having a direct social or personal end, or from any consideration of the part such purposes commonly play in major literary history.

On this, two general points might be made. One is that the more we look into the matter the more we see that all modern literary creation (in ways determined by the whole supporting culture) involves just such acts of self-creation and self-definition, a point it would be entertaining to develop with reference to some very respectable case like that of Milton, who had a good deal to say about the personal factor in high literary achievement, the noble infirmity of wanting to make a name for yourself, and so on. In American writing in particular, where Emerson, Whitman, Hart Crane remain archetypal presences, this motivational confusion of realms, of craftsmanship and soulmaking, has been of the central stuff of working tradition. In any event the question is not of totally disparate categories of performance, out of reach of each other's standards of valuation, but of different histories, or circumstances, or doctrines and conceptions, of "the self"; different working postures and strategies, adopted according to each writer's picture of his own and his audience's situation; different expressive intentions embraced and different effects sought, each having its own reasonable measure of virtue. The other general point is that writing meant to serve directly some social cause or personal end will do so more effectively by creating, so to speak, a broad or an intense imaginative field of reference and allusion, and will therefore also have its distinctive resources and precedents in past expressive tradition; for such fields of reference and allusion are not created out of raw sensation. If these are not literary resources and precedents, what are they?

The particular forms writing of this kind commonly uses are familiar enough to us: the open letter, the preachment, the apology, the parable or representative anecdote, the capitulatory brief, the tirade, the narrative or polemical exposé, the public prayer, the appeal to conscience, the call to arms. These are the literary forms, in fact, forms mostly of direct address designed not only to reach but in a sense to *create* a genuine audience, that *Soul on Ice* is written in; the forms, too, that for obvious reasons have traditionally been most available in the social community Eldridge Cleaver's writing emerges from and largely assumes. (By this I mean not only the black community but the larger national community—the community *manqué*, not so much fragmented as fundamentally unformed —which since independence has been the immovable obstacle in the path of high American ambition, in literature and out of it.) The rhetoric or style Eldridge Cleaver works in corresponds. It is, quite simply, a version of that long-established plain style of first-person deposition and affirmation in which so much of modern revolutionary polemic and testimony on the non-Marxist side has been cast. Rousseau, Tom Paine, Voltaire are among a sizable company of predecessors and models cited by the in fact quite noticeably bookish author of *Soul on Ice,* though a nearer source would be popular oratory and evangelical preaching. And it seems to me that in such cases an exercise of specifically literary criticism—formal, stylistic—is altogether appropriate, though it requires kinds of discretion and informed good sense that are not guaranteed possessions among graduates of our organized critical schooling. It strikes me as very much worth knowing, and worth saying in the right way, whether a writer like Eldridge Cleaver uses the received modes he has chosen to write in well or badly—and by "well" I mean adroitly, cogently, mind-openingly. It is a *critical* finding which, if reached in a way that makes sense to us, may provide a useful pragmatic measure of the present strength and tactical readiness of the whole collective movement of mind, conscience, social will, which the book in question speaks for, and out of.

But to remind ourselves that these modes and forms do also properly belong to the history of literature is only to point up the disregard of them that has somehow got institutionalized among us. How prominent *is* Tom Paine in English or American literary studies? I am not sure that much room is ever made for him, in Mr. Gilman's figure, on the shelves we regularly work from or send students to, or that we would quite know how to make the critical case for getting him up there. Yet Paine is one of the genuine masters of English prose in the plain or popular style, surely as much so as Burke is of its forensic opposite. But that style, too, is neglected as an object of inquiry; we would hardly know how to begin to talk critically about it. That being the case, we may have to agree, on practical grounds, that Mr. Gilman has a point; our common practice of literary criticism does not prepare us to deal very effectively with books like *The Rights of Man* or *Soul on Ice.*

In any event, since the matter applies a fortiori to Malcolm's autobiography, let us turn to that remarkable book.

No one can read very much of Malcolm's writing, more

precisely listen to the voice transcribed in the autobiography (dictated to the journalist Alex Haley) or the printed versions of his public speeches, without forming the sense of an extraordinary human being: fiercely intelligent, shrewdly and humanely responsive to the life around him despite every reason in the world to have gone blind with suspicion and hate, a rarely gifted leader and inspirer of other men. The form of autobiographical narration adds something further; he comes through to us as the forceful agent of a life history that was heroic in the event and has the shape of the heroic in the telling, a protagonist who, in Francis R. Hart's fine description, has himself created and now re-creates "human value and vitality in each new world or underworld he has entered."*

The power of Malcolm's book is that it speaks directly out of the totality of that life history *and* the ingratiating openness of his own mind and recollection to it. It seems to me a book that, *pace* Mr. Gilman, does not require any softening or suspension of critical judgment. In the first place it is written, or spoken, in a quick, pungent, concrete style, again the plain style of popular idiom, improved and made efficient by the same sort of natural sharpness and concentration of attention that gives life and color to the best of Mark Twain's recollective writing, or Franklin's, or Bunyan's. In the run of the narrative the liveliness of observation and recollection, the "histrionic exuberance" (Professor Hart again), are continuously persuasive, and incidentally confirm as elements of a true style Alex Haley's assurance that the book is indeed Malcolm's own and not a clever piece of mimicry or pastiche. The casually vivid rendering of other persons is worth remarking, a test some competent novelists would have trouble passing. People who were especially important to Malcolm—his strongminded half-sister Ella; the motherly white woman who ran the detention home he was sent to at thirteen, who was always kind to him and would call his people "niggers" to his face without a flicker of uneasiness; Shorty from Boston, who set him up in business; West Indian Archie, who "called him out"; or the tough convict Bimbi in Charlestown prison, strange

---

* "Notes for an Anatomy of Modern Autobiography," *New Literary History*, I, 3 (Spring, 1970).

little man of unexpected thoughts and arguments, who broke through the wall of rage and hate Malcolm was closing around himself—all these figures are precisely defined, according to their place in the story.

The grasp of the narrative extends in fact to whole sociologies of behavior. The Harlem chapters in general, with their explanation of hustling in all its main forms—numbers, drugs, prostitution, protection, petty in-ghetto thievery—offer one of the best accounts in our literature of the cultural underside of the American business system, and of the bitter psychology that binds its victims to it. Malcolm came to see very clearly how the habituations bred by ghetto poverty operate to destroy individual efforts to break out of it, and he could use that insight with force and point in his preaching. Most generally it is just this blending of his own life-story with the full collective history of his milieu and the laws of behavior controlling it that gives Malcolm's testimony its strength and large authority—and sets it apart, I think, from the many more or less skillfully designed essays in autobiography we have had recently from writers like Frank Conroy, Claude Brown, Norman Podhoretz, Willie Morris, Paul Cowan, David Mc-Reynolds, to mention only a few; sets it apart also from the great run of novels about contemporary city life.

But it is Malcolm himself, and his own active consciousness of the myth of his life's progress, that most fills and quickens the book, making it something more than simply a valuable document. His past life is vividly present to him as he speaks; he gives it the form, in recollection, of a dramatic adventure in which he himself is felt as the precipitating agent and moving force. It is not unreasonable that he should see himself as someone who has a special power to make things happen, to work changes on the world around him and also to change within himself; and thus finally as one whose rise to authority is in some sense in the natural order of things, the working out of some deep structure of fortune. That is my way of putting it; Malcolm himself, as a Muslim, of course uses other words.*

---

* So Borges: "A classic is that book which a nation (or group of nations, or time itself) has taken to read as if in its pages everything were pre-determined, predestined, deep as the cosmos, and capable of endless interpretation." *New York Review of Books,* August 13, 1970.

The force of this continuously active process of self-conception and self-projection is fundamental to the book's power of truth. It gives vitality and momentum to the early parts of the story, the picture of Malcolm's salad days as a Roxbury and Harlem sharpie, with conked hair and "knob-toed, orange-colored 'kick-up' shoes," the wildest Lindy-hopper and quickest hustler of all, delighting always in his impact on others—as in the interlude of his first trip back to Lansing, Michigan, to wow the yokels with his Harlem flashiness—finding satisfaction, too, in the names, the folk identities, that attach to him at each new stage: "Homeboy," "Harlem Red" or "Detroit Red," "Satan" in the storming defiance of his first imprisonment. Most decisively, this force of self-conception is what brings alive the drama of his conversion, and his re-emergence within the Nation of Islam as a leader and teacher of his people. For Malcolm's autobiography is consciously shaped as the story of an "education," and in so describing it I am not merely making the appropriate allusion to Henry Adams or the *Bildungsroman* tradition; "education" is Malcolm's own word for what is taking place.

Above all, the book is the story of a conversion and its consequences. We can identify in it various classic features of conversion narrative. A full detailing of the crimes and follies of his early life makes more astonishing the change of changes that follow ("The very enormity of my previous life's guilt prepared me to accept the truth"). In the central light of this new truth, particular events take on symbolic dimensions; they stand as the exemplary trials and challenges which the redeemed soul must pass through and by which it knows the meaning, feels the reality, of its experience. That meaning and reality, to repeat, are not merely personal. Grander historical patterns are invoked and give their backing to the story—the whole long history and tragedy of the black race in America; then, at the crisis, the radically clarifying mythology of the Black Muslim movement (a mythology which, to anyone willing to consider it objectively, has the character of a full-blown poetic mythology; a source, once you place yourself inside it, of comprehensive and intrinsically rational explanations for the life experience it refers to, that of the mass of black people in a historically racist society).

And always there is Malcolm's own fascination with what has happened to him, and what objectively it means. As if establishing a leitmotif, the climaxes of his story repeatedly focus on this extraordinary power to change and be changed that he has grown conscious of within himself and that presents itself to him as the distinctive rule of his life. Malcolm speaks with a just pride of his quickness to learn, to "pick up" how things are done in the world; of his readiness, even when it humiliates him, to accept schooling from those in possession of some special competence or wisdom; of a "personal chemistry" that requires him to find out the full vital truth of his own experience and that keeps it available to consciousness from that time forward. His curiosity about life is unquenchable ("You can hardly mention anything I'm not curious about"). He has a driving need to understand everything that happens to him or around him and to gain a measure of intelligent control over it; it is a passion with him to get his own purchase on reality.

It thus makes *narrative* sense, of a kind only the best of novelists are in command of, that he should discover his calling in life as a teacher and converter. Malcolm has his own theories for nearly everything that interests him—theories of language and etymology (he has an autodidact's sense of word magic, dating from the time in prison when studying a dictionary, page by page, in a folklorish fury of self-improvement, began quite literally to give him an extravagant new intuition of power and freedom, as of one suddenly finding a key to his enemy's most treasured secrets); theories about how Socrates' wisdom came from initiation into the mysteries of black Egypt and about the persecuted black philosopher Spinoza and the black poet Homer, cognate with Omar and Moor, and about who really wrote Shakespeare and translated the English Bible (it was that subtle tyrant King James himself) and why. Of course we can laugh at a lot of this from the pew boxes of a more orderly education, but I find myself impressed even in these odd instances with the unfailing rationality of the uses to which Malcolm put his thought, the intelligence even here of what really matters to him, which is the meaning of his life as a black man in the United States and the enormous responsibilities of a position of authority and leadership in which he can count on no help from the official, institutionalized culture but what he wrenches out for himself.

But it is, again, the prodigy of his own conversion that gives him the most direct confirmation of his beliefs; the awareness of himself as a man capable of these transforming changes that gives him confidence in his testimony's importance, that lets him say, "Anything I do today, I regard as urgent." The *Autobiography* was written to serve at once a religious and a political cause, the cause of the religion of Islam and the cause of black freedom, and it is filled with the letter of Malcolm's teaching. In the later chapters especially, more and more of the text is portioned out to explanations of essential doctrine and to social and political commentary and analysis. But here, too, it is a personal authority that comes through to us and makes the difference.

I should like to try to characterize this authority a little further. I first read Malcolm's autobiography when I happened also to be reading through the Pauline epistles in the New Testament; the chance result was a sharp consciousness of fundamental resemblances. Resemblances, I mean, to the voice and manner of the Paul who not only is teaching his people the law of the new faith (to which he himself is a late comer, and by hard ways) but who suffuses his teaching with all the turbulence of his own history and masterful personality. Two recent students of Paul's letters, Charles Buck and Greer Taylor, have commented on the singularity of this element in Paul: "a presumption of personal authority on the part of the writer which is quite unlike that of any other New Testament author." Malcolm, too, writes as the leader of a new, precariously established faith, which he is concerned to stabilize against destructive inner dissensions yet without losing any of the priceless communal fervor and dedication that have been released by it. So at every point he brings to bear the full weight of his own reputation and active experience, including his earlier follies and excesses, precisely as Paul does in, for example, the astonishing final chapters of Second Corinthians, full as they are of the liveliest and most immediate self-reference.* The tangible genius of both Paul and Malcolm as

---

* There are other parallels. Much of the time Paul is writing (as in Philippians and First Thessalonians) for the very particular purpose of

writers is to bring the authority of living personality, and of a dramatized self-mastery, into the arena of what is understood to be an argument of the utmost consequence; a matter of life and death for those who commit themselves to it.

Malcolm's concerns are of course civil and political as well as sectarian. In his last years he had become, and knew it, a national leader as important as Dr. King; a leader moreover who, as the atmosphere of the Washington March of August, 1963, gave way to the ghetto riots of the next summer, was trusted inside Harlem and its counterparts as the established black leadership no longer was. And the last academic point I want to make about the literary character of Malcolm's book is that in this regard, too, as a political statement, its form is recognizably "classic." The model it quite naturally conforms to is that of the Political Testament, the work in which some ruler or statesman sets down for the particular benefit of his people a summary of his own experience and wisdom and indicates the principles which are to guide those who succeed him. The historian Felix Gilbert has called attention to this rather special literary tradition in his study of the background of Washington's Farewell Address. It is necessarily, in the number of its members, a limited tradition; besides Washington's address Professor Gilbert mentions examples attributed to Richelieu, Colbert, the Dutch republican Jan de Witt, Robert Walpole, Peter the Great, and Frederick the Great, who wrote at least two of them. My argument is not that Malcolm was in any way guided by this grand precedent, merely that in serving all his book's purposes he substantially re-created it—which is of course what the work of literature we call "classic" does within the occasion it answers to.

---

freeing Christian worship from the so-called Judaizers; to ward off, that is, that one sectarian deviation within the practice of the new faith which was most likely to blight its ecumenical growth. So Malcolm, with the fresh changes, the broadening in his thought that took place in the last years of his life—changes crystallized by his characteristically intense and transforming response, traveling abroad, to the polyracial vision of the true Islam and the free cosmopolitan outlook of black Africa—was writing finally to free Islam in America from the constraining prejudices of Elijah Muhammad.

Malcolm himself refers to Paul in defining to himself the character of his experience. The violent circumstances of Paul's conversion deeply impressed him; he speaks of reading the account in Acts "over and over" in the Norfolk County Prison Library.

With *The Armies of the Night* it isn't necessary to go so
far afield for critical justification. Norman Mailer's standing as
a proper literary figure has been less and less in doubt in recent years, and this book's selection for national prizes and
awards was surprisingly well received in all concerned quarters. In fact a lot of readers who had doggedly stuck by Mailer
while he was producing one after another of the most com-
pellingly unsatisfactory books being published in a mountingly
unsatisfactory era fell on *Armies* with exaggerated noises of
approval; there was offputting talk about his finally proving
his claim to be the "best writer in America," and so forth. Yet
I think it is a masterly book according to its kind—and what I
would especially call attention to is the way it grows into its
power and eloquence (not transcending the occasion but responding to it, pursuing it, with an unstinting fullness of consideration) by adopting, or reinventing, a classic American
literary mode: the exploratory personal testament in which
the writer describes how he has turned his own life into a
practical moral experiment and put it out at wager according
to the chances, and against the odds, peculiar to his time.

Some of our best-known secular autobiographies have
made this their leading theme or action—Franklin's most
famously, Lincoln Steffens' in more recent times—and much
narrative fiction also builds on this format, which lies open to
a lot of latter-day civil mythology about the response to vocation, the testing of virtue, and the like. But Thoreau's *Walden*
is the formal precedent I was particularly reminded of in reading Mailer's book, neither of them being, strictly speaking, an
autobiography but the testamentary description of an episode
of such gathered intensity that the shape and logic of whole
life-histories may fairly be inferred from it. *The Armies of the
Night* was written out in a few weeks, as against the nine years'
gestation and seven rewritings that produced the *Walden* we
read, and it does not on the whole serve the writer's peculiar
work of language refreshment and generative sentence-making
as well as Thoreau's did. (Yet whose writing does do that work
in these days of, as Godard has defined them, grave and progressive semantic loss?) But I think it fairly compensates in
its greater practical spaciousness and hospitality of reference,
the common realistic abundance, so to speak, of its narrational

vocabulary. On this rich ground another American forerunner it brings to mind is *Roughing It* (itself underrated, critically) , a book that is also a pointedly personal and, though differently balanced, partly comic and partly tragic account of a great national *massenbewegung.*

In his earlier books some excess of personal insistence— willfulness, egotism, unregulated ambition—kept Mailer straining after more than he could satisfactorily deliver; more, it also seemed, than his found or improvised materials could intrinsically support. Yet the failures always seemed to be of execution rather than of imaginative purpose. He was a writer made as impatient by his own inventions as by everything else, in literature or out of it, that was offering itself for public acceptance; a writer growing more and more distrustful of the whole established occasion of literary making. He clung to the idea of The Novel as the great field of the fame he thirsted for and to the older idea of (as he still puts it in *Armies,* though with an ironic detachment) the writer's "responsibility to educate the nation," yet he seemed in the event to disbelieve in both the old novel and the old pedagogic rationale with an intensity that was sometimes the only halfway convincing sign of real originality, real seriousness. Critical reactions were fairly uniform in their disapproval. It was a reviewer's commonplace that Mailer belonged to publicity rather than to literature; that, as Benjamin DeMott put it, he was in hostage to the national cult of Success and the "belief in the sanctity of The Career," and that the "desire for triumph" was greater than any willingness to define an adequate cause to triumph in. Up through *An American Dream,* his last proper novel, these remained reasonable views. But one way of describing the formal strengthening and consolidation of Mailer's more recent books (I include *Cannibals and Christians* and that genuine tour de force, *Why Are We in Vietnam?,* but not those being done from the first on journalistic assignment) , books that have turned one reviewer after another right around from head-shaking to sober respect and praise, is that his time's history has, to say the least, brutally overtaken his private will to power. What is more, it has given that will legitimacy, in the consciousness of readers, as a kind of counterforce. Anything less strenuous or more temperate and circumspect would seem pathetically inadequate. The writer who is not fuming in apprehension and willful resistance may be the writer who, incredibly, has not yet really heard the bad news.

The public life of the past decade has not only given him subjects worthy of the most vehement ambition, it has had the effect also of justifying themes, attitudes, that earlier seemed freakish or fantastic. Mailer has been saying for years that the great contemporary subject was totalitarianism. Now we are all saying that, or something like it, and feeling it with a paralyzing oppressiveness. His obsession, as it used to seem, with conflicts of power and brute force, with pitting himself against rivals (not just other writers but more ferocious antagonists like Sonny Liston, the Kennedys, Lyndon Johnson), with combat to the death against some vast imaginary Thing called various names but most ominously "cancer," no longer strikes us as ersatz Hemingwayism but as a kind of nervy common sense; and we read him now with all the interest a witness-bearer deserves whose obsessions have been borne out by the explosion of actual events.

The Armies of the Night is directly and continuously about that world of totalitarian civil power that in our lifetime has clamped down on every natural life-agency, every human usage and custom of existence; that power which, in Mailer's words, not only exploits the present but consumes the past and gives every promise of demolishing whole territories of the future. The book is also, not unrelatedly, about egotism and the anarchic aggression of the immitigably self-enclosed against civil propriety, decency, equity, responsibility. This is the broad link to Thoreau's book that particularly catches attention. For in both *Armies* and *Walden* the use of the writer's own self-projected image or self-conceit—in large part through comic exaggeration and a broad yet dead serious social mockery—is tactically central. Mailer is not the first American literary talent to be accused of throwing itself away in egotistical rant: an aspect of Thoreau's writing, strong in the opening pages of *Walden* and even stronger in the first drafts, that not only Lowell but even Emerson perhaps never really saw beyond.

Each book is a very personal record, yet one which appeals again and again to a broad common awareness of the curious rhythms, urgencies, constraints of the self's engagement with life; each thus forms an objective argument on the individual revolutionist's great question, "what therefore is to be done?" In *The Armies of the Night* egotism becomes not an instrument of self-promotion and performative self-betrayal but a theme for discourse, a controlled element in the essential structure. If you don't see this fairly soon, the first chapters of *Armies* can strike you as exhibitionistic in the extreme, and you may not get past them. For egotism, Mailer knows, is itself a main part of that field of force that constitutes totalitarianism's stranglehold on the technocratic-capitalist order; it is that arrogance of self that nourishes the arrogance of bureaucracies and of those nations we call advanced; it is also, ironically, a main source of the only really effective opposition to it. One way or another, it is the force we live by.

In *The Armies of the Night* the narrative dialectic between private and public motives, self-regard and national crisis, is rich and continuous, and it enters the book altogether naturally; for Mailer comes into the Pentagon march not simply as observer and chronicler but as an active participant. In the rites of gesture-making and the risks of real danger he is equal in status to everyone else. (This is the element necessarily missing, except by subrogation, in his reports on the 1968 conventions and the moon shot.) This ironic back-and-forth sustains, for example, the comedy of those opening chapters, indeed of the whole first part of the book, in which Mailer is trying to fit himself into the demonstration in a way that will satisfy all his motives, all the psychic and moral not to speak of carnal pressures operating within him and around him. The old quasi-religious theme, so peremptory in our earlier literature, that it is our deepest moral task to do nothing that is not in harmony with our whole creaturely being crisscrosses the equally grand theme that the struggle for civil justice must supersede all other vocations and responsibilities.* In

---

* I sometimes think that the deepest function of "literature"—which exists by way of a refusal to serve directly either the Platonic imperatives of justice or the eschatological imperatives of sanctification yet achieves wisdom and full efficacy only by recognizing in some way their immense overbearing reasonableness—is to bear witness to the impossibility of reconciling these immense tasks except existentially, in living out, turning into a governing condition and fact of existence, their essential ir-

the process the narrative becomes a very anatomy of "bad faith" (and incidentally restores some richness of meaning to this jaded modern concept) : that faith-with-reasons, none of them pure, which is all we can reasonably count on being gifted with in our trial of life.

Let me try to give a little of the common flavor of this narrative dialectic, which is the book's power coil and the means of releasing the strong prose hymn it closes with. The main narrative begins with a telephone call summoning Mailer to take part in the upcoming demonstration, one that is going to be "different," it is promised, from all previous ones, a real open-ended confrontation. Immediately the back-and-forth of indecision begins. Something is being asked that "would not be easy to refuse but would be expensive to perform." Is it a challenge that has come in fatal response to a growing private conviction that he is curdling, going soft or stale as a vital agent; that none of his chosen projects has yet "cost him enough"? The affair will be dangerous, and a little "bubble of fear tilts somewhere about the solar plexus" that will grow as the days and hours pass and in the event burst inside him like an uncontrollable abscess. Yet there are interesting tactical problems, the romantic appeal of deploying small forces to outmaneuver great ones, perhaps the chance to save the whole demonstration from its own virtuous ineptness. He hears that Paul Goodman and Dwight Macdonald will be on hand, and he smells out the sour atmosphere of the instinctive loser, which he hates (metaphors of smell and taste, palatal sourness and sweetness, are major in the book's rhetoric) ; but Bill Coffin with his Ivy League bark of authority sounds like a birthright winner and in Robert Lowell there is the truly rarified air of one casually above and beyond ignoble apprehensions of winning and losing. Mailer distrusts these "idiot mass manifestations"; he has, moreover, genuine doubts about the morality of selective draft resistance; his own instincts, he feels again, are "conservative and warlike." Yet at news that

---

reconcilability. When we tire of the saints, Emerson remarked, Shakespeare is our city of refuge.

Mailer's own use of "existential" has been famously loose, yet I think this is the occupational truth his behavior as a writer has pivoted on at its best.

paratroopers are massing the old Wild Man rises within him,
the one who once "at the edge of paralysis" stood up to challenge Sonny Liston face to face, and in the throes of the experience that his wager of participation opens to him—panic, arrest, a touch of manhandling, common imprisonment—the
"nerve for adventure" that he has learned to trust as his truest
literary resource, though it always gets him into trouble, asserts
itself and takes command.

And there is also his career, his public image. He never
ceases, in the "personal history" that forms the first three-
quarters of the book, to be Norman Mailer the well-known
writer, who must consider first of all whether this event really
belongs to his own special obstacle-course of literary and moral
fortune. Is marching about in ill-organized and dubiously effective mass demonstrations an appropriate action for a serious
writer, especially a demonstration directed by the kind of un-
discriminating liberal right-mindedness of which the first
symptom is always soggy prose? On the other hand, can he
get around the fact that there is never any graceful way of
refusing the appeals of right-mindedness with a clear conscience? Well, then, why resist so remarkable a chance to try
out his "existential" act before so intent an audience, to be
Master of Ceremonies once more, to test himself on the latest
front line of contemporary reality, even if it means, as increasingly it seems likely to, missing the party he is scheduled
to attend in New York that night?

Yet suppose the event is not finally one he can absorb into
his literary ecosystem? Suppose he is really changed by it—
either profoundly violated, maybe killed, a victim if not of
paratrooper ordnance then of the sheer banality of too much
liberal virtue, or else forced to see that in the final cataclysm,
of which this demonstration may only be a first skirmish, he
will not be the romantic guerrilla leader and strategist of his
dreams but expendable, as shorn a lamb as any other? Vanity
plays its strong part; among other details it is suddenly revealed that a BBC television crew which he has consented to
have undertake a documentary on him is following him into
battle and will be there to film his final one-man assault on the
military police lines. And Honor, too, as the world measures
it; for in Lowell's company, in particular, he cannot put aside

the primitive claims of competitive comradeship *and* the stirring thought that in crossing into Virginia in what may be the opening engagement in a long civil war he will be marching with the ghosts of the Union dead.

All this is in the long first part of the narrative. In the structure of the book it is the private matrix that will be gradually burned away as the full objective dimensions of the event are revealed. The overpublicized framework of speculation about the kinds of truth possible to novels and histories doesn't seem to me to have any great theoretical importance or interest, but it functions well as a scaffolding for the basic movement of the narrative, which is from pugnacious personal comedy to prophetic witness and litany, with "the Protagonist" (as Mailer calls himself) increasingly subordinated to the high historical occasion. Certain passages of objective action and movement—the first climax of the march over the bridge, the oddly relaxed night bus ride to some obscure Virginia jail —are among the finest in the book; and at the end, in the moving evocation of the ordeal in the Washington jail of those Quakers whose resistance to totalitarian power becomes not just an afternoon's symbolic foray in front of television cameras but a life-and-death venture to the ragged edge of dehumanization and madness, Mailer is present only as an imaginative witness, asking unanswerable questions and offering his writer's metaphors of prayer and prophecy for those who have found a way through to the rare places of spirit that "no history can reach." It is they who may just possibly be able, as no one else yet has, to break the lethal pattern of present history and forge a new human beginning. The great Blakean metaphors of parturition and ambiguous new birth with which the book ends are treacherous to reawaken—and I notice that that exceptionally sensible critic, Conor Cruse O'Brien, has described these last pages as "the kind of nonsense which can be perpetrated by excellent writers when they take to wallowing in their own idea of their own culture"*—but to my American ear they have the heart-sinking beauty of an entire fitness to this fearful, intimately American occasion; it is hard not to feel that they form a climax which has been fully earned.

---

* *Albert Camus* (1970), p. 67n.

Of course a judgment like that is itself in hostage to the public circumstance that engendered the book. It may well be that the power of statement I have felt in *The Armies of the Night* I will not feel a few years hence, if somehow we do get out of the Vietnam War and our own spreading civil crisis without some transmogrifying catastrophe. Even so, as a work at least of personal witness, I think the book will keep its interest and vitality. For of these two books, Malcolm's and Mailer's, I think this finally can be said: they give us what our major literary tradition, as we find it in Franklin, Emerson, Whitman, Melville, Henry James, Robinson, Fitzgerald, the Stevens of the *Letters*, has always propounded and celebrated at the core, and what, moreover, since Tocqueville has been defined as the blessing of life most imperiled by the characteristic development of a mass exploitative society—and that is the saving counterforce of personality. To borrow a couple of famous cadences: in the midst of our immense depersonalization real personalities stand here, the indispensable mediators between consciousness and reality, between the life we still might learn to make and the life that bears down on us with the dead weight of all our past collusions. Real personalities— but of course only those who know the special impoverishment of life that comes with the loss of the poetry of human personality will know what it means for these two writers to have survived the violations of personal life and being our deadly era has made commonplace, and borne strong and truthful witness to them.

American Notes

Being and Growing: Cummings on Cummings

In the first of the six "nonlectures" delivered under his appointment as Charles Eliot Norton Professor of Poetry at Harvard and gathered under the title, *i*, EECummings identifies those of his writings—*EIMI, him, Santa Claus*, "perhaps twenty poems" and "half a dozen" essays—in which he finds his "stance as a writer most clearly expressed." The list is interesting in itself, but not more so than the principle of selection; it is characteristic of Cummings to pitch his scheme of evaluation and focus our attention on the figure of Man Writing. His second "outspokenness" makes the point again: "poetry and every other art was and is and forever will be strictly and distinctly a question of individuality . . . poetry is being, not doing." Now *i* is not all poetry, but it is unmistakably EECummings being himself. And in the sense (reversing his equation) that "being" is poetry, it is a very engaging production indeed.

To say, then, that it will not be one of the works by which his standing, different from his stance, will be measured is only to say that he understood the occasion for which it was designed. Invited to deliver the Norton lectures for 1952–1953, he took a lecturer's, or nonlecturer's, liberties. Being the best of talkers and an artful and illuminating reader, he talked and

Reprinted from THE NEW ENGLAND QUARTERLY, December, 1954.

he read, informally, disconnectedly, self-indulgently. A willing
but unavoidably staring audience of eight hundred is not the
optimum setting for the risks of sterner creation. He cheer-
fully announced that he was undertaking an "aesthetic strip-
tease." But true to that ceremonious art, he did not go "all
the way." We learn little that could not be guessed and is not
better known in the already published poetry and prose which
he has chosen to represent him again here. The passages on his
father and mother in the first nonlecture are lovingly spoken
and truly moving. Yet the poem, "if there are any heavens," on
which this nonlecture pivots says as much in its eighteen
verses; and the justly celebrated elegy, "my father moved
through dooms of love," introduces in that first line a dimension of feeling which has not been allowed to trouble the
serene recollections of *i*.

For all his show of outspokenness in *i*, Cummings is nothing if not reticent. Consider the third nonlecture, devoted to
"the mystery of transition from which" (out of the "longlost
personage" of an enchanted childhood) "emerged a poet and
painter named EECummings." The stages of this crucial event
are itemized: growing up in a happy time which declined no
gambits and had not heard of "security"; attending Harvard,
with a "glimpse of Homer," a "deep glance at Dante and
Shakespeare," and a taste of independence and truest friendship; discovering in succession Scollay Square, the future editors of the *Dial*, New York, Paris, and a war. The testimony is
not persuasive. If nobody should buy *i* but citizens whose lives
have followed this initial course, EECummings has a modest
best seller on his hands. Paris is traditionally a revelation to
the deprived New England eye, but it does not by itself transform the passionate pilgrim's lyric outcry into poems, into a
voice and a style, as individual and as accomplished as Mr.
Cummings' have always been. There is more than this, surely,
to be said about the genesis of a New England writer whose
climaxing sentences read like irreverent glosses on Emerson or
Thoreau ("all history's too small for even me"); whose "three
mysteries: love, art, and selftranscendence or growing," have
kept not only one poet and painter but a whole province literate and exalted; whose two long prose works, *The Enormous
Room* and *EIMI*, invoke repeatedly the sacred New England

master-texts of Bunyan and Dante; and whose sometimes embarrassingly callow "philosophy" crosses, in style, cracker-barrel pastoralism with conscientious imitations of demotic Somervillese.

This is not to imply that the explanation of his achievement will ever be easily given. By a triumph of inimitable voice Cummings survives all his resemblances. He is poised so obviously astride the Boston-Cambridge-Concord axis, the manner of the fathers is so much second nature to him, that the wonder is how he has managed for thirty years to escape the various fates which so many New England talents have succumbed to—the dissipation of impulse in conscientiousness; the too easily won, too quickly crystallized, too patronizingly received moral philosophy; the complicated and rarely surmounted barrier to self-fulfillment presented by so much literate eminence ("to our right occurred professors James and Royce; to our left transpired professor Taussig") ; the temptations to overhurried ripening and the seductions of predetermined ambition offered by that hothouse (or cold-frame) culture. The Norton lectures are valuable in showing us the other Cummings who might have been; for in the jolly corner of this six-part fantasia, among the Old Howard jokes, the affected verbosity, the talk of beauty's "immortal battle," the nose-thumbing and statue-fouling, we meet face to face the specter of inverted gentility which since Thoreau has haunted the overbred New England writer.

We meet him, and Cummings kills him again before our eyes. His weapon, we are surprised to discover, is discretion. Instead of talking on, after he had said the few things he had to say, instead of repeating or rephrasing himself, he spent at least half his time reciting poems. His recitations make up the bulk of the attractively published *i:* the select anthology of his own work and the little Golden Treasury of master lyrics to which he devoted the last third of each nonlecture—poems by Burns and Donne, Shelley and Keats, Swinburne and Chaucer, Charles d'Orléans and Walther von der Vogelweide, the ballad "Edward" and the "Ode. Intimations of Immortality from Recollections of Early Childhood."

Being recalled to such riches, we grant him his casual opinions. On a second look we may object that Cummings' principle of "fidelity to self" is too shrilly articulated, his myth of lovers reaching eternity too blandly pronounced. But no sooner is patience the least bit strained than he has turned abruptly from lecturing to reading, has sailed past us "deep in those heights of psychic sky" where his art transcends our unbelief and where he knows, and his craft and taste triumphantly proclaim, that "only the artist in ourselves is more truthful than the night." In the pinch our nonlecturer rises past romantic self-indulgence to the truthfulness of his own best writing: he knows that even the artist, though asserted to be "naturally and miraculously whole" in the "strictly illimitable country" of himself, is nevertheless "a man, a failure"; that he is only "*feelingly* illimitable"; and that—although his "only happiness is to transcend himself"—to grow is indeed his "every agony." In flashes of the nonlecturing, and steadily in the readings, the always surprising freshness, the durability, the high-spirited and deep-rooted resourcefulness of EECummings' work are made apparent to us once more. For this sufficient reason *i* is a certain blessing.

Memorial to a Golden Age

The Little Review Anthology has been compiled by one of the founders and permanent editors, Margaret Anderson, from the sixteen-year life-span of what was beyond doubt one of the best of all "little" magazines, on either side of the Atlantic. Its display of riches is breathtaking, the more so because accompanied by enough specimens of perishable junk to give the impression of a living magazine rather than a museum. Miss Anderson's original responsibility in bringing all this about was considerable. (Her good-tempered autobiography, *My Thirty Years' War*, is the kind of document that leaves you at once warm with admiration and green with envy.) Her account of the founding of *The Little Review* in 1913—that it was a "logical necessity"—is too modest. She writes, "It was the moment. The epoch needed it"—but of course by sensing that a new epoch of a very special kind had

Reprinted from THE NEW ENGLAND QUARTERLY, June, 1953.

dawned, she became in her way one of its significant guardians. Two passages in her lively *Anthology* indicate *LR*'s particular role. Ezra Pound, accepting the post of foreign editor, explained: "I wished a place where the current prose writings of James Joyce, Wyndham Lewis, T. S. Eliot, and myself might appear regularly, promptly, and together, rather than irregularly, sporadically, and after useless delays." And in a gracious letter for the final number in 1929, Eliot recalled that time when "*The Little Review* was the only periodical in America which would accept my work, and indeed the only periodical there in which I cared to appear."

Other little magazines, as Miss Anderson's collaborator, Jane Heap, summed it up, "had somewhat the same intellectual program, but the *Little Review* had the corresponding emotions." That eventually became its greatest danger as well, an indiscriminate passion for the *mystique* of Art, and some of the material "that would have been accepted by no other magazine in the world at the moment" would have been no great loss; the early numbers, as Pound observed, were "scrappy and unselective." Its beginnings were evangelical in the Chicago style of 1912–1913, Sherwood Anderson imploring the younger generation to "stand up and be counted among the soldiers of the new"; it ended somewhat after the editors had succumbed to their long-standing temptation to abandon "literature, drama, music, painting, sculpture" for "the psychology of those things," and for the "illuminations" exemplified by their unaccountably licensed contributor, the Baroness Else von Freytag von Loringhoven, she of the gold-painted bald head, who represented, or tried to explain, the "Art of Madness." But during, as Margaret Anderson acknowledges, the only one of its three main phases which wholly fulfilled her high ideal, *The Little Review* printed Eliot, Pound, Yeats, Hart Crane, Williams, Dreiser, Cocteau, Apollinaire, Hemingway; it devoted special issues to French Symbolism, to Henry James, to W. H. Hudson (that transmogrified New Englander), to Constantin Brancusi; and in its finest hour, in spite of the Society for the Suppression of Vice, the United States Post Office, the New York Court of Special Sessions, and the defection of Popovitch, son of the poetess-laureate of Serbia and the one printer in New York who had been eager for the job, it serialized *Ulysses* for three years, until the editors were arrested for publishing "obscene literature."

Quite properly the bulk of *The Little Review Anthology* is drawn from this 1917–1923 middle period. The selections adequately suggest *LR*'s variety and individuality. Only a few pieces by the star contributors are otherwise easy to find in anthologies. Williams' prose "Improvisations," Pound's "Study in French Poets," and a moving story called "Landscape with Trees" by one Carlos A. V. Kral (pseud.?) are outstanding items. Perhaps the prize recovery is Eliot's only known short story, "Eeldrop and Appleplex," from which two sentences must be added to the official canon ("There are evil neighborhoods of noise and evil neighborhoods of silence, and Eeldrop and Appleplex preferred the latter as being the more evil" and "With the decline of orthodox theology and its admirable theory of the soul, the unique importance of events has vanished": these from 1917). There is unsuspected talent in a Valentine-poem by Hemingway. A disagreement between Margaret Anderson and Pound about Marianne Moore is preserved in a valuable exchange on the nature of poetic statement and certain aspects of "Americanness." The sincerity of Emma Goldman's World War I "Letters from Prison" stands out among the watery imagism and pseudomodern sentimentality of many early entries. And there is the editor's challenging valediction, writing *finis* to her undertaking with as much swagger as she had carried it on: "Our mission was accomplished; contemporary art had 'arrived'; for a hundred years, perhaps, the literary world would produce only: repetition." It is an opinion, we may say, on which the final verdict is not yet in.

Van Wyck Brooks's Arcadia

Mr. Van Wyck Brooks's talents of evocation and indirection are well exercised in his new book, *The Dream of Arcadia*, subtitled "American Writers and Artists in Italy, 1760–1915."

Reprinted from THE NEW ENGLAND QUARTERLY, June, 1959.

Among the long file of observers, pilgrims, and expatriates who pass in review through his loosely strung succession of ten-page chapters are half the great names of our nineteenth-century literature; a vivid array of half-forgotten lesser notables well worth remembering, like Constance Fenimore Woolson, Charles Godfrey Leland, and Henry Blake Fuller; and a multitude of scholars, collectors, and fugitive practitioners of the plastic and graphic arts. So, too, a number of our pleasantest books are recalled in the picturesque circumstances that inspired them—*The Water Witch, The Marble Faun, Venetian Life* and *Indian Summer, Roderick Hudson* and *William Wetmore Story*, Mrs. Wharton's *Italian Gardens and Their Villas,* Berenson's *Italian Painters of the Renaissance.*

The book is a kind of postscript to the vast panorama of *Makers and Finders,* Brooks's "history of the literary life in America." It has, if the distinction may be made, a beguiling consistency—there is golden Italy and here are all these congenial Americans wandering through it—but no positive unity. One simply misses, but has learned not to expect from this author, the concentrated thrust of judgment or speculation that his rich materials would seem to require and that might give form and force to the ingenious mosaic of his presentation of them. It is not that the instinct or capacity for judgment is wanting. Arresting phrases are plentiful enough, such as that describing the occultist Leland "groping from the corner of one ruined conjecture to another." It is only that "Italy," literally for Brooks as imaginatively for Hawthorne a hundred years earlier, affords "a sort of poetic or fairy precinct, where actualities would not be so terribly insisted upon" as in the "America" out of which his various sojourners were all incessantly conscious of being transplanted: the actualities, in this instance, of the unending American struggle between the imperatives to self-expression, and to a new release of creativity, and the generating yet inhibiting New World conditions. Brooks does not choose to push his chronicle to the point, for example, which Henry James's life of Story occupies at once, of observing in so many words that what a Story's years in Italy and in the practice of sculpture and poetry amount to is not a "career" but a "case," the classic American case of underexposure and overcompensation.

The curious thing is that this is the kind of case which, in his recent memoir *Days of the Phoenix,* Brooks describes himself as having been "possessed by" as a critic—the miscarriage of talent and imagination in America, the foredoomed failure, the dissipated promise, the losing one's way as a creator and performer. He was mastered early on, like one of his many "victims of Italy" (but that again is James's phrase), by some Ruskinian vision of a social harmony in which creative talents, great or small, might flower without interference or malformation, each according to its natural capacity. I do not mean to ridicule this vision: it made *America's Coming-of-Age* a memorable manifesto, and it has inspired those recent books about Brooks's own life in letters and the lives of his friends —*Scenes and Portraits, Days of the Phoenix, John Sloan*—which more and more seem to me his own best contribution to our literature. In these books the dream of an ideal community of writers and artists, humanists and guardians, is substantiated by the natural abundance and sharpness of unforced recollection, of a history that is not ideologically manufactured but private and genuine; and they have in consequence a rightness of proportion, a harmony of emphasis and detail, such as his more ambitious but essentially synthetic *Makers and Finders* does not manage to sustain. This is Van Wyck Brooks's own fine "dream of Arcadia," of which the present volume is a welcome by-product.

Two Careers: Clarence King and Henry Adams

There has been a ready public for a biography of Clarence King—and a mental hazard for the writer attempting it—ever since *The Education of Henry Adams* put out its tantalizing intimations of the interest and possible symbolism of King's life. The rare promise, the precocity of actual accomplishment, the legendary charm and energy, the ominous unfulfillment

Reprinted from THE NEW ENGLAND QUARTERLY, December, 1958, and September, 1956.

and diminuendo—Adams outlined this drama, decreed its intensity, and insinuated an interpretation: that here was the representative American for a whole era of our history.

The first thing to say of Thurman Wilkins' *Clarence King: A Biography* is that it runs this hazard successfully and well deserves to find its public. His narrative is supported by thoroughgoing scholarship (bibliography and notes are most impressive) and also by a basic discretion and intelligence which the writing itself does not always do justice to but does not obscure. The interest of King's career proves as great as Adams claimed, though it is not altogether the same interest. It is, in the nature of Professor Wilkins' undertaking, an interest less decisively emblematic yet not less exemplary from a historical point of view. The best years of King's life were the years devoted to science and the scientific exploration of the Far West, culminating in his appointment in 1879 as first Director of the United States Geological Survey, and the account of these years is the most absorbing part of the book. Professor Wilkins is especially effective in communicating the excitement of going in for science—geology, paleontology, ethnography, mine engineering, surveying, mountaineering—in the 1860's and 1870's, in the days of Agassiz and Dana, Lyell, Darwin, and Edward Tylor, with the whole vast American West lying open for scientific (and economic) exploitation. We get a just impression of how the new prestige of science joined with the romantic attractiveness of virgin and frontier territories and the competitive scramble of the Gilded Age to set the course of King's career.

Not that everything about it is cleared up or put in order. Obscurities and enigmas remain. That they do remain is really one of the merits of this biography, for though the author suggests explanations for the progression of King's life, he does not straitjacket his subject but allows him the mysterious freedom of movement and change without which no characterization can persuade us. From the start, evidences of some fundamental instability go side by side with the signs of exceptional talent. King had an appetite for work, and had won for himself, by his middle twenties, a well deserved reputation for original research and for leadership in the field. But he was never able to surrender himself to the scientific vocation. Perhaps his successes came too easily and on too many fronts. He could outline, with striking self-assurance, intuitive solutions to the broadest theoretical problems—the origins of volcanoes, the age of the earth—but increasingly lacked the professional patience to put them thoroughly to the test. Repeatedly he would feel himself ready to quit "the analytical study of Nature and drink in the sympathetic side," and gives us in one way or another an impression of rather overindulging a desire to lead the Life Beautiful and make of his own existence a work of art and vessel of pleasure. Yet his relish for beauty and the amenities served a rather conventional imagination. He was disgusted by the schemes for Grant's Tomb, but what we are told of his own alternative design seems, despite La Farge's approval, scarcely less vulgar.

Early on in King's life the advance symptoms of chronic ill health—recurrent fevers, back trouble, nervous disorders—began to take toll of him. He squandered his physical powers in the exertions of fieldwork, and perhaps also his chances for psychological balance. Certainly that extraordinary capacity for working at full stretch was severely and prematurely diminished, though down to his last illness he would jump up from a sickbed and go thousands of miles on a speculative mining venture or in the hope of "striking some smashing blow" in theoretical science. But one senses also deeper disabilities. When he resigned from the Geological Survey in 1881, one feels him moved by more than simply the wish to make a private fortune. King was not a man for long-term commitments. In a way his career as a scientist was a brilliant prolongation of a student's enthusiasms; it was over, he had in effect "turned his back on it," as Professor Wilkins remarks, before he was forty. A knot of private needs—drawn tight perhaps by the possessiveness of a young and attractive mother, only sixteen when he was born and twice widowed before he turned twenty-five—gradually constricted his capacity for risk and perseverance. His mysteriously broken engagement to a charming Washoe girl, his restlessness and wandering, his conflicting predilections for Gilded Age elegance and for the primitive or derelict societies of the tropics and the frontier, his underground marriage at forty-six to a young black woman —it is part of Professor Wilkins' accomplishment to make all these things seem pieces in a coherent pattern, of which we lack only the key, the complete original.

Except here and there, as in the awkward business of getting started, Professor Wilkins has let the facts in the case of Clarence King tell their own story, a story which so manifestly reflects so many aspects of American life and sensibility between 1860 and 1900 that any sort of special pleading would have been a waste of breath. If he now wants to put us further in his debt, he might give us next a new edition of King's *Mountaineering in the Sierra Nevada*. His brief account of it bears out the claim that here is a classic of Western exploration, and an expression of the old New England temper *in partibus infidelium*, which should take its place in our literature along with Dana's *Two Years* and Parkman's *Oregon Trail*.

❊　❊　❊

In writing *Henry Adams: A Biography*, Elizabeth Stevenson has had a clear field, hers being (except for James Truslow Adams' short volume published in 1933) the first full-length portrait. On the whole she has acquitted herself well. Adams is not the most tractable subject for biographical treatment. There is the *Education*, not to be read as a true account of Henry Adams' actual life, yet looming in formidable judgment over any subsequent attempt to render a true account; there are his books, essays, and letters, providing an already full, subtle, and discouragingly articulate record of that life of the mind for its treatment of which any new biography is bound to be judged; and, to obscure the evidence, there is Adams' constitutional and lifelong habit of attitudinizing—over small matters and large, private affairs and public—the outward expression of a most perplexing inward man. An illuminating sympathy and a basic rightness of judgment in essential matters tide Miss Stevenson over these barriers; further, her book is, as a piece of writing, succinct, unpretentious, and thoroughly readable.

Adams himself remains her principal source. Except for two unpublished letters she draws only on materials made familiar by Ernest Samuels, Robert Hume, William H. Jordy, and other recent workers in the field. But her arrangement of these materials is skillful and creative; her selections from Adams' letters amount to a critical anthology of their concentrations and repetitions; and gradually a firm, credible, original likeness emerges, commanding assent and deserving the praise reviewers have given it.

Miss Stevenson is especially alert to the personal stake, the biographical element, in Adams' books; without exaggerating, she persuasively suggests the place of each in the successive equations of his life. As in her earlier study of Henry James (*The Crooked Corridor*), it is the ground on which life and work join that most interests her. And though her method of analyzing Adams' books can be awkwardly diagrammatic, it is usually justified in the result. On the *Life of Gallatin* and its value to Adams as a first full-scale "experiment in technique," she is concisely suggestive. She does justice to the problem of the novel *Esther*, its disturbing mixture of buoyancy and desolation, the possibility that Marian Adams never knew of it. When Miss Stevenson misses the mark, she usually makes the necessary correction herself. Of the inadequacy of her description of the theme of the nine-volume *History of the United States During the Administrations of Jefferson and Madison* as "the fall of a young and naïve society from a too high, a too ideal theory of government to a more realistic and less heroic conception," her full chapter on the *History* is evidence enough; the analysis there is rather labored and inelegant, yet in the end it delivers a fair and unstinted suggestion of the *History*'s range, weight, and intensity as a work of speculative imagination.

Perhaps her best contribution to our understanding of Adams' work is her demonstration (performed with an economy which has graced none of the recent academic studies) of a certain fixity of interest, a unity of apprehension and expressed concern, from the sophisticated Civil War letters written in his early twenties to the last theoretical essays of 1908–1909. All his best work, the *Mont-Saint-Michel* as well as the *History*, is addressed to what the author defines as Adams' fundamental subject at every stage: society, the social order, "man fixed firmly in the political, social, and economic condition of life" —and thus, in due course, history. Even his "autobiography," as Miss Stevenson reminds us in a well-chosen phrase, makes sense only as "a study of history"; if Adams in his preface reached back for parallels to Augustine, Rousseau, Franklin, we more properly look forward to the Toynbee era, and Adams does not suffer in the comparison.

It is at this point, on the significance and direction of Adams' work in his chosen profession and its weight and place in the history of thought, that the present book falls short. To say this is no great disparagement. The critical essay that will do justice to Adams' achievement has yet to be written; Mr. R. P. Blackmur's struggles to write it testify to its difficulties as well as its attractions. For both in his concerns and in his capacity to express them Adams stands apart among postcolonial American writers. The generative moral values and conceptions in the best of our classic literature—such as are with us yet in our ordinary ideas of what is good, so that we have found James rather more congenial than Adams—are personal integrity and spiritual vitality; what Emerson's era meant by "self-culture"; what is permitted to individual men, or what may be struggled for, in a society apprehended as free, essentially pliable (which is not to say unbrutal), and materially abundant, within a pluralistic universe. But Adams (for whom, as Miss Stevenson puts it, the highest good would have been to be "used" by a purposeful and organized society "all of a long, productive, unsubjective life") was too "fretful" and "impatient" to find satisfaction in self-culture. In his best work he takes another stance: he figures in our literature as a fairly unique observer-moralist of the outward, public, historical circumstance of American life, and as our first conscious, objective, systematic analyst of mass society. Where he properly belongs as a writer is in the company of Tocqueville, Burckhardt, Ortega, Jaspers even, writers whose achievement is to have combined a prophetic apprehension of the special character of democratic and technological society and a new insight into the form and meaning of modern history.

As early as 1863 Adams was saying: "I have learned to think De Tocqueville my model, and I study his life and works as the gospel of my private religion." This was barely a year after he had responded to the strategic threat posed by the

Merrimac with prophetic excitement: "I tell you these are great times. Man has mounted science, and is now run away with." Halfway through his work on his own *History*, in 1884, he wrote Francis Parkman that the more he labored, the more confident he grew that "Democracy is the only subject for history," a pronouncement which he expanded in the absorbing last chapter of the ninth volume: "Should history ever become a true science, it must expect to establish its laws, not from the complicated story of rival European nationalities, but from the methodical evolution of a great democracy." (The well-known quotations are all in Miss Stevenson's book, but she does not reconstruct the pattern they make.) And if Adams' opportunities for testing and refining his insights were fewer and his capacities that much less trained than Tocqueville's or Burckhardt's, there is in his work a compensating facility and boldness (whatever we think of the analogies between history and science) in carrying historical analysis into the realm of philosophic principle and grounding it, as he did, in problems of knowledge. Perhaps this is because he came to his work from within the American situation, which was for Tocqueville and Burckhardt the very harbinger of mass society, the model for better or worse of the universal democratic future, a concept seeking material embodiment. If Adams' point of departure is more abstract than theirs, and his line of advance more precarious and problematical, this is indeed a measure of his Americanism.

As with Emerson, upon whose relation to European thought the same kind of judgment may be passed, Adams' forcing of analogies among different modes of knowledge, different categories of experience, could be a source of irrelevance and of error, but also of original insight. In measuring natural "force" and human adaptation, or educability, Adams looked back to classic nineteenth-century inquiries into the "moral" relationships of nature and mind. But in making history and the philosophy of history his field of speculation, he looked forward to a later development, still unformed and barely conceived, but more creative, more profoundly searching and consequential than the factitious effort to make history a positive science: the development of an understanding of "history" as a unique category of relationships; a distinct existential dimension; the newest and least charted of the symbolic forms of knowledge and behavior ("Phases of Matter," the carryover determinist in Henry Adams called them); a field in which the newest conjunction of empiricism and rationalism, of statistical description and prophetic commitment may take place, leading perhaps to a new philosophic definition of human freedom (as it is in large part through the dimension of "history" that theology has been restored to intellectual respectability and practical use). This is the nature and direction of Adams' achievement, and it gives him his place among the makers of the modern imagination. Miss Stevenson has not pushed her study this far, but as his biographer she has done her job well in opening a way of approach.

The Nineties—And After

In his fine essay on Stephen Crane, the novelist Ralph Ellison characterizes the literary situation of the 1890's in the United States in these words: "Despite the prosperity and apparent openness and freedom of the society, it was as though a rigid national censorship had been imposed—not by an apparatus set up in Washington, but within the center of the American mind. Now there was much of which Americans were morally aware but little which they wished to confront in literature, and the compelling of such confrontation was the challenge flung down by Crane to history." This, broadly, is the theme of Larzer Ziff's stimulating new book, *The American 1890's*, which he has subtitled "Life and Times of a Lost Generation." His starting point is that by the nineties the literate classes in America lived in one way but preferred to express themselves in another and that the serious writers of the day were beset by a problem of truth of the commonest sort, the problem of bridging "the chasm which yawned between private experience and public literature."

With poetry almost a "suppressed instinct" (Henry Ad-

Reprinted from AMERICAN LITERATURE, March, 1967.

ams' phrase) prose fiction provided the arena—that is, if discussion is limited to "imaginative" literature—in which this struggle for truth and re-engagement began to be fought out. Professor Ziff shows in the rich detail of broken careers and wasted opportunities how disabling this struggle proved to be. It had already driven Howells into compromises that neutralized the encouragement he was prepared to give younger successors; it had driven Henry James and Mark Twain into the different but curiously related forms of "literary absenteeism" that made both men "inaccessible," Ziff effectively demonstrates, to the rising generation. The works and days of this generation are surveyed principally in terms of a common effort to produce what is called at one point "the novel of social forces," though psychological truthfulness was a parallel aim. Professor Ziff tells his melancholy story with tact and humor and with a flexible critical sympathy; he is not tied down to dogmatic conceptions of "realism" or any other rigid standard of merit.

It is a virtue of his confidently argued book that its best chapters are on what nearly everyone will agree to be its most important particular topics. The description of Crane's brief progress and of Dreiser's shocking advance into candor in *Sister Carrie* are solid additions to critical understanding. The chapter on the newspaper ambiance of writing in the nineties is the best account I know of this notorious forcing-bed (and rack) of American literary ambition. The chapter on literary magazines is more perfunctory—and with regard to the author's concern with historical links between the nineties and better-provided times to come, his omission of Mosher's *Bibelot,* with its openness to uncommon European developments, is notable. A more distressing omission is of Thorstein Veblen, whose name does not appear in the book. Yet if there was one work of "penetration" (an announced standard) that triumphed over the national censorship of the 1890's, it surely was *The Theory of the Leisure Class*, which Howells greeted with enthusiasm as a work of satire. It seems to me also that the whole effort to identify a "Midwestern Imagination" is seriously defective. The sheer diversity of this vast section defeats Professor Ziff's method of tying a topic up in a taut single chain of suggestive details and insinuations; and as to these one must question a whole series of indicated assumptions, such as that the whole of the Midwest was settled out of New England, that the Midwest which nourished writers was a region of farms and scattered villages ("rural America," "the Great Plains homestead") and not one of county seats, state capitals, and river and lakeshore cities-on-the-make, or that "society" in the Midwest was "servantless"—a very odd notion indeed.

More generally, since the book's argumentative force and skill will recommend it to good students, should not two primary historical judgments be strongly queried? Professor Ziff refers to the next decade, 1902–1912, as in the wake of the defeats of the nineties' writers the "dreariest" in American literary history. Is this really the case? Precisely by comparison with the nineties, these next ten years hardly require apology; it is the decade of *Belchamber, The Souls of Black Folk, The House of Mirth* and *Ethan Frome, Three Lives* and *The Making of Americans, The People of the Abyss* and *Martin Eden, Mont-Saint-Michel and Chartres* and the *Education, Mr. Crewe's Career, Together, The Jungle, The Miller of Old Church,* and *Jennie Gerhardt,* of Robinson's and Pound's poetry, Willa Cather's first stories, Huneker's criticism, and the extraordinary creative resurgence of Henry James. Much of this work, however, is by more patient and resolute contemporaries, classmates, so to speak, of Professor Ziff's somewhat restricted cast of characters. I suspect that the unit of the decade is simply unsuited to the description of a generation's experience.

More important is the matter of the book's blunt closing assertions that it was the struggles of the writers of the nineties which opened the way to the renaissance of 1912 and after. These assertions may roughly fit the American publishing data. But that is just what is unsatisfactory about them: they are wholly restricted to the American scene, as if the immediate reasons why one thing follows another in American literary history have ever been exclusively or even primarily American. The plain fact is that there was a renaissance in literature and other arts in the United States after 1912 because there had been, and still was, one in Europe. The immediate creative context for Eliot, O'Neill, Hemingway, Hart Crane, even for Sherwood Anderson and William Carlos Williams, was established by Frenchmen, Irishmen, Russians; by Baudelaire, Maupassant, Ibsen, Joyce, Ford, Turgenev, *et al.* Furthermore, with regard to specifically American influences, one might just as reasonably argue that the pathos of broken careers and blighted promise in the 1890's (itself not only an American phenomenon) chiefly served to foster a note of histrionic self-pity which crept into nativist criticism in the 1920's, as with Van Wyck Brooks's studies of Twain and James, or the famous *Green Hills of Africa* disquisition on the something that "happens to our good writers at a certain age."

I am moved to add that the virtues and faults of this lively book—both considerable—seem to me typical of the present state of American literature studies. *The American 1890's* is not really a work of systematic historical definition so much as an exercise (in this instance of a quite superior order) in retrospective journalism, or in a new kind of market-conscious antiquarianism in which the generally familiar materials of some poignant past episode are reassembled as museum exhibits are assembled, for show and for quick consumption more than for any thoroughgoing attempt at original elucidation. Compare this book, for example, with the tougher virtue, the bolder commitment to a primary effort of critical recovery and renewal, of an older work it somewhat resembles in design, Kazin's *On Native Grounds.* I do not mean that Professor Ziff's book was not worth doing, only that it would have been worth doing even better, with a critically firmer purpose and on a broader front. American literature studies really must decide anew what their fundamental purposes are, what range of consideration and understanding is required of them, what kinds of truth and knowledge they have first of all to serve. "Literary interpretation must be systematic," M. René Girard has written, "because it is the continuation of literature." Admittedly it is rather too often the continuation of literature "by other means," but if it is to earn its way as a special department of scholarship, it can hardly settle for any lesser task.

The Case of Wallace Stevens

The point of departure for Helen Hennessy Vendler's close-woven essay on Wallace Stevens* is the critical judgment that the best of Stevens is in those longer poems—from "Sunday Morning" in 1915 to "An Ordinary Evening in New Haven" of 1949–1950—which mark off the main intervals and developments of his extraordinary career. This judgment has the support of Stevens himself, who spoke at various times of how the sustained attention to a single subject which is required by the long poem is what most fully "liberates" imagination, for the reader as well as the poet, and "naturalizes" it in a freshly organized world of discourse. The critical commentary Mrs. Vendler offers is intelligent and acute in its perceptions. Moreover it springs from a personal sympathy that does not fail to communicate the rich charm and pathos, and the spells of declamatory grandeur, that Stevens rose to again and again in these brilliant poems. From first to last, *Harmonium* to *The Auroras of Autumn* and beyond, "he mutter spiffy" (as John Berryman's dream song has put it, not spitefully), and it is a first virtue of this study to keep that poetic spiffiness in full view.

Mrs. Vendler is especially good in characterizing Stevens' style and its progressive transformations. She writes tellingly of the "elaborately mannered movement of thought" that, in one tonality or another, is at the basis of Stevens' rhetoric; of a delicate "drift" of moods, and of curiously poignant debates over the meaning of certain unaccountable perceptions and "forms half-glimpsed," the "presences" that attend the seasons and chromatic variations of the mind's wavering life among phenomena (Stevens' great subject); of the lavish accretion of metaphors which are "extremely provisional in their species, but quite permanent in their genus"; of the virtuoso play of "appositions and qualifications," making an elegantly "in-

---

Reprinted from AMERICAN LITERATURE, May, 1970.
* *On Extended Wings: Wallace Stevens' Longer Poems* (1969).

cremental" style, with corresponding "oscillations of rhythm";
of the special extensions of these strategies which give "The
Man With the Blue Guitar" its "rigid and flawless structure"
of alternating stasis and flow, and "Notes Toward a Supreme
Fiction" its freer and grander harmony; and, movingly, of
"the great and remote poetry of Stevens' old age, so unlike any
other poetry in English." Her discussions continually send us
back to the poems and concentrate a sense, lovely to renew, of
their distinguishing solemnity and poise. What handsomer
service can commentary perform?

This being so, it may be ungrateful to express regret that
Professor Vendler's study stays so much inside its designated
task. (And couldn't a less audibly devout title have been found
for it?) Yet at this stage in our long assimilation of Stevens'
poetry something more is wanted, particularly if a certain
atmosphere of coterie veneration that has been thickening
around him in the universities is to be kept under control.
The lack of reference to wider contexts than are provided by
touchstone allusions to, say, Shelley or Keats may produce
something like an effect of inflation or at least dislocation in
the table of judgment. Readers immersed in American literary
history, for example, are likely to have felt something deeply
familiar in the recurrent behavior of Stevens' longer poems,
bringing a different set of resemblances to mind. Can we not
recognize in his compositional trick of turning philosophic
formulas and issues into the elements of an abstract drama of
moods and mental states a fresh version of that subjectivist
rhetoric which Emerson first mastered in American writing?
The whole elaborate back-and-forth in later Stevens between
"imagination" and "reality" recalls nothing so directly as the
shadowy interplay in Emerson of "Power" and "Fate" as argu-
ment-framing themes; and the result is much the same kind of
subtle and fluent pageant, radically idealizing, of autonomous
mental gestures and symbolic hypotheses.

To place Stevens' achievement in full relation to the
Emersonian set of so much subsequent American writing (and
American art) is not only to reach a more precise sense of the
provenance of his style. It may also serve to situate that nagging
further impression set down in Berryman's little poem—an
impression hardly to be admitted in a critical brief that makes

its corroborative appeal almost exclusively to poets of the class of Wordsworth, Milton, Spenser—of an "odd something . . . something . . . not there in his flourishing art." Professor Vendler acknowledges a "narrowness," a persistent abstraction of experience into diagrammatic soliloquy; but, to take a major case, in explicating "Notes Toward a Supreme Fiction" she makes no mention, and gives no indication of feeling the absence, of that fourth section that Stevens once regretted not having gone on to write, a section to be called "It Must Be Human." There is an issue of imaginative grasp and equity here that must be faced with Stevens; a sense of a particular limitation (a built-in tautology of argument and syntax together) that we do not feel in the greatest poetry, including that of other Anglo-American moderns like Yeats, Eliot, Hart Crane, not less capable of transcendental heightenings but holding a fuller, more direct purchase on the body of human life and passion. Stevens' letters, in the great collection published by his daughter in 1966, seem to me wonderfully revealing in this regard, binding the poems far more intimately than one had suspected to a lifelong regimen, toughly and artfully persisted in, of personal endurance and self-restoration; but Professor Vendler does not make much use of them, except in points of interpretive detail.

The point, of course, is not to put Wallace Stevens down or discourage absorption in him but to identify more precisely the odd grandeur of his achievement—of which, as Lowell remarked of Emerson's peculiar eloquence, the one thing that may not be said is that it was not noble. This central critical task is one which Professor Vendler's book, where one agrees with it and where one disagrees, both encourages and advances.

The Case of Hart Crane

The critical purpose of R. W. B. Lewis's new book, *The Poetry of Hart Crane,* is set out modestly enough in the Preface. It is "to follow the development of Crane's poetry," and simultane-

Reprinted from THE MASSACHUSETTS REVIEW, Autumn, 1968.

ously "to chart the career of Crane's imagination," in such a way as "to open, not to close" discussion of the poet's achievement. This plan makes good sense, given the present facts of the case—the imperfectly realized character of much of Crane's work; the confusions generated by his vivid and aggressive poetic personality; the corresponding absence of any critical consensus, even on the point of his relative importance. An impression has persisted, ever since magazine publication of certain poems in 1922 and 1923, that Crane's might conceivably be the strongest talent in American poetry after Eliot's, but it remains an impression only. A gesture of commemoration like Robert Lowell's "Words for Hart Crane" still catches us by surprise; we hardly think to assimilate it into the classical convention of the master poet's elegy for an acknowledged peer.

Academic scholarship has kept *The Bridge* in view: in recent years there have been, besides journal articles, L. S. Dembo's book-length analysis (1960) and Alan Trachtenberg's historical study of the poem's chief symbol (1964), and Roy Harvey Pearce's *The Continuity of American Poetry* (1961) has reminded us of the long line of American precedents for the poem's "epic" intention. But the effective character of the poetry itself, the basic questions of whether it is alive ("Are you too deeply preoccupied to say if my verse is alive?"—Emily Dickinson's challenge to Higginson is poetry's eternal challenge to criticism) and how it comes by that core of poetic life, have never really been put front and center. Professor Lewis has good reason to offer his study as introductory.

Beyond doubt his task has been a difficult one. The critical effort to deal comprehensively with any important modern writer imposes at least a double obligation. What is needed is not only a reasonably tactful description of the work and the career but also the postulation of some appropriate framework of historical assumptions, so that what is truly individual in that work can be more objectively felt and grasped and its specific virtue more precisely identified. At present, despite much fertile speculation, this kind of historical framework has not been secured for modern literature. Only recently has a corpus of discussion recognizing the continuities that link

Romanticism and modernism come into being; we have only just reached a point of loose agreement that such continuities not only exist but are of decisive importance, and we have hardly begun to grasp how they are constituted or to sort out the ways in which they affect performances. So an exploratory study of the work of one poet can be broadly useful, perhaps serve as a model for retrospective criticism in the modern period in general (as does, for example, Herbert Howarth's absorbing *Notes on Some Figures Behind T. S. Eliot* of 1964), without at all having to persuade us that it is the last word on its subject. It can satisfy whether or not it compels acceptance of all its particular interpretations and judgments.

If then I think Professor Lewis's intelligent, detailed, strenuously informed and mooted book is, as a work of literary criticism, more of a calamity than otherwise—a book likely to stand in other readers' way rather than promote understanding —it is not simply because of disagreements with particular critical findings and certainly not because of the very high valuation put on Crane's poetry in general. Rather it is because the book's argument, for all its roominess (it is 420 pages long!) and its incidental insights, lacks an essential fitness to the felt character of its subject. Too often it is as if the critic had not yet really *listened* to the poetry he discusses. Further, the book is chatty and voluble where it needs to be circumspect and verbally precise; it is a rackety, noisy book, as if the thought that a writer's job, in criticism as in anything else, includes tightening the contraption of his argument until he has made it both efficient and durable had not seriously been entertained. And this is a pity, because in incidental passages *The Poetry of Hart Crane* manages to say a lot of good things about its subject, clarifying by its undaunted sorties into explication and paraphrase a good deal that may previously have seemed obscure.

How are we to explain a miscarriage of this kind, with a critic of evident intelligence and force? We are told in the Preface that several chapters took form in a series of academic seminars and lectures. Is that the explanation? Is the book as a whole one more instance of how classroom presentation in the prevailing American manner, evangelically diligent in its will to remove obstructions and gain converts and prizing talk for its own time-filling and communion-establishing sake, has its final issue in erratic and wasteful treatises that are at once overurged and undermeditated? Professor Lewis's would not be the first. One can sympathize with the teacher-critic in such a case, thinking of him in conference groups where students who no doubt test in the top one percent nationally in "verbal aptitude" may nevertheless be struck dumb, or rattled into astonishing irrelevance, by the commoner sorts of metaphor and tonal irony. But the unfortunate truth is that classroom remarks, however ebullient, are not criticism, nor is the machinery of classroom explication any substitute for that fuller imaginative acquaintance without which talk about poetry will never get beyond the clatter of opinion-mongering. Richly figured poems on complex themes of human experience occupy the imagination slowly, and they require for "understanding" a kind of attention and patience, an incremental weighing of alternatives, for which the shallow routines of class discussion may be a positive hindrance.

Or is it Professor Lewis's critical method that keeps—necessarily, I think—breaking down? The main run of his commentary takes the form of a narrative retelling or paraphrase of events alleged to be taking place in the poems under examination ("As 'Voyages VI' opens, the poet finds himself. . . . He had, against all the warnings of 'Voyages I,' embarked on the dangerous love-journey. . . ."). It is a method that is bound to produce falsification. Because it must use words and phrase-cadences other than the poet's own, it establishes a pseudo-particularity that invariably departs from the metaphoric and imaginative particularity of the poems themselves; it thus regularly changes—reduces, makes grotesquely prosaic and literal—their created meaning. The whole painstaking analysis of "Voyages," forty pages long, founders on this kind of literalism. It founders specifically on the unwarranted assumption that these six poems are "about" an actual love affair and that their turns of argument are to be referred directly to the successive episodes in that affair. That the sequences of Crane's relationship with E. O., among others, contributed to the emotional sequences of these precisely and beautifully figured poems is of course hardly to be doubted. What, simply, one disbelieves is the critic's gossip-column literal-mindedness in assuming that the poems tell the story of that relationship.* That accomplished poetry is not, primarily, veiled biographical testimony is something Professor Lewis clearly knows but cannot seem to keep in mind.

The more serious trouble with this method of narrative paraphrase is that Crane's important poems are not for the most part narrative in structure and cannot be *retold*. Rather they are lyrical and associative; they project a succession of appearances and apparitional events ("Now no cry, no sword / Can fasten or deflect this tidal wedge, / Slow tyranny of moonlight . . .") that are positioned and addressed in such a way as to produce an ordered, psychologically reasoned succession of emotional tones. Images and metaphors are the chief means of establishing the first succession; idiom and syntax (or variations in them, vocative ironies) are the complementary means of establishing the second. What therefore is properly required of the intensive critic of Crane's poems is not narrative restatement but phenomenological and rhetorical analysis, leading to a more precise identification of the achieved theme. This in fact, or at least the phenomenological part of it, is the principal critical assumption in a recent monograph by Jean Guiguet, *L'Univers poétique de Hart Crane* (1965), and it is why Professor Guiguet's "examen des éléments constitutifs" in the poet's work, scarcely a fifth as long as Professor Lewis's book, is so much more satisfactory as a critical introduction. In the fitness of its address to its subject, Professor Guiguet's little study is both an immediately useful contribution to critical understanding and a convenient reminder of how work of this kind is most profitably done.

Criticism cannot, after all, take the place of reading poems and should not try to. What it can do is encourage reading, listening, a second time and a third and so on, by conveying assurances that getting this poet's work into one's mind *will* have its rewards.

Professor Lewis's book does offer a provocative general description of Crane's achievement, and though we may feel that this description only begins to explain the authority

---

* A disbelief confirmed in Susan Jenkins Brown's *Robber Rocks: Letters and Memories of Hart Crane, 1923–1932* (1969).

Crane possesses, it does promote discussion along serviceable lines. Hart Crane is presented as essentially a poet of *vision*. More particularly, *vision*, at once poetic and religious, is defined as the determining subject of the important poems, the leading symbols of which—*The Bridge* included—are taken to be symbols primarily of vision, of poetic imagination, achieved or broken. Crane is thus seen as the most important modern heir, along perhaps with Stevens, of the high Romantic program for poetry, the poetry of Blake, Keats, Shelley, Whitman; and the critic's persistent concern is to identify "the traditional and Romantic cast of Crane's imagination." Professor Lewis seems to have drunk deep of the heady waters of recent Yale scholarship in Romantic and modern poetry; we notice in the Preface that Professor Harold Bloom is cited as a guide and collaborator in shaping his interpretations.

Now beyond question this is a proper historical perspective for Crane, whose positive borrowings from Blake and Keats, Longfellow and T. S. Eliot, among others, go considerably beyond the haphazard record of them this volume offers. Professor Lewis's effort of definition needs, however, to be extended further. As it stands it is liable to much the same kind of objection as Professor Bloom's spirited readings of the major Romantics often are. This is simply the objection that for the English and American poets in this tradition, although the establishing of "vision" is of such importance that again and again we find it celebrated in and of itself, it is also and equally a means to further ends which are, to say the least, not less important in determining the power and virtue of the poet's actual statement.

First of all (to put aside the bothersome question whether even for Romanticism "poetic vision" and "religion" are simply different names for one thing), visionary experience is prized because it can open the way to new, regenerated forms of human association. The revival of common sympathy and respect for the Romantic undertaking in poetry is a happy circumstance of recent academic criticism, but frequently the emphasis on the centrality of the poet's own visionary act has been at the expense of the civil and historical radicalism—itself religious in character—that animates the Romantic consciousness. Such emphasis thus subtly endorses, I think, that separatism of consciousness, that secular individualism and elitism, which is the curse of our established intellectual life, though who knows but that a new era and a rising generation, working by more truly democratized covenants, are not doing away with all that?

A phrase from Hart Crane's late poem, "The Broken Tower," describing "the visionary company of love," has become a slogan for this view of Romantic tradition. Characteristically, however, the two nouns in this striking phrase are neglected; the talk is all of *vision* and only incidentally, if ever, of the forming of a *company* in the bond of *love*. But for Hart Crane, as for Blake or Whitman, vision gains its extraordinary value for men because it is a means to the achieving of something beyond itself and greater than itself, and that is love; the regeneration of fundamental human relationships under a new civil dispensation; the binding of being to being, and only incidentally of eye to object, which in this deeper sense of the "Word" of creation remains to Christian tradition what the New Testament says it is: of the virtues available to man, the greatest.

With *The Bridge* a relative inattentiveness to any note but the ecstatic-affirmative is less distorting, this note being dominant in most of the poem's climaxes. Also the length of *The Bridge* precludes line-by-line restatement, so that its larger design is more satisfactorily displayed. I agree, though, with Alan Trachtenberg's careful argument (*Kenyon Review*, November, 1967) that the specific social and historical content of the poem is excessively disregarded.* So, in general, is the degree to which, in building up the poem, Crane borrowed from that aroused preoccupation with the special character and destiny of "civilization in the United States" that governs so much of our twenties writing, and so much of the best of it. Not only Crane's choice of subject but the scale of his ambition and the confidence with which he first set to work were backed by the special urgency this high theme had for the American literary mind of the 1910's and 1920's. The choice, after all, of a great traffic-bearing feat of metropolitan engineering as

---

* I commend this review for its very different judgment of the merits of Professor Lewis's book, which it finds "excellent" and "important."

the chief symbol for a poem also full of destructive, dehumanizing examples of machine-age enterprise and continental expansion makes a substantial difference; it points to a more complex conception of the country ("Cathay," "Atlantis") toward which the poet's imagination moves in *The Bridge* than simply, as Professor Lewis identifies it, "the country of vision."

The odd effect of Professor Lewis's preoccupation with the precarious moment of pure vision is that although his book is full of extravagant commendation, he somehow makes Crane's poetry seem less interesting and accomplished than it really is. The critical argument seems fairly deaf to Crane's remarkable command of a species of generously affirmative irony that enables him to ground his praise of visionary ecstasy in a truthful consideration of actual constraints and thwartings. In passage after passage this irony (and self-irony, as it must be for a poet in the Romantic tradition) enters as the conclusive sign of poetic intelligence and wisdom. Professor Lewis, however, pretty regularly ignores it; more precisely, he detects it sporadically but understands it as a kind of intermediate tonality which must be "altogether transcended" in the achievement of true poetic greatness. Every reference to the apparatus of transcendent vision is therefore taken straight, and the poet's precise and deliberate ironic extravagances are regularly accepted as confessions of faith. The "grail of laughter" made out of "an empty ash can" with which Crane closes his charmingly ironic valentine to Charlie Chaplin—charming because the poem's tones are so tactfully adjusted to the licensed sentimentalities of Chaplin's art and the special range of responses it sanctions—can only be the Holy Grail itself, the sacred object of an "overwhelming visionary affirmation." The more harshly ironic opening of "The Wine Menagerie," where every strained word reinforces the sense of grotesque and pathetic self-delusion, is swallowed off as purest elixir; predictably, the single "overtone" the critic picks up in the poem's first line—"Invariably when wine redeems the sight"—is the "Eucharistic."

One must stop with these two examples of a way of reading individual poems that controls and directs the whole superabundant argument. Professor Lewis, we begin to see, is preaching a sermon. What he wants of literature is "some promise of moral and spiritual beauty," and what he watches for in Crane's poems is the leap "to the phase of final rejoicing," the effect of which will be "to redeem the fallen world." When he wishes to praise a poem in the highest terms, he speaks of it as reproducing "one of the oldest and greatest of theological formulae," and he means to hold us in our pews until we pray ourselves into agreement. But this is parsonage criticism. Where a hundred years ago it would be asked whether or not the poet "believed," and fifty years ago whether he was "optimistic or pessimistic," the critic now considers whether or not he has affirmed redemptive vision. Such commentary cannot be proved either right or wrong, except perhaps when it leads to establishing, as a rubric for the description of Crane's significant growth as a poet, the theme of an "escape from irony." It is merely irrelevant; it is not in the nature of the thing being examined; the questions it intrudes concern not so much the erected sequences of the poet's work as the exigencies of the critic's own will to faith. One can only comment that it was Crane's freedom from this kind of doctrinaire irrelevance and presumption, his indifference to the satisfactions of "theological formulae," that regularly saw him through to the completed argument, the architectural (and musical) resolution, of his best poems. And it is just this steadiness of artistic purpose and intelligence that seems to me at the core of his remarkable achievement and the reason why, along with the imaginative scope and power he reaches out for, his best poems live in the mind as they do.

The sources and configurations of that achieved poetic "life" remain the proper object of critical elucidation, and my impatience with Professor Lewis's book is intensified, I hope not perversely, by the indications here and there that he does recognize the most important factors in its creation. The religious element in Crane's will to expression is surely one of these factors. But for all the emphasis on Crane as a poet of religious apprehension, there is surprisingly little discussion of the specific character of his religiousness—its relation, for example, to erotic affirmation—or even of the traditions of religious consciousness he appears to have been most familiar with. (It should be clear that modish references to "that enor-

mous cultural event known as the death of God" tell us nothing about the poet's own intellectual circumstance.)

For example, Crane's sympathetic interest in Christian
Science, his mother's desperately adopted faith, is briefly
mentioned but not pursued. Yet much in his way of defining
his creative ambition—his postulation (it is quoted by Professor Lewis) of certain "fields of added consciousness and
increased perception" as "the actual province of poetry" or his
concern with something he called "thought-extension"—will
be familiar to anyone having in mind not only the vocabulary
of Christian Science but the greater and freer traditions from
which Christian Science literalistically derives: the broad
tradition of post-Reformation theosophy and the potent
spiritual optimism of evangelical, new-light Protestant thinking in general. Long ago, Coleridge (*Biog. Litt.,* chap. ix)
described the remarkable debt owed by modern poetry and
philosophy to these ebullient, open-minded popular traditions,
though remarking also on the existence of "a sort of secret and
tacit compact among the learned" to ignore their value and
interest. The case of Hart Crane is interesting historically for,
among other reasons, the evidence it offers of their continuing
vigor and generative power.*

The further question with Crane—it is the same question
that faces us in the greater and more complex case of Yeats—is
how such motives and resources were turned into accomplished poems. Professor Lewis shows that he is aware that
this, too, is a question criticism should properly focus on: i.e.,
Crane's achievement of what Yeats called, at various stages of
his own advance to greatness, a new "intensity of pattern," a
"passionate syntax for passionate subject matter," a specifically
poetic gain in "self-possession and power." A footnote late in
the present book speaks of "the quality of encompassing finality
that marks Crane's phrase-making power," and a few pages
later "finality" is again put forward as the word to describe

---

* A power on which more and more poets of the present time have been
drawing: an essay might be written, for example, on the presence of Jakob
Boehme in contemporary American verse, from Kenneth Rexroth's *The
Signature of All Things* to the latest volumes of Robert Bly, James Wright,
Robert Kelly, and on the implicit resistance to the Boehmist antipathy to
nature in Gary Snyder's ecological poetry.

his rhetoric at its most "stunning." A critical study that started here, and that would thus supplement M. Guiguet's phenomenological description with as thorough an assessment of Crane's compositional artistry and of its failures in those poems which, by this measure, are not so much disordered as unfinished, would be worth having. It would not have to be a long study. But it would have to begin from a surer understanding of what is critically appropriate. (It could do worse than build on the brief account of Crane's working methods—"a kind of creative opportunism"—in Philip Horton's fine biography of 1937, and, more broadly, on the remarkable characterization of Crane in Robert Lowell's *Paris Review* interview of 1961: ". . . less limited than any other poet of his generation. There was a fulness of experience . . . The push of the whole man is there.") As much as ever in the past, our criticism, for all its accumulated sophistication, needs first of all a more disciplined and submissive sense of primary task. It needs what the greatest criticism has always worked by and what has made it a source of renewal as well as clarification for the literature it serves, and that is a self-denying ordinance against mere self-expansive cleverness and erudition. Nothing else, I think, can prevent the kind of wastefulness and irrelevance exemplified by this well-intentioned study.

Index

ABOUT THE AUTHOR

WARNER BERTHOFF joined the faculty of Harvard University in 1967 as a professor of English. He taught at Bryn Mawr from 1951 to 1967 and has been a visiting professor at Minnesota, California (Berkeley), Columbia, Pennsylvania, Catania (in Sicily) and Warsaw. He will be Fulbright-Hays Lecturer at Rome for 1972. He was born in Oberlin, Ohio, graduated from Harvard College, and served in the U.S. Naval Reserve during World War II. His books include *The Example of Melville* and *The Ferment of Realism: American Literature, 1884–1919*. He lives with his family in Concord, Massachusetts.

PS121 B53
+Fictions and eve+Berthoff, Warner

0 00 02 0197396 3
MIDDLEBURY COLLEGE